Pelican Books

The Age of Keynes: A Bi

D1143858

Robert Lekachman was born in New York City in 1920 and received his A.B. and Ph.D. degrees from Columbia University, where he taught for eighteen years. He left Columbia in 1965 to accept a position as Chairman of the Department of Economics at the State University of New York at Stony Brook. He has been spending this current year at the Harvard Law School as a Fellow in Law and Economics. When he returns to Stony Brook he will make use of his experiences to teach a new course in law and economics which will try to trace the impact of legal institutions upon the distribution of income, wealth and power in American society.

Apart from *The Age of Keynes* he has written a *History of Economic Ideas* (1959) and edited five collections on assorted economic themes, and he has been a 'compulsive scribbler' for periodicals, general and grave. He conducts a monthly page on the state of the economy for *Dun's Review*, a business periodical, and has recently contributed to the new *International Encyclopedia of the Social Sciences* and has written an introduction to the forthcoming reissue of the *Temporary National Economic Committee Hearings of the 1930s*.

Robert Lekachman's principal objective at the moment is to return economics to the real world of greed, power and inequity and to discourage the continued fascination of the profession with other-worldly mathematical models.

Robert Lekachman

The Age of Keynes

A Biographical Study

Penguin Books

For Jack Lekachman

Penguin Books Ltd, Harmondsworth,
Middlesex, England
Penguin Books Australia Ltd, Ringwood,
Victoria, Australia

First published in the U.S.A. 1966
Published in Great Britain by Allen Lane The Penguin Press 1967
Published in Pelican Books 1969
Copyright © Robert Lekachman, 1966

Made and printed in Great Britain by
Hazell Watson & Viney Ltd, Aylesbury, Bucks
Set in Monotype Garamond

Contents

Prelude

More than a generation has elapsed since either Great Britain or the United States has suffered the mass unemployment, idle factories, business failures, mortgage foreclosures and black despair which once were the inseparable companions of apparently inevitable business-cycle depressions. For the majority of Americans and Britons under the age of forty, the Great Depression of 1929–33 is one of history's set pieces rather than an unpleasant personal recollection or a prophecy of similar future events. The word *depression* itself has lapsed from the popular vocabulary and very nearly from the technical lexicon of the professional economist. In its place is *recession*, and most people expect their recessions to be brief, gentle and infrequent.

We base our expectations upon our recent experience, and what most of us have enjoyed during our working lives has been uninterrupted employment, steady promotions, gratifying increases in earnings, larger houses, bigger cars, vacations in distant lands and varied leisure in this one. For their part American businessmen have come to anticipate that each year's sales will exceed its predecessor's record and each earnings report will tell a happier tale of dividends and earnings than ever before. Old economic records topple annually. And as the population increases and its average living standard continues to ascend, the makers of everything from baby oil to burial caskets are investing and will continue to invest in new machines, new factories, and the research and development calculated to stimulate demand and output still further. These wagers upon future markets are themselves a powerful impetus to economic growth – an important component of the total demand for goods and an essential element of the steady progress which is now taken almost for granted by public officials, businessmen and ordinary citizens.

The balmy economic weather of the 1960s has enabled the Internal Revenue Service to collect an additional $7 billion* or so a year out

* In American usage, a billion is equal to a thousand million.

of a gross national product which in 1966 will undoubtedly exceed $700 billion. As a pleasant consequence, Presidents and Congresses in recent years have toyed with attractive choices among different varieties of tax reduction, subsidies to states and cities, and expansions of social services. Of course, economic heaven on earth has not been attained. The agenda of national need has not dwindled to zero. Even in prosperous America, forty million people are poor, and some of our urban slums are worthy rivals of Caracas's and Calcutta's. Although unemployment afflicts only one out of every twenty or twenty-five workers, its incidence is cruel in urban Negro ghettoes and rural backwaters. The prospect if not the presence of automation urges us to take a new look at our education system, our unemployment compensation arrangements, and our very definitions of work. Polluted streams, auto junk yards and highway billboards evoke severe reservations about the reality of America the Beautiful.

The list could readily be extended, but the point is this: none of these problems is new. The novelty in the present definition of economic necessity, the break from the past, is in the visibility of these persistent blemishes upon the face of a rich society. Now that the sad cycle of boom and bust has been tamed, now that many Americans have the means as well as the wish to diffuse prosperity and amenities throughout the community, the challenges to public policy have taken a new turn.

Whether in fact Americans will use abundance to eliminate poverty and convert a frequently crude and crass material culture into a genuine civilization is possibly the leading public issue of this generation. But it is worth the emphasis of repetition to say that the primacy of the issue is related to the tamed ferocity of the business cycle and the new American chance to look at the nation's natural and urban environment.

This is a great advance, founded upon a great achievement. What has happened to relieve the citizens of advanced nations from the idleness and misery of depression? The change is one of public policy, above all of the financial programmes of American national administrations. The contrast between the old economic policy and the new is between that article of public faith which consisted in esteem of the federal budget as an objective in itself and the modern analysis which employs taxing and spending as technical instruments of administrative action. There was a time, not so very long ago, when a President who submitted to his Congress a January budget which was in open deficit faced severe criticism from conventional business and financial minds. In those days only a few heterodox economists, the shame of their profession, supported behaviour which flouted the financial moralities so scandalously. Usually a President who did introduce an unbalanced budget endeavoured to justify his malfeasance by declarations of dedication to government economy, personal belief in balanced federal budgets and assurances of rapid progress towards evening the national accounts.

Today by contrast a chief executive, even in a time of continuing economic prosperity, can boldly offer his constituents a major tax cut deliberately designed to *increase* an existing deficit. Moreover, he can expect the general approval of professional economists, alert politicians and sophisticated businessmen. Although all of this is quite recent history, the efficacy of the new instrumental approach to federal finance has already been tested by the continuation of what by early 1966 was already the longest peacetime economic expansion on record.

How does it happen that a nation long accustomed to regarding public finance as simply an extension of personal finance has suddenly achieved the vision that although personal thrift may indeed be consistent with the Puritan ethic, public frugality or public lavishness should be expressions not of national morality but of intelligent attempts to maintain, increase or restore general prosperity?

Particularly in an unintellectual nation, such shifts do not come readily. They require both educative experience and theoretical formulation. During the last four decades, the prime educative experiences through which many Americans have passed have been three: the horror of the Great Depression, the new hope of the New Deal, and the widespread prosperity attendant upon the vast military expenditures of the Second World War. All the same, experience, however exemplary, is an inadequate teacher. By itself the most that it can accomplish is the creation of dissatisfaction with existing conditions and existing justifications of their continuation. To rage at the miseries of depression and the inadequate policies of Herbert Hoover in 1931 was not nearly enough; one needed also a set of reasons for advocating alternative policies. As Keynes always believed, it is truly ideas that are decisive for good or evil.

The New Economics of the 1960s is the triumph of an idea. And the idea itself is above all the product of the creative genius of a single man – John Maynard Keynes as he was christened; Lord Keynes,

Baron of Tilton, as he came to be. This is a book which attempts to tell the story of the man whose brain conceived the idea. Accordingly, it is an account of his education and career, of his teachers, friends and associates – the Cambridge of G. E. Moore, E. M. Forster and Lytton Strachey; the Bloomsbury of Virginia Woolf, Clive Bell and Duncan Grant; the King's College economics of Alfred Marshall and A. C. Pigou; the worlds of art, rare books, high finance and public administration, in all of which Keynes was a familiar.

This book is also the biography of a mind, an effort to trace the events and the influences which converted the inventive pupil of conventional economics into the most influential heretic of his age. The economics which Keynes learned and then taught at Cambridge until the 1930s was the economics which everybody who counted at Cambridge believed. And such was the University's prestige that what Cambridge economists thought good, lesser economists in the English-speaking world dared not controvert. It is a measure of Keynes's unorthodoxy that the economics which he preached in his masterwork, the 1936 *General Theory of Employment, Interest and Money*, split Cambridge opinion, outraged former teachers and colleagues of the moment, and set in motion an ideological quarrel among economists which lasted a decade at least. Revolutions in the minds of theorists are only slightly more common than revolutions in general opinion. Much of Keynes's fascination for his contemporaries was his capacity to advocate radically opposed ideas at different periods in his life. Most theorists consider themselves fortunate if during their careers they grasp and expound one major conception of their subject. For Keynes one was a small number. His mind was powerful, flexible and inventive, a trio of qualities infrequently found in each other's company.

Moreover, unlike most men of abstract thought, Keynes was not a resident of ivory towers. When he wrote economics, he hoped to convert his colleagues but even more he wanted to operate upon general educated opinion, and above all he longed to divert public officials from mistaken policy to enlightened action. He chafed at the obstinacy of slower men, he never suffered fools gladly, and he regretted the time it took to convert his peers. Nevertheless, even in his own lifetime, he enjoyed far more success than most men in bending his hearers and readers to his intellectual will.

Keynes died in 1946 of a heart attack quite probably accelerated by his prodigious labours in the Treasury during the Second World War and the intricate negotiations for a large American loan to Britain which he conducted in the winter of 1945. In the twenty years which have followed his disappearance from the scene, a long Keynesian epilogue has been played out in the economic policies of the United States, Great Britain, and the remainder of the Western world. That epilogue too is part of the life and influence of this remarkable Englishman.

It has been said that we are all Keynesians now. In the main this is a justified if slightly hyperbolic claim. It is the final victory of a new idea to become the common, everyday property both of the learned and of the laity, the mental furniture of businessmen, politicians and professors. Such has been the fate of Keynesian thought.

This result contains a touch of irony. Keynes himself was the sort of restless, responsive intellectual who adjusts his theories to the changing shape of the outside world. He was no closet philosopher. If Keynes had survived into the 1960s, he would surely be busy inventing a new and better post-Keynesian doctrine, directed at eliminating poverty and gross inequality of income distribution and improving the quality of English and American daily life.

The General Theory would not have been Keynes's last word. But there is no cause for ingratitude at the gifts which Keynes lived long enough to offer his countrymen and the rest of the world. The chapters which follow this one will recite the tale that can be told of the life, times, thought and triumph of the greatest economist of his age.

Keynes and Keynesian Economics

The 1880s were a watershed in British economic history. Until that decade Britons took for granted a British economic pre-eminence among trading nations from which many benefits flowed. The long British lead in the mass production of inexpensive textile and metal products had accustomed the nation to an annual surplus of exports over imports. The favourable balance of payments which resulted not only sufficed for the country to purchase from other nations much of the food and raw materials which nourished the workers and supplied the factories; it also generated a flow of profits and dividends which prudent Englishmen invested at home and abroad. By the repeal of the Corn Laws in 1846, the nation had finally settled the issue of free trade versus protection, and from the middle of the century onward, Britain persistently bought her food in the world's cheapest markets. Her own farmers might grumble, but to no avail; for free trade was founded upon impeccable economic reasoning and supported by the United Kingdom's manifest commercial benefit from the free flow of trade, so that protection stood little chance in a nation of exporters and importers. Indeed, such was the weight of the British example that for a time in the third quarter of the nineteenth century other European nations themselves were influenced by free trade doctrine.

Great Britain's prosperity might have been the envy of the world, but it was an extremely unevenly dispersed prosperity. Wealth was concentrated, savings among the prosperous were considerable, and wages were low. British arrangements were sympathetic to substantial capital accumulation; they were only moderately beneficial to working-class standards of life. Keynes later judged the 1870–1914 period in these terms:

While there was some continuous improvement in the daily conditions of life of the mass of the population, Society was so framed as to throw a great part of the increased income into the control of the class least likely to consume it.... This remarkable system depended for its growth on a double bluff of deception. On the one hand, the labouring classes accepted from ignorance or powerlessness, or were compelled, persuaded or cajoled by custom, convention, authority and the well-established order of Society into accepting a situation in which they and Nature and the capitalists were co-operating to produce. And on the other hand the capitalist classes were allowed to call the best part of the cake theirs and were theoretically free to consume it, on the tacit underlying condition that they consume very little of it in practice.[1]

In other words the social equilibrium was the consequence of a combination of relatively weak labour unions, a more or less chronic labour surplus, and aggressive, self-confident employers. Predictably, wages were low and profits were high. It was the character of the capitalist class which made this situation tolerable even to ordinary workers. British capitalists were frugal, thrifty and industrious. Their saving habits released large sums of money for further investment, increased productivity, and in the long run at least expanded the flow of consumer goods. In Keynes's judgement what made the social scene calm was the general acceptance of these conditions as a part of the order of nature.

Doubtless there were plenty of social reformers and no dearth of hope that in due time the condition of the poor would be improved out of present recognition. But recognition of the possibility of improvement was entirely consistent with confidence in the institutions which had thus far ensured Victorian prosperity: free trade, the international gold standard, and *laissez faire* in domestic affairs. They had benefited many. They would benefit more. It was a state of mind not less realistic than the somewhat similar American vainglory of the twentieth century.

Still, by 1883, the year of John Maynard Keynes's birth, unexpected new challenges to British economic dominance were visible. Europe's Germany and North America's United States were competing with the U.K. in Latin America, Asia, the Union of South Africa and Australia in textiles and metal products as well as in an array of novelties like typewriters, canned meats, small tools, sewing machines and apples in barrels. As one of the period's historians has put it, 'By the nineties the "Made in Germany" label and the photograph of the American millionaire had become powerful foci of English resentment.'[2] Far from evincing proper reverence for British leadership, German and American businessmen displayed a disgustingly aggressive competitive spirit, and they employed advertising with a skill and ruthlessness unmatched by their more complacent English rivals. It was an English economist, H. S. Foxwell, who 'remembered proudly that he was taught as a child never to buy a product that was advertised'.[3] It was the same Foxwell who in 1917 remarked that 'most of our best people never, or very rarely, advertise'.[4] Possibly, the 'very rarely' represented the austere moralist's concession to the spirit of the age.

The challenge to British leadership succeeded. By 1914 the United States by a wide margin and Germany by a smaller one exceeded the British output of coal, iron and steel, and pressed hard over a wide range of industrial products. The Germans had a commanding lead in optical instruments, pharmaceuticals and chemicals. The Americans assumed an equally significant superiority in automobiles and electrical equipment. What was especially disquieting was the British failure to hold the country's own in the products of the newer technologies.

In retrospect all of this was clear, and even at the time signs of alarm were numerous and vociferous. Nevertheless, for the middle classes of Britain, prosperity on the whole continued right up to the eve of the First World War. Although the British share of world markets might have been shrinking, the absolute volume of exports continued to rise. Moreover, many a Victorian family enjoyed the benefits of the dividends and interest from past investment. The private income, the allowance to a scholarly or artistic child, and the small inheritance described in Victorian memoirs testify to a financial ease based on the fortunate commercial adventures of the past. One famous instance illustrates the condition. In his charming biography of his great-aunt, Marianne Thornton, E. M. Forster recalls that when she died in 1887, she bequeathed him £8,000. The interest on this sum was to be employed in the education of her legatee, and the principal was to be his at age twenty-five. As Forster gratefully notes, that Victorian inheritance made an important difference in his life:

Thanks to it, I was able to go to Cambridge – impossible otherwise, for I failed to win scholarships. After Cambridge I was able to travel for a couple of years, and travelling inclined me to write. After my first visit to India and after the First World War the value of the £8,000 began to diminish, and later on it practically vanished. But by then my writings had begun to sell, and I have been able to live on them instead. Whether – in so stormy an age as ours – this is a reputable sequence I do not know. Still less do I know how the sequence and all sequences will end, with the storms increasing. But I am thankful so far, and thankful to Marianne Thornton; for she and no one else made my career as a writer possible, and her love, in a most tangible sense, followed me beyond the grave.[5]

Marianne Thornton's money dated all the way back to the death of her father, Henry Thornton, Member of Parliament, banker and author of a remarkable essay on *The Paper Credit of Great Britain*. Henry Thornton died in 1815, and it is far from fanciful to credit his final balance sheet with two important assets: *Howard's End* and *A Passage to India*.

John Maynard Keynes was born into the Victorian world of the prosperous. His family's home at 6 Harvey Road, Cambridge, has been described as a 'tall Victorian gothic house, which still retains many of the William Morris influences of the time of his parents' marriage'.[6] Each of the three children of the marriage achieved a distinguished career, Geoffrey as a physician and an editor of William Blake, and Margaret as a pioneer social worker, particularly among the aged. The parents were no less remarkable than their children. John Neville Keynes, who inherited a moderate competence from his father, John Keynes, entered Cambridge as the winner of a scholarship in mathematics. First as a scholar and tutor and then as an administrator, he spent his life happily as well as usefully at Cambridge. For a generation or more his *Scope and Method of Political Economy* was a standard work on the methodology of economics. As registrar of the University between 1910 and 1925, he was in effect Cambridge's chief administrative official. Of his father as an administrator, his most famous child was to say:

For thirty-three years he was one of the best administrators there ever was and during those years the University was a better place in my judgement than it has ever been before or since. Perfect order and accuracy without a shadow of pedantry and red tape, the machine existing for the sake of the University and not the other way round as it sometimes seems to be now. He really helped to create a framework within which learning and science and education could live and flourish without feeling restraint or a hampering hand, and he combined this with himself possessing learning and science and education at the highest level – which no one now seems to be able to do.[7]

The letters between father and son attest to a warm relationship throughout their mutual lives. Family reading, holidays in common, and intelligent parental interest all played their part.

Cambridge was equally prominent in the life and affections of Florence Brown, who married John Neville Keynes in 1882. Her father, the Reverend John Brown, D.D., and a man of advanced views, sent his daughter to Newnham College and enabled her to become one of the earliest female graduates of Cambridge. In the last years of the nineteenth century, Mrs Keynes, who would much later serve as mayor of Cambridge, pioneered in a variety of projects designed to assist the unfortunate, among them a Juvenile Labour Exchange, a pension scheme for the community's aged, regular assistance to workhouse families, and improvements in the treatment of the tubercular. Her work was both the harder and the more necessary because of general public penuriousness in the assistance of any of the Victorian era's numerous social casualties. Victorian England lagged far behind Bismarck's Germany in the creation of the social services which an industrial community urgently needed.

The family at 6 Harvey Road lived in 'moderate circumstances but solid comfort, the house well staffed with domestic servants'.[8] For a Victorian academic family, 'solid comfort' implied a good deal more in the way of amenities than an ample domestic staff. It meant travel in Europe, theatre- and concert-going, books and periodicals in quantity, and naturally the very best schools and universities for the children of the home. In some respects this was the sort of life which only the really affluent are today in a position to enjoy.

It was proper, therefore, for the young Maynard to attend Eton before he matriculated at Cambridge. Now, it is possible to compile a long list of eminent Englishmen whose lives at school were miserable. George Orwell's bitter account of his Eton days is in a familiar vein; misery at school is one of the recurrent themes of English memoirs and novels. However, it is a theme to which Keynes contributed nothing. At Eton his life was happy, successful and productive of lasting attachment to the school. The quality of Keynes's early triumphs foreshadowed the achievements of his adulthood.

In the exclusive, somewhat snobbish context of the English public school, the pupil who wins favour among his contemporaries is frequently an athlete, much less often a gifted student, on occasion an incipient politician, but always someone who suits the tone and the temper of the ruthless company of the young. As an athlete Keynes was not especially gifted, although he participated in the Eton Wall Game, and rowed enthusiastically on the river. Of his cricket prowess, he himself judged that 'if the theory and history (*not* the practice) of cricket were included in Trials I would do well in the subject'.[9]

The qualities which earned Keynes eminence at Eton were those of intellect, managerial capacity and personal charm, not those of muscle and coordination. As a scholar he did everything easily and well. His tutor judged Keynes 'to have the power of being interested in everything...at the same time he seems incapable of doing anything in a dilettante manner'.[10] This appears no more than a fair comment on a fifteen- or sixteen-year-old who was capable of winning in the same school career mathematical prizes, citations for high performance in the classics, and praise for the varied papers and essays he presented to the Eton Literary Society. All subjects appeared grist to the young virtuoso's mill: Bernard of Cluny, the character of the Stuarts, the differences between East and West – to take only three instances. Those who taught him classics foresaw a great future in classical scholarship. His mathematical tutors were no less confident of his future in their subject. He himself appeared almost equally interested in everything and began a notable, varied collection of books while he was at Eton as an expression of his tastes.

Still, even though Eton was more sympathetic than many other public schools to achievements of the mind, Keynes could scarcely have won the esteem of his schoolmates solely on the basis of intellectual pre-eminence. The fact was that he possessed unusual gifts of leadership in the bargain. He seems naturally to have assumed the management of undergraduate societies, and his charm of person and conversation made him popular as well as successful. Thus, he easily won the highest honour Etonians accord their fellows: election to Pop, the student society which acted as part of the government of the school. The evidence suggests that the unusual blend of original thought and effective action which distinguished Keynes in maturity evidenced itself in his adolescence at Eton.

As Keynes approached the end of his years at school, he wavered between two of Cambridge's largest and most distinguished colleges, King's and Trinity. He finally selected King's, which he entered in 1902, aged nineteen, primarily as a mathematician but with his other interests still very much alive. Eton and King's College have had a long historical connection, and Keynes's Eton reputation preceded him at the University. One of his biographers observes that he 'quickly established at King's the ascendancy that he had achieved over his contemporaries at Eton'.[11] At the University Union Society, a debating organization which has given their first lessons to a good many of England's political leaders, Keynes blossomed as a polemical speaker. In due course Keynes became president of the Society. As an adult Keynes was always a political maverick, unable to perceive in either the Liberal or the Labour Party sufficient merit to warrant his consistent support. As a Cambridge student, he spoke warmly in one debate against party government, which he considered hostile to the rule of intelligence – a portent of things to come.

Indeed, Keynes's interests both as a debater and as a scholar were rapidly becoming more political and less mathematical. This was fortunate, one of his later colleagues and admirers judges, because 'by the exacting standards of Cambridge he was not in that narrow superlative class which alone can hope to achieve fame in the field of pure mathematics'.[12] Cambridge's standards at the time were not far from those of the Nobel Prize committee. Keynes had his consolations; in 1904 he won a prize for an essay on 'The Political Doctrines of Edmund Burke'. His vocational interests turned more and more to the civil service. The British civil service, after the Victorian innovation of selection by competitive examination, was a promising career for the most gifted of English university graduates. The administrative grade at Whitehall has consistently offered careers of influence, public position, and generous financial compensation – in substantial contrast to the American civil service. Thus, it was entirely natural for someone of Keynes's talents and background to consider a government career as an alternative to an academic vocation.

In Keynes's case the civil service was especially appealing because at graduation he had not quite fully decided to become an economist. At Cambridge he came to economics relatively late, but he was speedily recognized by his principal teachers, Alfred Marshall and A. C. Pigou – holders in turn of the University professorship in economics – to possess extraordinary aptitudes. Marshall had this to say in a letter to the elder Keynes: 'Your son is doing excellent work in Economics. I have told him that I should be greatly delighted if he should decide on the career of a professional economist. But of course I must not press him.'[13] Despite or perhaps because of Marshall's praise, the father had his doubts: 'I am afraid Marshall is endeavouring to persuade him to give up everything for Economics.'[14]

But this was scarcely likely. Cambridge had far too much to offer in diversion and variety. Keynes's friends and intimates and Keynes himself shared much wider interests than simple political economy. The friend whose rooms were above Keynes's said this of him:

Hospitable, receptive, intellectually impish, nipping up the staircase with his latest purchase from David, hurrying off at five o'clock to McTaggart's philosophy lecture at Trinity, almost as grown up as Gaselee, almost as good a bridge player as Spens, admittedly the inferior of Furness in Rabelaisian wit, yet in the sum, because he could do (or say) nearly any-thing, superior to them all. If he couldn't find it at King's, there was Trinity and Lytton Strachey. If it wasn't to be had at Trinity, there was the wide world without.[15]

The name Lytton Strachey is a clue to a significant part of Keynes's life. The pre-First World War Bloomsbury group had its origins in Vanessa and Virginia Stephen, the daughters of Leslie Stephen, Victorian pundit and agnostic, and equally in Lytton Strachey and his Cambridge circle at the time of Keynes's attendance. The group first around Strachey and then around Strachey and Keynes were members of an exclusive set with a long Cambridge history of secrecy, called simply the Society. Harrod has dated the official beginning of the independent London life of the Bloomsbury circle as 1908, when Vanessa Stephen (later Vanessa Bell) and Virginia Stephen (later Virginia Woolf) were enabled by the death of their father to establish an independent household. Hence Keynes was actually involved in the prehistory of London's Bloomsbury group, for he met at Cambridge according to his own account Leonard Woolf, Lytton Strachey and Clive Bell, three of the most active members of the group,* as well as E. M. Forster, a sympathetic but elusive participant.

The interests and talents of these gifted individuals were extremely varied. They were united by certain common qualities, among them exceptional cleverness, great articulateness, extraordinary personal sympathy, and a doctrine. The doctrine was formally enunciated in print in 1902, at the close of Keynes's first Cambridge year. The book was the philosopher G. E. Moore's *Principia Ethica*. According to Keynes, Moore completely ejected all other influences, among them those of McTaggart, Dickinson and Bertrand Russell.[16] As Keynes

* Bell disputes Keynes's recollection of their Cambridge meeting. See his *Old Friends* (London: Chatto & Windus, 1956).

summarized Moore's teachings, they were exceptionally appealing to the spirited young:

Nothing mattered except states of mind, our own and other people's of course, but chiefly our own. These states of mind were not associated with action or achievement or with consequence. They consisted in timeless, passionate states of contemplation and communion, largely unattached to 'before' and 'after'. Their value depended, in accordance with the principle of organic unity, on the state of affairs as a whole which could not be usefully analysed into parts. For example, the value of the state of mind of being in love did not depend merely on the nature of one's own emotions, but also on the worth of their object and on the reciprocity and nature of the object's emotions, but it did not depend, if I remember rightly, or did not depend much, on what happened, or how one felt about it, a year later, though I myself was always an advocate of a principle of organic unity through time, which still seems to me only sensible. The appropriate subjects of passionate contemplation and communion were a beloved person, beauty and truth, and one's prime objects in life were love, the creation and enjoyment of aesthetic experience and the pursuit of knowledge. Of these love came a long way first.[17]

As a doctrine this was highly aristocratic and highly personal. It assumed a society sufficiently stable and satisfactory in its social, financial and political arrangements to enable the practitioners of Moore's ethics to devote all their time to the acquisition of desirable states of mind. Since worldly activity of any kind tended to diminish the possibility of success in acquiring these states of mind, Moore's disciples appeared to need substantial private incomes – from a series of Marianne Thorntons.

As Keynes himself perceived in his 1938 recollections, this was an odd faith for an economist ceaselessly occupied with public affairs, the fortunes of his own College, and his private financial speculations. Moore scarcely considered a speculative preoccupation one of the desirable states of mind. Yet in his own career, Keynes was as much a man of action as a man of thought. The mature Keynes could not help but realize that 'There are many objects of valuable contemplation and communion beyond those we knew of – those concerned with the order and pattern of life amongst communities and the emotions which they can inspire.'[18] Still, even in his fifties, Keynes judged that 'This religion of ours was a very good one to grow up under. It remains nearer the truth than any other that I know. . . . It was a purer, sweeter air by far than Freud or Marx. It is still my religion under the surface.'[19] However, for the maturer Keynes, Moore became a religion of Utopia, not a set of precepts to guide his worldly life. Keynes did not refrain from adding, 'It is remarkable how wholly oblivious he managed to be of the qualities of the life of action and also of the pattern of life as a whole. He was existing in a timeless ecstasy.'[20]

Among such friends and such ideas Keynes lived at Cambridge. They suffice to point the difference between him and the conventional specialist. All the same, lacking a private fortune and possessing an active temperament, he had to choose some financially adequate vocation. At Cambridge he had performed respectably but not brilliantly in his mathematical examinations, and in any event his interests were less in pure mathematical theory than in the applications of mathematics to probability. Thus, he temporized: he decided to postpone writing the prize dissertation which was then the prerequisite to election as a lifetime fellow of King's College and to take instead the civil service examinations. On these he placed second.

The candidate who came in first chose the most desirable opening, a position in the Treasury, the most powerful and interesting of government departments, which then as now exercised control over appointments to lesser branches of administration, collected taxes and supervised expenditures. For his part Keynes accepted the only other possible position which attracted him, a job in the India Office. Such are the vagaries of competitive examinations that in those which decided Keynes's immediate fate, he got his worst grades in the economics section. His comment was, 'The examiners presumably knew less than I did'.[21] Although the work of the India Office was not excessively arduous, Keynes may have exaggerated when he alleged that he divided his day between study of *The Times* in the morning and disposal of his personal correspondence in the afternoon. Hence the India Office never struck Keynes as his final resting place. While he was still a public employee, he worked on the dissertation on probability which he planned to submit to King's in the expectation of winning a fellowship and moving into an academic career.

Never short of self-confidence (less charitably, Bell called him 'cock-sure'), Keynes was much annoyed when he was not elected. His embarrassment was only temporary. Still eager to recruit a promising student, Alfred Marshall saved the situation by offering him a lectureship in economics at £100 a year, financed by Marshall himself at this time and later by his successor, A. C. Pigou. Although this was less than adequate income even at early-twentieth-century prices and Keynes had no assurance that a revised version of his fellowship dissertation would achieve its object, he decided all the same to resign from the India Office and return to Cambridge. All turned out well. Elected a fellow of King's College in 1909, he had a secure academic base as long as he wanted one for the rest of his life. From 1909 until 1915, when he entered the Treasury service, Keynes's occupation and responsibilities were at Cambridge, but he continued to spend much time, especially during the ample University vacations, with Duncan Grant and Lytton Strachey, travelling in such places as Scotland and the Orkneys, Italy, Spain, Greece, Turkey and Egypt in the spacious fashion of his class and period.

Keynes's departure from London involved no loss of his Bloomsbury associations. Although it anticipates chronology, it is worth telling one Bloomsbury story as an illustration of what friendship implied to Keynes and his circle. It is best told in the words of a survivor of the original Bloomsbury group. The events detailed occurred at the very outset of the First World War:

Maynard told me that he had succeeded in raising enough money for Ferenc Berkassy to leave England the night before. The banks were all shut owing to a moratorium and Berkassy was anxious to return to Hungary to fight against Russia. War had not been declared between Britain and Austria-Hungary until the morning after Berkassy left.

I said that I thought Maynard should have refused to find the money on the double grounds that he was sending a friend to his death and strengthening the enemy forces.

Maynard disagreed violently. He said he had used every argument to persuade Berkassy not to go – but having failed to persuade him, it was not the part of a friend to impose his views by force, or by refusing help. He respected Berkassy's freedom to choose though he regretted his choice. My second argument was ridiculous: what was one man in a score of millions? I agreed that friendship was more important than patriotism, but asked if he would restrain the friend who contemplated suicide, or would he lend him the money to buy poison? Maynard replied that in certain circumstances he would lend him the money – if it was a free choice, made by a sane man, after due reflection, for compelling causes.[22]*

---

* E. M. Forster has put this position in an extreme form: 'I hate the idea of causes, and if I had to choose between betraying my country and betraying my friend, I hope I should have the guts to betray my country.... Love and loyalty to an individual can run counter to the claims of the State. When they do – down with the State, say I, which means that the State would down me' ('What I Believe', *Two Cheers for Democracy* (London: Edward Arnold, 1956)).

Keynes had energy enough for Bloomsbury and economics as well. In the years before the First World War, he was constructing a reputation within Cambridge and beyond it. In King's College he may have been teaching, according to his later claim, more than half the University's economics students. The claim is less impressive for the circumstance that in 1910, for example, only nine men and three women were specializing in the subject. It is more impressive when we note that between 1907 and 1914 Cambridge graduated such noted economists as Walter Layton, Hugh Dalton, Hubert Henderson, Gerald Shove, Claud Guillebaud and Dennis Robertson. Keynes lectured and conducted individual supervisions. His lectures touched on the subjects where his expertise was already considerable – money, credit and prices.

The barbarous slogan, 'Publish or perish' had not yet poisoned the University atmosphere. Still, in 1909 Keynes's 'The Method of Index Numbers' won him the Adam Smith prize, and he appeared in the most important technical periodical, *The Economic Journal*, with a major article entitled 'The Recent Economic Events in India', one of the fruits of his two-year service as a bureaucrat. Nevertheless, his reputation outside of Cambridge was sufficiently fresh that his appointment to the editorship of *The Economic Journal* at the tender age of twenty-eight caused some astonishment and perhaps dictated the appointment of an editorial committee of grave elders to counsel the fledgeling. For his part Keynes ignored the committee and made his own editorial decisions – including rejection of unsatisfactory articles by the eminent.

Whatever deficiencies in general reputation may have existed were soon repaired. In 1913 Keynes was appointed to the Royal Commission on Indian Currency and Finance, just about the time when his first major book, *Indian Currency and Finance*, was published.* His service on the Commission – he was only thirty when he was selected – extended three benefits. In the first place, much of his policy prevailed, especially his preference of a gold exchange standard over a gold coin standard. Moreover, this was Keynes's first practical opportunity to demonstrate one of his great strengths, an unusual capacity to apply economic theory to practical problems. Finally, Keynes encountered for the first time a number of prominent per-

---

* Still a standard reference, the volume was an interesting anticipation of two favourite Keynesian roles: the monetary reformer and the inventor of novel techniques in economic management.

sonages of later importance to his career, among them Austen Chamberlain and Basil Blackett of the Treasury.[23]

Thus, when war came Keynes – though a young man of thirty-one in a country which venerated age – was well enough known and strategically enough placed to anticipate a public role of some significance. All the same the wheels of administration ground but slowly, and he was not immediately summoned by an alert government. Thus it was that his first public service was analytical and private. Keynes's initial comments on war finance, 'War and the Financial System, August, 1914', appeared in the September, 1914, *Economic Journal* and must have been written almost immediately after Britain's entry into the conflict. It and a sequel in the November issue showed considerable grasp of the issues, particularly the probable necessity of some international regulation of gold movements. Conceivably Keynes's professional judgement was better than his personal judgement. One of his friends recalls a remarkably optimistic prognosis of the war's duration:

... Maynard went on to talk about the war. Much to my surprise, I discovered that he was extremely optimistic about the larger issue. He told me that he was quite certain that the war could not last more than a year and that the belligerent countries could not be ruined by it. The world, he explained, was enormously rich, but its wealth was, fortunately, of a kind which could not be rapidly realised for war purposes: it was in the form of capital equipment for making things which were useless for waging war. When all the available wealth had been used up – which he thought would take about a year – the Powers would have to make peace. We could not use the cotton factories in Lancashire to help our Navy blockade Germany; Germany could not use its toymakers' factories to equip her armies.[24]

The Treasury summoned Keynes at the start of 1915. He was co-opted to work with Sir George Paish, whose official position was Adviser to the Chancellor of the Exchequer and to the Treasury on Financial and Economic Questions. Much of the economic aspect of the conduct of the war passed through Treasury hands, but as far as Keynes himself was concerned, his sphere of responsibility became largely external. Considerably before the United States Government initiated its series of loans to Great Britain, the latter – departing from an historical policy of outright subsidy of her continental allies in European conflicts – extended loans to France and Italy. The terms on which these loans were contracted, the arrangements by

which borrowers could draw upon them, and the relations between
Allied and British demands upon painfully scarce resources all fell
within the purview of Keynes's work. The control system which he
invented was later adopted by the United States in its financial relations with Great Britain after the American entry into the war.

Another of Keynes's responsibilities was in the acquisition of
scarce foreign currencies. Here his nerve and mastery became
legendary. There was, for example, the occasion when he scraped
together with much ingenuity a small supply of Spanish pesetas.
Congratulated on his *coup*, he coolly informed his well-wisher that he
had already sold the entire hoard of pesetas in an effort to break the
market. The gamble succeeded, and Spanish currency as a result
became considerably less scarce and substantially less expensive.

Keynes's possibly unique combination of the guts of a burglar and
the intellect of a first-class economist gained their official reward. By
the last year of the war, he had reached a rank equivalent to that of
Assistant Secretary, and in the Treasury hierarchy only the two Joint
Permanent Secretaries were his superiors. In 1917 he was named a
C.B. (Companion of the Bath), a pleasant, if in Keynes's opinion
belated, token of official recognition. Although in 1919 Keynes was
still a young man, the Treasury found it entirely natural to nominate
him as its financial representative at the Paris Peace Conference. The
appointment was to have momentous effects upon Keynes's reputation and career.

SOURCE NOTES TO CHAPTER I

1. J. M. Keynes, *The Economic Consequences of the Peace* (London: Macmillan,
1919).
2. Herman Ausubel, *In Hard Times* (New York: Columbia University Press,
1960).
3. Ibid.
4. Quoted in ibid.
5. E. M. Forster, *Marianne Thornton* (London: Edward Arnold, 1956).
6. E. A. G. Robinson, 'John Maynard Keynes' in Robert Lekachman (ed.),
Keynes's General Theory: Reports of Three Decades (New York: St Martin's, 1964;
London: Macmillan).
7. Quoted in Sir Roy Harrod, *The Life of John Maynard Keynes* (London: Macmillan, 1951).
8. Ibid.

9. Quoted in Robinson, op. cit.
10. Quoted in ibid.
11. Ibid.
12. Quoted in ibid.
13. Quoted in Harrod, op. cit.
14. Quoted in ibid.
15. Quoted in Robinson, op. cit.
16. See J. M. Keynes, 'My Early Beliefs', *Two Memoirs* (Village Station, N.Y.: Kelley, 1949).
17. Ibid.
18. Ibid.
19. Ibid.
20. Ibid.
21. Quoted in Robinson, op. cit.
22. David Garnett, *The Golden Echo* (London: Chatto & Windus, 1953).
23. Robinson, op. cit.
24. Garnett, op. cit.

For those who hoped that the Paris Peace Conference would write a treaty motivated not by revenge but by a spirit of reconciliation, the outcome of the protracted negotiations was disastrous. Soon enough Keynes was to arrive at this conclusion and, characteristically, to declare his feelings publicly. Indeed, his service at the Conference and its immediate sequel registered a transformation of Keynes's situation. Up to the Conference, good judges considered him a brilliant, possibly the most brilliant student of Marshall and Pigou, as well as a rising young Treasury official with promise of reaching the very heights of public management. In 1919 he was famous – or notorious – neither for startling theoretical departures from the work of his masters nor for strikingly heterodox public policy postures. The Peace Conference started Keynes on a life of controversy terminated only by his death. The controversies were to span economic theory, economic policy and the politics of England and other countries.

There is little mystery in the sequence of events. Early in his Paris service, Keynes came to a depressing evaluation of the prospects. He was convinced that the eminent negotiators Lloyd George, Woodrow Wilson and Georges Clemenceau were well advanced on the road to an unjust and unworkable treaty. It was an enterprise with which he did not care to be associated long, especially since the extended strain of the negotiations and above all the collapse of hope for a reasonable settlement took their toll of the uncertain health of a man who from childhood had subjected a frail constitution to heavy stress. He seems to have contemplated resigning fairly early. In a 1 June 1919, letter to his parents, he expressed his feelings openly:

Partly out of misery for all that's happening, and partly from prolonged overwork, I gave way last Friday and took to my bed suffering from sheer nervous exhaustion. . . . My first idea was to return to England immediately, but General Smuts, with whom I've been working very intimately for changes in their damned Treaty, persuaded me that it was my duty to stay on and be available for the important discussions of these present days, declaring that one can only leave the field of battle dead.... I dragged myself out of bed today to make a final protest before the Reparations Commission against murdering Vienna, and did achieve some improvement.[1]

General Smuts delayed Keynes's departure only briefly. On 5 June he conveyed his intentions to Lloyd George, at the time still prime minister:

I ought to let you know that on Saturday I am slipping away from this scene of nightmare. I can do no more good here. I've gone on hoping even through these last dreadful weeks that you'd find some way to make of the Treaty a just and expedient document. But now it's apparently too late. The battle is lost. I leave the twins* to gloat over the devastation of Europe and to assess to taste what remains for the British taxpayer.[2]

Resignation of public office implied for Keynes the freedom to speak his mind, and in two months during the summer of 1919 he composed an indictment of the Versailles settlement in his *Economic Consequences of the Peace*. His publishers put it in the bookstores by Christmas of the same year. What Keynes wrote inevitably exposed him to the charge of pro-German sympathy. His own definition of his aim was rather different: 'My purpose in this book is to show that the Carthaginian Peace is not *practically* right or possible.'[3] Keynes's burning indignation at the stupidity of his superiors took the shape of one of the century's great polemics.

The volume is composed of three significant elements, of which the one which achieved the greatest notoriety was the least important. This was Keynes's acid character sketches of the major participants. The flavour of the series is suggested by Keynes's comments upon Woodrow Wilson:

The first impression of Mr Wilson at close quarters was to impair some but not all of these illusions. His head and features were finely cut and exactly like photographs, and the muscles of his neck and the carriage of his head were distinguished. But, like Odysseus, the President looked wiser when he was seated; and his hands, though capable and fairly strong, were wanting in sensitiveness and finesse. The first glance at the President suggested not only that, whatever else he might be, his temperament was not

---

* The 'twins', or as Keynes sometimes called them, the 'heavenly twins', were Lords Cunliffe and Sumner, British representatives on the Reparations Commission who believed in the infliction of huge reparations obligations on the Germans.

primarily that of the student or the scholar, but that he had not much even of that culture of the world which marks M. Clemenceau and Mr Balfour as exquisitely cultivated gentlemen of their class and generation. But more serious than this, he was not only insensitive to his surroundings, in the external sense, he was not sensitive to his environment at all. What chance could such a man have against Mr Lloyd George's unerring, almost medium-like sensibility to every one immediately round him? To see the British Prime Minister watching the company, with six or seven senses not available to ordinary men, judging character, motive and subconscious impulse, perceiving what each was thinking and even what each was going to say next, and compounding with telepathic instinct the argument or appeal best suited to the vanity, weakness, or self-interest of his immediate auditor, was to realize that the poor President would be playing blind man's buff in that party. Never could a man have stepped into the parlour a more perfect and predestined victim to the finished accomplishments of the Prime Minister. The Old World was tough in wickedness anyhow; the Old World's heart of stone might blunt the sharpest blade of the bravest knight-errant. But this blind and deaf Don Quixote was entering a cavern where the swift and glittering blade was in the hands of the adversary.[4]

Nor was this the end of the description. According to Keynes, Wilson was not only a 'blind and deaf Don Quixote'; he was simultaneously and somewhat remarkably 'like a Nonconformist minister, perhaps a Presbyterian. His thought and his temperament were essentially theological not intellectual, with all the strength and the weakness of that manner of thought, feeling, and expression.'[5] Even at that Keynes excised from his account some of his most biting comments upon Lloyd George, only, as it turned out, to publish them later in another form.

It was this aspect of his book which *The Times* attacked in stately measures:

How came it ... that the man who could write the pages of incisive portraiture, not to say caricature, that fill the chapter on 'The Conference', came to hold the position of technical adviser to one of the most technical Departments of State? How, unless his bias had been throughout akin to that of the conscientious objector, could he place the Allies persistently on the same moral level as Germany in regard to the war? ... Indeed one of the striking features of Mr Keynes' book is the political inexperience, not to say ingenuousness, which it reveals. Yet he sits in judgment upon and condemns severely, as statesmen and as men, the French and British Prime Ministers and the American President. He draws portraits of them in which only those who know his subjects more intimately can distinguish the true from the false.... Mr Keynes may be a 'clever' economist. He may have been a useful Treasury official. But in writing this book, he has rendered the Allies a disservice for which their enemies will, doubtless, be grateful.[6]

The reference to the conscientious objector was a scarcely veiled comment on Keynes's own objections on grounds of conscience to the principle of conscription, and his assistance to friends compelled to justify their own conscientious objections to war itself before special tribunals.

Although *The Times* intoned in its best tradition, general opinion was nearer acclaim than condemnation. In his sketch of Keynes, Schumpeter declared that the book, not least the character sketches, 'met with a reception that makes the word success sound commonplace and insipid ... the book is a masterpiece – packed with practical wisdom that never lacks depth; pitilessly logical yet never cold; genuinely humane but nowhere sentimental; meeting all facts without vain regret but also without hopelessness: it is sound advice added to sound analysis'.[7]

If it was to be expected that these sharp accounts of the eminent would attract the most public attention, it was probably equally predictable that a second aspect of the volume should attract least general comment. At a time when others were celebrating victory, Keynes was making a sober assessment of just how precarious had been the equilibrium of economic and political forces even in prewar Europe. It was his judgement that the key institutions of Europe between the Franco-Prussian War and 1914 were exceedingly fragile, among them the apparently stable social structure, the international division of labour, the truce between labour and management, the apparently automatic gold standard, and the assumption of automatic economic progress. These had been the comfortable foundations of the society of 6 Harvey Road. War had shattered them. Possibly the wisest peace settlement could not restore them. Evidently the Treaty of Versailles was not the wisest of settlements. Hence the post-war outlook was very grim. Keynes was to recur to this diagnosis again and again. It contained in it the germ of the doctrine of secular stagnation which became popular in the United States during the 1930s.

The heart of Keynes's argument, however, was an economic demonstration that the reparations provisions of the treaty were utterly unrealistic. To this demonstration feelings of revenge or indulgence towards the Germans were equally irrelevant. Keynes's powerful reasoning influenced both events and the author's own public reputation. As Keynes analysed it, Germany's pre-war prosperity rested on three pillars: a substantial overseas commerce in which her merchant marine, foreign investment, manufacturing exports and the overseas connections of her merchants all played a role; the exploitation of coal and iron deposits and the industries which employed these materials; and a transport and tariff system which efficiently expedited the objectives of German production and export. But, Keynes pointed out, the Versailles Treaty aimed at the destruction of all three of these pillars at precisely the time that it imposed tremendous reparations obligations upon a curtailed territory and a weakened economy.

How did Versailles damage German overseas commerce? In several ways. Germany was forced to cede the bulk of her merchant marine to the triumphant Allies. She was compelled to surrender not only political title to her overseas colonies but, what was more damaging, the private assets that German citizens held within these territories. Yet Germany was to remain responsible for the debts of her former possessions. German private property in Alsace and Lorraine could be liquidated at the discretion of the victors. Finally, the allied Reparations Commission was empowered to demand payment of up to $5 billion, 'whether in gold, commodities, ships, securities or otherwise', *before* 1 May 1921, quite independently of the reparations settlement proper.

If anything, the peace treaty struck even severer blows at the iron and coal foundation of German industrial strength. Two territorial arrangements diminished German coal resources. The Saar basin, subject to a later plebiscite, was ceded to France. Upper Silesia, the source of twenty-three per cent of German hard coal, was transferred to Poland. Next, out of these substantially depleted resources, Germany was required to make good the estimated French war damage losses in her northern mines, and to supply France with seven million additional tons annually for ten years, Belgium with eight million tons for the same period, Italy with an initial 4·5 million tons, and Luxemburg with an amount equal to the pre-war annual consumption of German coal in that principality. In sum, the Allies demanded deliveries of something like twenty-five million tons of coal each year. If Germany honoured these commands, she would have about seventy-eight million tons left for her own use. But her pre-war coal consumption was on the order of 139 million tons annually. Thus, faithful fulfilment of the treaty's coal provisions implied something like the industrial crippling of Weimar Germany. And the outcome was the likelier because France recovered Lorraine, the source of seventy-four per cent of Germany's pre-war iron ore. After Versailles, Germany was compelled to buy that ore from France with French francs or gold – no easy job for a bankrupt nation.

Finally, a number of clauses were aimed at transport and tariffs. Although Keynes evaluated them as comparative pin-pricks, they included special tariff concessions to Poland, Luxemburg, Alsace and Lorraine, and restraints upon Germany's power to vary her own general tariff level. The German Government was thus deprived of the chance to control an influx of luxuries and semi-luxuries into a land which simply could not afford them.

To Keynes's way of thought, all these provisos were bad enough. But they were still little more than preliminaries to a massive reparations impost. On the reparations issue, public discussion and political argument had been unrealistic from the outset. Many newspapers and some politicians wanted the Germans to pay not only for the damage which they had inflicted on invaded French and Belgian territory but also for damage inflicted by land, sea or air – compensation, in other words, for shelling, bombing and submarine sinkings. England, after all, had not had the good fortune to be invaded by the Germans. This clamour broadened into something like a demand that the Germans assume the entire cost of the war to the winning side.

As Keynes reiterated, quite apart from issues of justice and the allocation of war guilt, Germany was quite incapable of even approximating such a scale of payment, particularly after her losses of territory and raw materials. In Keynes's opinion, it was fair enough and possible enough to ask the Germans to compensate the winners for the direct damage that their armies and navies had inflicted. This total was modest only by comparison with some of the wilder numbers advanced by the more belligerent. Keynes's own estimate, possibly a trifle on the low side, allocated $750 million to Belgium, something like $4 billion to France, $2·85 billion to Great Britain (largely in compensation for submarine sinkings), and $1·25 billion to the other Allies. This total of $8·85 billion was less than a quarter of the total which the makers of the Versailles Treaty imposed upon Germany.

How much could Germany actually pay? The answer, argued Keynes, depended on an analysis of how any nation meets its obligations to another country. A country could remit in gold and silver. It might transfer ships or foreign securities in its possession. In German circumstances, it might realize the value of property abroad. Finally, a debtor nation might depend upon the saleable value of the commodities and services which its merchants and exporters were able to persuade British, French and American importers to pay gold or foreign currency to obtain.

Of such assets and opportunities Germany was notably short in 1919 and 1920. Her total stock of gold was only $300 million, less than the minimum needed to assure the stability of her paper currency. The merchant marine left in German hands might have sold for another $600 million. Foreign securities were valued at somewhere between $500 million and $1·25 billion. Possibly another half-billion dollars' worth of German private property in Latin America and elsewhere might have been converted to reparations.

To have liquidated all of these assets would have further damaged German productive capabilities and raised only a small fraction of the necessary amount. Clearly, then, Germany could meet the bulk of her obligations only by running a highly favourable balance of payments, by selling substantially more to the rest of the world than she purchased from the rest of the world. Once more the outlook was extraordinarily bleak. In the last pre-war year, 1913, Germany's actual commodity balance had been negative. Like any advanced industrial nation, she had supplemented her income from sales of merchandise with interest and dividends on her investments and earnings from financial and mercantile services. Worse still, of her major commodity exports, several were intensely competitive with those of British manufacturers, who showed an understandable reluctance to yield their customers to the defeated enemy. The two nations were rivals in iron, machinery, coal and woollen and cotton goods. There was some room for manoeuvring in Germany's situation. As the loser, she could limit her imports and diminish the consumption of her own people. But major savings could be realized only if food and raw material imports were curtailed. Severe dietary restrictions could only lessen the efficiency of the working population and raise the costs of German manufactures. If raw materials were restricted, German factories would necessarily produce fewer finished products.

Taking all these factors into account, Keynes considered it likely that Germany could pay at the most something like half a billion dollars annually – the interest at five per cent on a capital sum of $10 billion, coincidentally close to his estimate of the direct damage inflicted by the German armed forces. Over this conclusion endless quarrels raged during 1920, but of Keynes's general finding that the demands upon Germany were excessive, events in the 1920s gave copious testimony. For the Germans did not pay. Probably they could not pay. In December, 1922, and January, 1923, Germany was declared in default. Before January's end French and Belgian troops initiated the occupation of the Ruhr. By September, as the sequel to German passive resistance, the mark had declined in value to virtual worthlessness. In the classic description of the period, housewives took baskets of money to market and returned with small loaves of bread.

At this juncture the United States stepped in. On 15 December 1923, President Coolidge convoked the Dawes Commission and charged its members to formulate a workable schedule of reparations payments. Issued on 9 April 1924, the Dawes Plan proposed to stabilize German currency by reorganizing the Reichsbank under Allied supervision. What was more important, it sharply revised the amount of annual reparations payments downwards, and sweetened the whole proposition for the sullen Germans by offering a foreign loan, more than half of it American.

This was not the end of revision. German dissatisfaction even with these manageable obligations resulted in a new series of negotiations, culminating in the Young Plan of 1929, which reduced German indebtedness to $8 billion payable over fifty-eight and a half years at 5·5 per cent interest. The cream of the historical jest remains to be identified. Throughout the decade of the 1920s, American leaders stoutly maintained that German reparations payable to the European Allies and European war debts owed to the United States were absolutely unrelated financial phenomena. Our position was clear though misguided: if the Germans defaulted, the French, the Italians and the English were not a jot less responsible for prompt payments to their American creditors. The classic expression of the sentiment is the Coolidge pronouncement, 'They hired the money, didn't they?'

What was really happening made a mockery of the legalities. Since neither Great Britain nor the United States displayed any wish to facilitate the sale of German exports within their borders, since the

Allies persistently demanded German payment of reparations, and since the Americans firmly insisted upon Allied repayment of war loans, only one resolution of these conflicting attitudes was even temporarily possible. One more series of loans might do the trick. So it was that the final element of the financial farce was supplied: Americans furnished funds to the Germans, who used the proceeds to meet their reparations payments to the European Allies, who in turn transferred what they received from the Germans to the Americans in fulfilment of their war loan obligations. As long as the United States was willing to make gold loans to Germany, therefore, the shaky structure of inter-Allied war debts and German reparations could stand. Just as soon as Americans tired of this expensive sport, the structure was certain to collapse. Thus, when American loans to Germany began to dry up during our own Great Depression, Germany promptly defaulted in 1931, and Herbert Hoover was compelled in June of the same year to declare a twelve-month moratorium on all government debts and reparations payments. By June, 1933, only Finland was continuing to make full payment of the interest on her debt to the United States.

History cannot be re-run. Hence the question remains arguable whether, if the Versailles Treaty had been as magnanimous from the outset as Keynes urged or as relentlessly Carthaginian as Clemenceau demanded in the name of France, Hitler might never have mobilized German resentment and come to power. It is as certain as these things can be that the Allies incurred all the enmity which a ruthless settlement might properly have earned them, but secured little credit from later revisions of the treaty. Germany was neither weakened enough by severity nor reconciled enough by generosity to become a peaceful member of European society.

Keynes was blamed, most notably by Etienne Mantoux,[8] for Allied weakness towards German belligerence during the 1920s and 1930s, and for the specific failure of the United States to join the League of Nations and associate herself with her former allies in the supervision of Germany. In part Mantoux's criticisms were justified. There is no doubt that Keynes's arguments were widely employed by the revisionists during the immediate post-war decade. It is probable that Keynes helped generate the guilt about Versailles which increased British hesitancy to deal with the Hitler government. On the narrower issue of American membership in the League of

Nations, Mantoux seems to have overstated his case. The fundamental reservations upon which Henry Cabot Lodge and the majority of the Senate Foreign Relations Committee insisted had been the fruits of deliberations which commenced in July, 1919. The reservations themselves were offered to the Senate in September and November, all of these dates preceding the publication of Keynes's book. Wilson's unsuccessful tour on behalf of the League also occurred before Keynes was heard.[9]

Keynes was now a private citizen. Indeed, the publication of *The Economic Consequences of the Peace* enraged official opinion quite sufficiently to make it certain that Keynes would be isolated from government affairs for a long time. It is a curious fact that although Keynes was to occupy a position of very considerable influence during the Second World War, at the Bretton Woods Conference in 1944, and in the post-war negotiation of the $3·75 billion American loan to Britain, he never again occupied a government post which carried with it administrative responsibilities as extensive as those entrusted to him as a young man by the British Treasury.

There was, of course, his fellowship waiting for him at King's College. To this he accordingly repaired. But Keynes was not suited by temperament, taste or income for the unrelieved academic life. About half of his week he typically spent in Cambridge. He did a certain amount of lecturing, never more than eight performances in an academic year; he supervised the weekly essays of the best young economists King's could supply; and he conducted the affairs of his Political Economy Club. This last, a somewhat alarming institution, was to play its part in the formation of the Keynesian school and the education of young Keynesians. Of the operations of this club, E. A. G. Robinson, a member who became a colleague of Keynes, gave this account:

It was essentially an undergraduate club. Dons, both economists and others who ... were interested in kindred problems might come. If Keynes had a visitor, more particularly from abroad, he would often bring him. But the papers in nine cases out of ten would be read by undergraduates or young researchers. ... To the undergraduate of the early twenties, I can say from experience, Keynes' club was fascinating but alarming. Fascinating because here one heard Keynes, a large part of the Faculty, and all the best of one's rivals discussing in realistic detail all the real and most urgent problems of the world. Alarming because if one read a paper one was likely to find one's undergraduate efforts (I speak from painful memory) being dissected by a visiting Mr Hawtrey, destroyed by the full power of Frank Ramsey's dialectical analysis,* and when one had maintained one's position to the best of one's ability for some three hours, Keynes would sum up in friendly but utterly devastating fashion – I learned a certain sympathy with the prisoners waiting for the judge's black cap. Alarming because if it was not one's turn to read the paper, one must draw a number from the hand of the Secretary, and take one's turn on the hearthrug to discuss a paper on a subject about which one might well feel an embarrassing ignorance in the presence of some of the most critical minds of Europe. But a wonderful training, because in Keynes' presence there were certain forms of nonsense that one did not enjoy perpetrating once, and remembered for life not to perpetrate a second time.[10]

Since King's College was the place above all others to learn economics, and Keynes was the man to teach the subject, the Club and even Keynes's half-time presence on the scene meant that Keynes influenced the prominent economists of the 1930s and 1940s as did no other Cambridge economist of his generation. Keynes could always be certain of an indulgent hearing for the most outrageous of his novelties from a group whose opinions came to count more and more in the world of economics.

As Robinson's reminiscence implies, Keynes's influence upon the young was by no means entirely a matter of personal amiability. That Keynes cherished his friends every testimony agrees. That he would take endless trouble to alleviate their personal, legal and financial problems many have recorded. That he could be the most charming of conversationalists none denied. Clive Bell was not alone in considering him the cleverest man he had ever met. But like any aristocrat, particularly of the Bloomsbury variety, he tended to separate his friends and his pupils sharply from the rest of the world. Pretension he abhorred, and if ever he 'could be surprisingly tolerant of honest stupidity',[11] the stupid needed to be unassuming and preferably young. Another former student of Keynes's in the 1920s compares the Keynes 'known to the general public chiefly as a merciless critic of the – only too plentiful – economic errors and follies of the financial and political leaders of the period' with the Keynes known to his pupils for a 'kindly restraint which was in marked contrast not

---

* R. G. Hawtrey's prestige as a student of finance was unrivalled during the 1920s. Ramsey's mathematical and philosophical brilliance became Cambridge legend. No severer judges were to be found.

only to the practice of other brilliant dons but also to the scathing savagery which he showed to similar failings on the part of leading figures'.[12]

During the 1920s Keynes was a part-time Londoner as well as a Cambridge don. In London he pursued quite successfully a series of financial speculations which placed him in a comfortable position. He accepted an increasing number of financial directorships and acquired a grasp of city of London practices which few theoretical economists command. He continued to see his Bloomsbury friends, although less frequently than in earlier years, and there was some apprehension in Bloomsbury that Maynard had been seduced by the attractions of the world of affairs from the single-minded pursuit of personal relations.

One new personal relationship of significance did alter Keynes's life. In 1921 Diaghilev opened a new season of ballet in London. London audiences, among them Keynes, flocked to the performances which were especially graced by the return to the company of Lydia Lopokova. Enchanted by ballet, Keynes was no less enchanted by the ballerina. It was a good deal to ask of a woman to give up a triumphal career and become an English wife, especially since she was married, though separated, at the time. Undeterred by such obstacles, Keynes courted his Lydia, introduced her to his Cambridge friends, overcame their doubts about the propriety of marrying a 'chorus girl', helped secure his prospective bride's divorce, and on 4 August 1925, solemnized their union at the St Pancras Central Registry Office. No less an authority than Mrs Alfred Marshall, the economist's widow, later termed the marriage 'the best thing Maynard ever did'.[13]

There was still another aspect to Keynes's crowded life. To his direct influence as an economic scholar and teacher he added a powerful journalistic pen. He wrote much for the English *Nation and the Athenaeum*, a journal of generally Liberal opinion, and when it merged with the somewhat similar *New Statesman* in 1931, Keynes went on the combined board of *The New Statesman and Nation*. Keynes had easy access to *The Times*, *The Guardian* and other periodicals favoured by the serious and the influential.

The character of Keynes's opinions is conveniently available for examination in one place. His 1931 *Essays in Persuasion* were culled almost entirely from articles and essays which Keynes composed for general audiences between 1919 and 1931. The five sections in which the volume is divided fairly represent the range of Keynes's interests as an economic commentator.

The opening group of five essays reiterated and amplified Keynes's earlier analysis of the reparations settlements. Although they added little to the full-dress argument of *The Economic Consequences of the Peace*, they had their influence on the successive revisions of the economic clauses of the Versailles Treaty.

More needs to be said about the discussion of inflation and deflation, which was the principal concern of the second group of essays. To begin with, despite his later reputation, Keynes was far from favouring inflation. No proponent of inflation was likely to say, as Keynes did, that 'Lenin was certainly right. There is no subtler, no surer means of overturning the existing basis of Society than to debauch the currency. The process engages all the hidden forces of economic law on the side of destruction, and does it in a manner which not one man in a million is able to diagnose.'[14]

Although he perceived the dangers of inflation, Keynes was still an economic expansionist. The other interesting feature of this section of his collection was the election manifesto which Keynes composed in May, 1929, for his old Liberal friend and enemy, Lloyd George. Lloyd George's key economic proposal was a development or public works programme to cost £100 million annually and to employ 500,000 men. With the knowledge of Keynes's reasoned theoretical position of seven years later, his earlier argument makes interesting reading. Essentially, it was an assault upon the Treasury position that 'Whatever might be the political or social advantages, very little additional employment can, in fact, and as a general rule, be created by State borrowing and State expenditure'.[15] It is a matter of record, as well as of wonder, that this peculiar doctrine, which postulated something like a fixed capital fund susceptible only of diversion and never of enlargement, dominated equally the policies of Conservative Chancellors of the Exchequer like Winston Churchill and Labour holders of the office like Philip Snowden. Indeed, the latter was perfectly capable of arguing that in time of 'grave industrial depression', expenditures had to be curtailed, not enlarged. His moral was identical with the most banal Conservative platitude: rigid economy was essential on pain of financial collapse. This was Herbert Hoover's view; it was equally the 1932 conviction of that Franklin Delano Roosevelt who virtuously attacked Hoover for his inadvertent budget deficits and cried, 'Let us have the courage to stop borrowing to meet continuing deficits. Stop the deficits.'[16]

In 1929 Keynes was not yet ready to mount a full-scale theoretical assault upon such foolishness, but he did make effective use of analogy and common sense. If, he argued, the Treasury's analysis were correct, then it 'must apply equally to a new work started by Morris or Courtaulds, to any new business entailing capital expenditures'.[17] But this was an opinion that nobody held, for nobody believed that additional *private* capital expenditure was simply a diversion from alternative uses and never an addition to output and employment. As Keynes put it, 'If it were announced that some of our leading captains of industry had decided to launch out boldly and were about to sink capital in new industrial plants to the tune, between them, of £100 million, we should expect to see a great improvement in employment. And, of course, we should be right.'[18] Hence somebody's reasoning must be awry. Didn't the capitalists divert funds from other productive enterprises just as surely as any expansionary programme initiated by a government? The Treasury view inescapably conflicted with common sense and common observation.

Even on its own premises, it was guilty of logical error. For one thing, the Treasury neglected to include in its calculations sources of finance which could readily expand total production and total employment. The savings now transferred to the unemployed simply to sustain them in unhappy idleness could as readily be used to 'equip the country'. Again, net foreign lending might be reduced and the funds thus released devoted to domestic expenditure. It all came down, maintained Keynes, to a 'broad, simple, and surely incontestable proposition. Whatever real difficulties there may be in the way of absorbing our unemployed labour in productive work, an inevitable diversion of resources from other forms of employment is not one of them.'[19]

In the same period, Keynes was accorded an unusual opportunity to advance the case for public works in an official capacity. In 1929 he was made a member of the Macmillan Committee on Finance and Industry. This blue-ribbon committee* was instructed 'to enquire into banking, finance and credit, paying regard to the

---

* Its members included labour leaders like Ernest Bevin, bankers like R. H. Brand, politicians like Reginald McKenna, bureaucrats like Gordon Ismay, and professors like T. E. Gregory.

factors both internal and international which govern their operation, and to make recommendations calculated to enable these agencies to promote the development of trade and commerce and the employment of labour.'[20] The hearings, which lasted into 1931, enabled Keynes to wring from Montagu Norman, the powerful governor of the Bank of England, the reluctant admission that unemployment was the likely consequence of the interest rate policies that the Bank of England considered it appropriate to follow. Here is a characteristic exchange:

KEYNES: So it is of the essence of the case that the Bank Rate should have an important effect; that when it is raised it should have an effect on the direction of unemployment. That is what you want. Am I right?
NORMAN: Yes, I should think it was. .... [21]

Keynes's own testimony before the Committee was generally judged a *tour de force*. In it he concentrated upon remedies for unemployment. At the centre of these remedies was the policy which later was called pump-priming, the notion that an injection of government investment will serve to stimulate private investment sufficiently to allow of a subsequent cessation of government emergency spending. On this point Keynes was more optimistic than he was to become:

Government expenditure will break the vicious circle. If you can do that for a couple of years, it will have the effect, if my diagnosis is right, of restoring business profits more nearly to normal, and if that can be achieved, then private enterprise will be revived. I believe you have first of all to do something to restore profits and then rely on private enterprise to carry the thing along.[22]

Keynes was not able to persuade his colleagues to endorse sentiments so heterodox, and in consequence the conclusions of the Macmillan Committee's *Report* were cautious and conventional, though within their limits sensible. Keynes felt able to sign the report, and attached to it an Addendum which he persuaded five of his colleagues, among them Ernest Bevin, to join him in signing. This highly unorthodox postscript opposed wage reductions as a cure of unemployment and proposed in their stead higher tariffs and enlarged government spending. Wisely, the heretics couched their novelties in decorous language:

45. For these reasons and also because relief would be given both to the Budget and to the balance of trade, it would seem that restrictions on im-

ports and aids to exports would run well in double harness with the other class of remedy which we next discuss, namely, schemes of capital development. For it is obvious that the whole of the resources required for capital development at home are necessarily found within the country, and as a result of our own efforts and sacrifices, except in so far as their effect is to diminish our net foreign surplus. . . . [23]

Within the *Essays in Persuasion*, the third section centred on Britain's return in 1925 to the gold standard under the auspices of Winston Churchill, at the time Conservative Chancellor of the Exchequer. 'The Economic Consequences of Mr Churchill', a scintillating piece of polemical writing, demonstrated to the writer's satisfaction at least that the government was making a serious mistake by returning to the gold standard at a dollar valuation of the pound which made British costs and prices too high for effective competition in international markets. The worst of the error, in Keynes's estimation, was the disruptive sequel which the poor initial decision entailed. The government tried to reduce wages and prices in order to make export industries competitive with their foreign rivals. The General Strike of 1926, the doldrums into which British foreign trade subsequently fell, and the high unemployment which marked the remainder of the decade are all testimonials to the acuteness of Keynes's analysis. Keynes's judgement of Churchill, as usual, concerned both personality and policy:

he [Churchill] was committing himself to force down money wages and all money values, without any idea how it was to be done. Why did he do such a silly thing?

Partly, perhaps, because he has no instinctive judgment to prevent him from making mistakes; partly because, lacking this instinctive judgment, he was deafened by the clamorous voices of conventional finance; and, most of all, because he was gravely misled by his experts. [24]

Which is to say that while Churchill was naïve and uneducated, the experts were well-informed and stupid.

The fourth section, in three notable essays, presented Keynes as a political observer. His 'A Short View of Russia', written in 1925 after he visited the country on his honeymoon trip, was undoubtedly wrong about the survival powers of Communist regimes, but it was unmistakably clear about Keynes's own reasons for detesting Marxist doctrine and the Russian manifestations of that doctrine:

How can I accept a doctrine which sets up as its bible, above and beyond criticism, an obsolete economic textbook which I know to be not only scientifically erroneous but without interest or application for the modern world? How can I adopt a creed which, preferring the mud to the fish, exalts the boorish proletariat above the bourgeois and the intelligentsia who, with whatever faults, are the quality in life and surely carry the seeds of all human advancement? Even if we need a religion, how can we find it in the rabid rubbish of the Red bookshops? It is hard for an educated, decent, intelligent son of Western Europe to find his ideals here, unless he has first suffered some strange and horrid process of conversion which has changed all his values.[25]

The economic Keynes had by no means swallowed up the Bloomsbury Keynes.

His 'The End of Laissez-Faire', written in 1926, attained at least equal celebrity. In this essay Keynes fell readily into a typical posture. He had, he proclaimed, no doctrinaire attachment to *laissez faire*, but he did have an anxious care for personal liberty. Therefore, he disliked

... doctrinaire State Socialism, not because it seeks to engage men's altruistic impulses in the service of Society, or because it takes away from man's natural liberty to make a million, or because it has courage for bold experiment. All these things I applaud. I criticise it because it misses the significance of what is actually happening; because it is, in fact, little better than a dusty survival of a plan to meet the problems of fifty years ago, based on a misunderstanding of what some one said a hundred years ago.[26]*

The proper approach for a libertarian and humanitarian was the discovery of ingenious ways of solving economic problems within the framework of liberty and within the institutions of market capitalism. The conclusion was true Keynes: 'The next step forward must come, not from political agitation or premature experiments, but from thought.'[27] Keynes's own thoughts ran in terms partly of new organization and partly of new policy. On the first score, he stated a belief that 'progress lies in the growth and the recognition of semi-autonomous bodies within the State – bodies whose criterion of action within their own field is solely the public good as they understand it'.[28]

Perhaps astonishingly, the institution that Keynes had particularly in mind as the agent of progress was large business corporations,

* The plan Keynes had in mind was the nationalization of basic industries, and the person misunderstood was, with some oddity of chronology, Karl Marx.

which, 'when they have reached a certain age and size ... approximate ... the status of public corporations rather than that of the individualistic private enterprise'.[29] Forecasting accurately the increasing separation of management and ownership in the giant corporation, Keynes thought that managers would come to esteem more highly 'the general stability and reputation of the institution' than 'the maximum of profit for the shareholders'.[30]

As far as public experiment was concerned, Keynes thought the three most promising fields were unemployment, savings and investment, and population policy. In 1926 Keynes was willing to settle for 'the deliberate control of the currency and of credit by a central institution ... and ... collection and dissemination on a great scale of data relating to the business situation'. Somewhat vaguely, he plumped for the solution of investment and savings disequilibriums by 'some co-ordinate act of intelligent judgment'.[31] Of one point he was certain: 'private judgment and private profits, as they are at present', could not do a job adequate for the needs of the community.[32] On population, Keynes was prepared to go no further than the statement that each country 'needs a considered national policy about what size of population, whether larger or smaller than at present or the same, is most expedient'. In the longer run, considerations of eugenics might become controlling: 'The time may arrive a little later when the community as a whole must pay attention to the innate quality as well as to the mere number of its future members.'[33]

In his personal politics, Keynes remained rebelliously uncommitted. In 'Am I a Liberal?', the text of an address that he delivered at the Liberal Summer School at Cambridge in 1925, he started with the question of how he could be a Conservative. Conservatives are dull and unexciting, they pursue 'no ideal', and they aspire to 'no intellectual standard'. What about the Labour Party? Keynes granted the party a superficial attraction. But in the end, membership was impossible for such as Keynes because the Labour Party was a 'class party, and the class is not my class'. As a realistic matter, Keynes continued, 'If I am going to pursue sectional interests at all, I shall pursue my own. When it comes to the class struggle as such, my local and personal patriotisms, like those of every one else, except certain unpleasant zealot ones, are attached to my own surroundings. I can be influenced by what seems to me to be Justice and good sense; but the *class* war will find me on the side of the educated *bourgeoisie*.'[34] Since the intellectual elements in the Labour Party were not likely ever to run the show, and the group would thus be led by the unintelligent, Keynes could not affiliate himself with it.

More by elimination than by positive choice, then, Keynes declared himself willing to be a Liberal, that is, if the Liberal Party could be turned into a 'party which shall be disinterested as between classes, and which shall be free in building the future both from the influences of Die-Hardism and from those of Catastrophism, which will spoil the construction of each of the others'.[35] The party of Keynes's aspiration would discard *laissez faire* and old-fashioned individualism. It would be pacifist, interventionist in economic affairs, and enlightened in its attitudes towards birth control, contraception, marriage and divorce. Keynes's comparative innocence of how the politics of a democratic community is actually conducted released his creative imagination but afforded little prospect of concrete results.

The final section of the *Essays in Persuasion*, 'The Future', contained an interesting essay composed in 1930 on the economic outlook two generations thence. Keynes adopted a cheerful view of the future and refused to be oppressed by the troubles of the present. 'Do not let us overestimate the importance of the economic problem,' he urged, 'or sacrifice to its supposed necessities other matters of greater and more permanent significance. It should be a matter for specialists – like dentistry.' Possibly displeasing both professions at a stroke, Keynes concluded, 'If economists could manage to get themselves thought of as humble, competent people on a level with dentists, that would be splendid'.[36]

Such, then, was the Keynes of the 1920s: slightly anarchist in character, aristocratic in his preferences, rational in his outlook, ingenious in his remedies, friend of no orthodoxy, foe of human stupidity in every form.

The last fifteen years of Keynes's life were associated with a great intellectual and a great political event. The first was *The General Theory of Employment, Interest and Money*, and the second was the Second World War and its immediate aftermath. The famous Keynes, the Keynes the public of England and the United States came to identify, was the Keynes who placed himself in the centre of the world stage between 1936 and 1946. On the threshold of Keynes's fame as a prophet of our time, it is convenient to pause and ask again what manner of man had emerged by the beginning of the 1930s from the moderately unconventional life and the exceptional intellectual performance of a fortunate Englishman.

Consider first the man's personal qualities. Every picture represents Keynes as ugly – from childhood to middle age. But those who knew him swore that the photographs lied. The face was so mobile, the smile so magnetic, the eyes so penetrating, and the voice so hypnotic that no one in Keynes's presence could think of him as a homely person. Although he was plain in appearance to the point of homeliness, nature had made the appropriate amends in other directions. For Keynes as a person was more than intellectually gifted. As a friend he was intensely loyal and capable of evoking the same sentiment from all who knew him well. No doubt his commitments to individuals had their intellectual sanction in the doctrines of G. E. Moore and the group judgements of Bloomsbury. But the attachments were also matters of emotion. The quality of the friendship which Keynes and his circle treasured set the opinions and the approval of private friends far above the applause of official opinion.

One friend recalls the occasion when Keynes invited two of his powerful associates in government to dinner and discovered inconveniently late that his Bloomsbury companions had drunk up the champagne he had planned to serve. Said the friend, 'He took it well enough. His sense of values appeared to be intact.'[37] It was Clive Bell once more who approvingly remembered that when Maynard and Lady Keynes came to visit the Bells just after his elevation to the peerage had become public. 'He was downright sheepish. "We have come to be laughed at", he said.'[38]

These were intimates, to be treasured above the pitiful remainder of the human race. But Keynes had an almost equally delicate sense of the wider fellowship of the talented, living and dead. This was the focus of his essay, 'The Great Villiers Connection', 'from whom', Keynes noted, 'are descended all the ambitious fascinators, with so much charm of countenance and voice and so hard a little nut somewhere inside, who were the favourites and mistresses of our monarchs in the seventeenth century and of the parliamentary democracy ever since'. The essay commenced as a review of a book on heredity, and speedily turned into a loving recital of the 'cousinship of Dryden, Swift and Horace Walpole', who themselves owned a common ancestor in John Dryden; of the great Verney connection; and of the lineage of the Macaulays, the Huxleys and the Churchills. 'This is,

A.K. – 3

indeed, the true blood-royal of England,' said Keynes.[39] Snobbery, no doubt, but snobbery of the least offensive variety, which treasures achievement rather than wealth or social position. As Schumpeter said of him, Keynes himself belonged in 'spiritual kinship with the Locke–Mill connection'[40] – a connection which has ever exalted close thought, admission to favour by merit alone, and genuine achievement.

Keynes's patriotism, which began with friendship and widened to his peers of all ages, applied more generally to England and Englishmen. Schumpeter's comment was fair: 'Keynes' advice was in the first instance always English advice, born of English problems even where addressed to other nations.'[41] Thus, Keynes readily shifted ground on tariffs in the Macmillan Committee *Report* and elsewhere out of a sober consideration of British interests. Not entirely consistently, he preferred these interests to a doctrine of free trade, which he continued to value highly on intellectual grounds.

Or there is the case of the four articles which he wrote in March, 1933, for *The Times*. In these articles Keynes was aiming consistently at one objective: a programme capable of lifting the world from depression. But he started with the condition of Britain and was led by his analysis of what *she* needed for recovery to advocating policies applicable to the remainder of the world. His sentiments were generous, and no doubt these policies would have benefited the countries sensible enough to apply them. Still, it all started with British needs and British circumstances.

Keynes was subject to one of patriotism's less pleasant corollaries, provincialism, or to use Schumpeter's word, 'insularity'. The quality is prominent in Keynes as an economist; he shared to the full the Cambridge tendency to regard economics as an English if not a Cambridge monopoly. It went beyond economics. By Clive Bell's austere standards, Keynes's taste in pictures and literature was both limited and poor. Bell cited with remembered horror Keynes's likening of David Low's cartoons to the work of the great French draughtsman Daumier. Even as a bibliophile of resource, Keynes concentrated on English editions. He seems to have been comfortable in no language other than his native tongue.

Keynes's loyalty extended to institutions as well as to persons. By all accounts he valued few honours as much as his election to the governing board of his old school, Eton. His handling of the finances of King's College after the First World War, initially as second bursar and later as first bursar, was a miracle of affectionate attention to the College which he cherished. As first bursar (from 1926) Keynes pursued so imaginative and fruitful an investment policy that some £30,000 of unrestricted funds which were available at the beginning of his tenure had grown to some £380,000 by the time of his death.[42] As treasurer of the Camargo Ballet Society, Keynes was able in 1932, not the most propitious of years, to unite its resources with the Vic–Wells Ballet and the Ballet Rambert. Of his efforts the critic Arnold Haskell wrote, 'I do not suggest that Mr J. M. Keynes is the new Diaghileff, he has other work which he might mistakenly regard as more important, but he has succeeded with tact and energy in centralising the available talent, a gigantic task; and to that extent the season is very much his.'[43] Still another felicitous invention of Keynes's was Cambridge's Arts Theatre and the attractive restaurant still associated with it.

In the glitter of Keynes's successes as an organizer of cultural and educational institutions, it is possible to forget that from the 1920s onwards he held important positions in organizations more suitable for an eminent economist. In 1921 he became chairman of the National Mutual Insurance Company. He was a director of the Independent Investment Company for a time and later of the Provincial Insurance Company. His touch was golden. In Robinson's words, 'About his flair for investment there can be no doubt. The prosperity of the National Mutual, of his College, of the Royal Economic Society, of his own finances, all bear ample witness.'[44]

Conceivably Keynes was the most versatile economist in England since the days of that seventeenth-century intellect of all work, Sir William Petty.* The variety was partly, like Petty's, a matter of occupational role. In his sixty-odd years of life, Keynes was a civil servant, government adviser, diplomat, journalist, book collector, farmer, editor, financier and promoter, as well as a teacher and economist. The man, like the boy, was never a dilettante. He was as professional in the supervision of his farm at Tilton as in the management of King's College finances. He took as many expert pains to get value in first editions as to speculate profitably in foreign currencies.

For Keynes versatility was also a principle and an outlook. The

---

* Petty was, among other things, an inventor, linguist, friend and student of Thomas Hobbes, sailor, professor of music, vice-principal of Brasenose College, Oxford; army doctor, experimental shipbuilder, Irish expert, writer and political economist.

myriad occupations were the outward sign of that steady and indes-
tructible Keynesian conviction that the human reason could successfully ameliorate the human condition. A struggling ballet like a
struggling nation required the thoughtful attention of an uncom-
partmentalized intellect. In the dark year 1933, Keynes gave characteristic expression to this passionate belief in rationality:

If our poverty were due to famine or earthquake or war – if we lacked
material things and the resources to produce them, we could not expect to
find the Means to Prosperity except in hard work, abstinence, and invention. In fact, our predicament is notoriously of another kind. It comes
from some failure in the immaterial devices of the mind, in the working of
the motives which should lead to the decisions and acts of will, necessary
to put in movement the resources and technical means we already have.
... Nothing is required and nothing will avail, except a little, a very little,
clear thinking.[45]

In other words the cure for irrational behaviour is – rational thought.
Perhaps it is not astonishing that Keynes, like Mill, Jevons and his
own father, was attracted to the problems of logic and probability.
At any rate Keynes produced his own *Treatise on Probability* as one
more token of the abiding taste of English economists for this style
of investigation.

The description offered thus far of Keynes's qualities appears to
define more the intellectual than the economist. Certainly Keynes
shared the intellectual's characteristic belief in the importance of
ideas. The last sentence of *The General Theory of Employment, Interest
and Money* is justly famous: 'But, soon or late, it is ideas, not vested
interest, which are dangerous for good or evil.'[46] He shared as well
the intellectual's enjoyment of sheer verbal virtuosity. In Keynes the
taste evidenced itself not only in the sensitive literary style of *The
Economic Consequences of the Peace*, the obituary article on Alfred
Marshall, the *Essays in Biography*, and much of the journalism, but
also as a delight in conversation upon almost any topic, whether or
not he was thoroughly briefed about the merits of the opposing
position. Needless to say this readiness of comment occasionally
irritated the critical, especially since Keynes as frequently as not
would advance his opponents' better arguments as his own the very
next day. If initially he argued for victory, in the end he argued for
truth.

It is possible to be an intellectual without being an economist and at least equally possible to be an economist without being an intellectual. Subsequent chapters will assess Keynes's virtues as an economist. Suffice it to say here that his qualities as an intellectual did not desert him when he wrote economics. In fact they were joined to several formidable specialized talents. One was a complete command of some of the branches of economic theory, above all monetary doctrine and the principles of international trade. Another was an extraordinary grasp of the facts of the financial market. And a third was a superlative skill in exposition.

A fourth gift was possibly the most important of all. This was an exceptional ingenuity in the formulation of workable schemes and challenging expedients. One of the most consistent objects of Keynes's interest as an economist was currency reform. From his pioneer investigation of India's gold exchange standard just before the First World War, through his recommendations of the 1920s in *A Tract on Monetary Reform* and elsewhere for greater flexibility in administering the gold standard and his international currency schemes of the 1930s in *The Means to Prosperity*, to his plans for the International Monetary Fund at the Bretton Woods Conference in 1944, Keynes devoted himself to the creation of an international currency standard which would protect the civilized world from inflation at a price lower than internal economic sluggishness and high unemployment. If at times Keynes appeared hostile to the gold standard and on other occasions sympathetic to its continued life, the apparent inconsistency was not in Keynes's objectives. He was willing always to employ the most feasible means to a desirable objective. Since inconsistency has often been a charge levied against Keynes, it is worth quoting Robinson's answer:

it is difficult not to be impressed by the consistency of his main strategic objectives: the full employment of resources; the achievement of balances of payments for all countries by methods that would not be inconsistent with full employment; as a means to this, a system of exchange rates that would combine the short-term virtues of fixity and predictability with the long-term virtues of flexibility; and, as a means to full employment, low interest rates. . . . A careful study of Keynes will, I believe, show him to have been remarkably consistent in his strategic objectives, but extraordinarily fertile in tactical proposals for achieving them.[47]

In the best sense, he possessed a full measure of the intellectual's confidence in his capacity to produce alternative ideas. The confidence lies behind the succession of Keynes plans which appeared during the 1920s and 1930s. Keynes had solutions for domestic unemployment, reparations, gold, the financial system, the state of the exchanges and the level of tariffs. He could as easily advance a highly technical scheme to diminish gold shipments as a readily comprehensible device to pay for the Second World War.

Even his major intellectual difficulty was a defect of a virtue – his exaggerated confidence in the power of reason, his excessive faith in the willingness and the capacity of human beings to hearken to logic. It was always exceedingly difficult for Keynes to estimate justly the power of prejudice, emotion, malice and mental laziness in human affairs. Such a man was likely to be astonished at the ability of his fellows to produce what he hated most, 'muddle'. Such a man was unlikely, while he drew breath, to flag in his efforts to substitute beautiful clarity for ugly confusion.

SOURCE NOTES TO CHAPTER 2

1. E. A. G. Robinson, 'John Maynard Keynes', in Robert Lekachman (ed.), *Keynes's General Theory: Reports of Three Decades* (New York: St Martin's, 1964; London: Macmillan).

2. Sir Roy Harrod, *The Life of John Maynard Keynes* (London: Macmillan, 1951).

3. J. M. Keynes, *The Economic Consequences of the Peace* (London: Macmillan, 1919).

4. Ibid.

5. Ibid.

6. Quoted in Robinson, op. cit.

7. J. A. Schumpeter, *Ten Great Economists from Marx to Keynes* (London: Allen & Unwin, 1952).

8. See P. Mantoux, *The Carthaginian Peace, or the Economic Consequences of Mr Keynes* (New York: Scribner, 1952).

9. On points of chronology, see Robinson, op. cit.

10. Ibid.

11. Ibid.

12. George Wansbrough, quoted in ibid.

13. Quoted in Harrod, op. cit.

14. J. M. Keynes, *Essays in Persuasion* (London: Macmillan, 1931).

15. Ibid.

16. The opening pages of William E. Leuchtenburg, *Franklin D. Roosevelt and the New Deal, 1932–1940* (New York: Harper & Row, 1963).

17. Keynes, *Essays in Persuasion*.

18. Ibid.

19. Ibid.

20. Committee on Finance and Industry, *Report* (London: H.M.S.O., 1931), June 1931, Cmd 3897.

21. Committee on Finance and Industry, *Minutes of Evidence* (London: H.M.S.O., 1931) I, 216; quoted in Harrod, op. cit.

22. From Committee on Finance and Industry, *Report*, I, 419; quoted in Harrod, op. cit.

23. Committee on Finance and Industry, *Report*, I, 421, quoted in ibid.

24. Keynes, *Essays in Persuasion*.

25. Ibid.

26. Ibid.

27. Ibid.

28. Ibid.

29. Ibid.

30. Ibid.

31. Ibid.

32. Ibid.

33. Ibid.

34. Ibid.

35. Ibid.

36. Ibid.

37. Clive Bell, *Old Friends* (London: Chatto & Windus, 1956).

38. Ibid.

39. J. M. Keynes, *Essays in Biography* (London: Macmillan, 1933).

40. Schumpeter, op. cit.

41. Ibid.

42. See Harrod, op. cit.

43. Quoted in Robinson, op. cit.

44. Ibid.

45. J. M. Keynes, *The Means to Prosperity* (London: Macmillan, 1933).

46. J. M. Keynes, *The General Theory of Employment, Interest and Money* (London: Macmillan, 1936).

47. Robinson, op. cit.

Friends and enemies of Keynesian economics tend to agree that *The General Theory of Employment, Interest and Money* is one of a very small number of really influential twentieth-century books. What makes a book important? In economics it is reasonable to term a book truly significant if after its appearance, economists think differently, students are presented with a fresh set of textbooks, politicians hear unexpected voices, and, perhaps most important of all, the public at large comes to expect a different set of government policies and a transformed attitude towards the exigencies of personal economic existence – employment, social security, education and health care. Of most books written by economists it can be said that the world would have been no different if their authors had refrained from swelling the copyright tide. A book that makes a difference is a rare phenomenon indeed. Our perception of ourselves was permanently altered by Sigmund Freud's *Interpretation of Dreams*. The history of race relations in the United States was influenced by Gunnar Myrdal's *An American Dilemma*.

The proposition that *The General Theory* belongs in such company is translatable into another claim: that Keynes rewrote the content of economics and transformed its vocabulary. It is hard to exaggerate the liberating impact of his achievement upon public policy. Keynes informed the world that fatalism towards economic depression, mass unemployment and idle factories was wrong. He demonstrated that intelligent action, deploying known tools of analysis in unconfined ways, was perfectly capable of marrying once again human needs and human resources. He did one thing more: he formulated the theory which justified his recommendations.

Once Keynes had spoken, the cynical citizen no longer had to expect of distinguished economists analyses as little addressed to current necessity as A. C. Pigou's remarks, in the middle of the Great Depression, to the Macmillan Committee. When he was asked to explain why unemployment was so high, Cambridge's distinguished professor of political economy could extend no aid more useful to his fellow citizens than a diagnosis that 'the relative demand for labour in different occupations has altered, and the transfers of labour appropriate to those alterations have not taken place'. There was little hint in Pigou's remarks of any novel solution. If unemployment existed the efficacious remedies were in the hands of ordinary workers and their trade unions. All that workers needed to do was shift jobs and locations judiciously and accept lower wages if necessary, and unemployment would disappear. The point was made explicitly in the following dialogue:

CHAIRMAN: Would you necessarily create vacancies ... by the reduction of wages?
PIGOU: I think you would to some extent.
CHAIRMAN: If wage rates were reduced, you think there would be an increased demand for labour?
PIGOU: Then, I think there would be an increased demand for labour.[1]

Pigou's remarks were not those of a reactionary. Indeed, his general preferences were egalitarian rather than elitist. Nevertheless, his understanding of economic theory assured him that even in a deep depression some industries would hire more men and women, and *no industries* would employ fewer men and women, if only real wages were reduced. Such was the theory. It was cold comfort to workers who in the real world were willing enough to accept jobs at practically any wages higher than zero.

Pigou represented sound economic opinion. Even D. H. Robertson, who, as it will appear later, saw deeply into the savings and investment mechanism, allied himself in the end with his friend and senior colleague. Here is a sample of his testimony to the same committee:

CHAIRMAN: Do I understand your view is that wages in this country are at present in excess of the economic value of the work?
ROBERTSON: Of what the economic value of the work would be if there were full employment.[2]

Thus, once more a leader of his profession committed himself to the conclusion that the route to full employment in 1939 ran through a series of wage reductions terminating in a lower average level of wages.

As for 'practical' men, it is necessary to recall only the views of their dean, Sir Montagu Norman, governor of the Bank of England and chief manipulator of its bank rate. In 1930, as many times earlier, it was possible for him to say that raising the bank rate was beneficial to the nation, for 'I think that the disadvantages to the internal position are relatively small compared with the advantages to the external position'. When he was asked quite sensibly how industry and ordinary workers at home benefited from the maintenance of the 'external position', Sir Montagu's answer, while undeniably patriotic, was hardly explanatory: 'This is a very technical question which is not easy to explain, but the whole international position has preserved for us in this country the wonderful position which we have inherited, which was for a while thought perhaps to be in jeopardy, which to a large extent, though not the full extent, has been re-established.'[3]

Small wonder that Ernest Bevin, no economist but a trade-union leader close to the situation of his constituents, was moved to ask Sir Montagu whether just possibly financial policy as managed by the Bank of England might have something to do with unemployment. But he got precious little in the way of admission from the imperturbable banker. In view of England's economic situation, one might justly have joined Bevin in asking just what had been 're-established'.

As a member of the Committee, Keynes himself had to work very hard to wring from Norman the admission that the bank rate had significant effects upon domestic employment. He was unable to shake another expression of the conventional wisdom of the period, this one from Sir Richard Hopkins, a Treasury official, who, in the presence of mountains of unused resources, still held firmly to the conclusion that state-supported schemes of capital development must 'make a hole in the capital which is available for the purposes of the community'.[4]

Such was the 'practical' wisdom of the erudite and the powerful in the desperate decade of the 1930s. Right or wrong, entrenched opinion is no more readily altered than vested interests are diverted from their objectives. What this chapter endeavours to do is explain how Keynes fused economic events and economic analysis into a new doctrine which ultimately produced a partial persuasion of vested interests and a nearly complete conversion of educated opinion.

For Englishmen the First World War was a shattering experience, not alone because of the brutal casualties suffered (by comparison the Second World War was an 'easy' war) and not even because of the decline in England's world position which victory brought in its train. Worst of all, the war put in question the old certainties of the pre-war era. Peace, progress, a stable social order: these could never again appear so feasible as they did in the England of the prosperous between 1870 and 1914. It was the precariousness of this new and deteriorated world which Keynes caught in the opening pages of *The Economic Consequences of the Peace*. In these pages he did more; he suggested that the apparently stable pre-war world was itself an unstable compound of good luck, sound arrangement and accidental deception. Before the war Europe prospered because a very complex division of labour and the delicate mechanism of the international gold standard just sufficed in a peaceful universe to permit modestly growing prosperity. Even at that, class relationships were tense and uncertain. As Keynes described pre-war Europe:

The new rich of the nineteenth century were not brought up to large expenditures, and preferred the power which investment gave them to the pleasures of indiscriminate consumption. In fact, it was precisely the *inequality* of the distribution of wealth which made possible those vast accumulations of fixed wealth and of capital improvements which distinguished that age from all others. Herein lay, in fact, the main justification of the Capitalist System. If the rich had spent their new wealth on their own enjoyment, the world would long ago have found such a regime intolerable. But like bees they saved and accumulated, not less to the advantage of the whole community because they themselves held narrower ends in prospect.[5]

Thus, even before 1914 the situation of capitalism was unstable, for social harmony demanded concord between economic classes whose interests were in reality opposed. A trifle more belligerence or a little more knowledge on the part of the labour unions and their leaders, a slight relaxation of puritanism on the side of the capitalists, and the whole uneasy arrangement would have collapsed. Even if war had not intervened, the world of 1870–1914 could not have persisted unaltered.

But if European economic relationships were so fragile even before 1914, what ought to be said of them after four years of senseless consumption of human life and material treasure? By rearranging frontiers and impoverishing the losing Central Powers, the Versailles

Treaty badly upset the pre-war division of labour among the major trading countries. The intricate network of Allied war debts and German reparations placed an intolerable strain upon the international gold standard. In some countries the threat and in others the actuality of inflation assaulted the foundations of thrift and violated the tacit treaties between workers and capitalists. If ever it was plain that capitalism, unguided and unsupported by intelligent government action, must founder, it was plain to Keynes at least in the 1920s.

These reflections of Keynes's had their importance in his later thought. Insofar as *The General Theory* is to be interpreted as giving *càrte blanche* to intelligent government action, the roots of *The General Theory*'s position can be identified in this 1920 polemic against the stupidity of the politicians and the wickedness of the treaty of peace. It did not take a worldwide depression to convince Keynes that capitalism contained strong tendencies towards instability.

Keynes's next book expanded his recommendations for improved financial policy. His *Tract on Monetary Reform*, published in 1923 and dedicated 'humbly and without permission to the Governors and Court of the Bank of England, who now and for the future have a much more difficult and anxious task entrusted to them than in former days',[6] fairly represented Keynes's willingness to innovate – to evaluate anew arrangements and policies which had outlived their time. The *Tract* was a specialized work, designed primarily for other economists. In it Keynes started by professing himself willing to leave 'Saving to the private investor' and 'Production ... to the business man'. The difficulty was that neither could operate efficiently 'if the money, which they assume as a stable measuring-rod, is undependable'. In fact, continued Keynes, 'Unemployment, the precarious life of the worker, the disappointment of expectation, the sudden loss of savings, the excessive windfalls to individuals, the speculator, the profiteer – all proceed, in large measure, from the instability of the standard of value'.[7]

If ever the charge was justified, the allegation that Keynes was a congenital inflationist unfairly describes the Keynes of the *Tract*. From his sketch of the menace of inflation, Keynes inferred a moral. The lesson was this – preservation of nineteenth-century economic values was utterly inconsistent with happy-go-lucky monetary policy:

it is not safe or fair to combine the social organisation developed during the nineteenth century (and still retained) with a *laisser-faire* policy towards the value of money. It is not true that our former arrangements worked well. If we are to continue to draw the voluntary savings of the community into 'investments', we must make it a prime object of deliberate State policy that the standard of value, in terms of which they are expressed, should be kept stable; adjusting in other ways ... the redistribution of national wealth, if in course of time, the laws of inheritance and the rate of accumulation have drained too great a proportion of the income of the active classes into the spending control of the inactive.[8]

But even in this context Keynes identified evils worse than unstable currency units, undesirable as these might be. Thus, although 'inflation is unjust and deflation is inexpedient', still 'deflation is, if we rule out exaggerated inflations such as that of Germany, the worse; because it is worse, in an impoverished world, to provoke unemployment than to disappoint the *rentier*'.[9]

In contrast with *The Economic Consequences of the Peace*, the tone of the *Tract* was quiet and unpolemical. All the same the final sixty-five pages consisted in a severe assault on a venerable icon, the gold standard itself. At the very time when England was about to return to gold, Keynes's position was sufficiently bold. In part Keynes was rebelling against the comfortable position of economists that appropriate adjustments would follow, in time, after the restoration of gold to its sovereign position. The trouble was this: '*In the long run* we are all dead. Economists set themselves too easy, too useless a task if in tempestuous seasons they can only tell us that when the storm is long past the ocean is flat again.'[10] The first sentence has entered the English language as a cogent expression of an attitude towards economic policy.

Intellectually, Keynes's case against the gold standard focused on the differences between the nineteenth and the twentieth centuries. It was no longer plausible to expect the gold standard to produce both a stable relationship between the pound sterling and gold and a firm, unchanging level of domestic prices. The largest of the new elements in the economic equation was the post-First World War tendency of the United States to absorb gold. Hence what was emerging was essentially a dollar standard, managed by the Federal Reserve authorities. In Keynes's words,

gold now stands at an 'artificial' value, the future course of which almost entirely depends on the policy of the Federal Reserve Board of the United

States. The value of gold is no longer the resultant of the chance gifts of Nature and the judgment of numerous authorities and individuals acting independently. Even if other countries gradually return to a gold basis, the position will not be greatly changed. . . . The actual value of gold will depend, therefore, on the policy of three or four of the most powerful Central Banks, whether they act independently or in unison.[11]

In the circumstances, a realistic English policy should 'allow gold back only as a constitutional monarch, shorn of his ancient despotic powers and compelled to accept the advice of a Parliament of Banks'.[12] Best of all, in Keynes's judgement, would have been a continuation of an openly managed system of currency. But if this was politically impossible, then a much modified gold standard was preferable to the old pre-war metal tyranny.

As always Keynes's advocacy was based upon an attachment to English interests and a conviction that these were best pursued by intelligent public control rather than with a doctrinaire reliance upon blind market forces. Thus, faced with an unavoidable choice between stabilizing the international value of the pound sterling and maintaining the level of domestic prices, he opted unhesitatingly for the second possibility. To Keynes, if not to the English Government, it was plain that the pains of deflation were too severe and the penalty inflicted upon active members of the community too large to permit of any other choice. Keynes's detailed recommendations for the domestication of the gold standard are now primarily of archaeological interest. What was striking once again was Keynes's cool willingness to act the iconoclast. Commented Harrod, 'People were profoundly shocked at the idea of abandoning the sheet anchor of stability constituted by the Gold Standard'.[13]

Once more Keynes had taken the unpopular view. It is time, however, to make a reservation. Although Keynes expressed minority opinions on such public issues as reparations, European reconstruction and currency, he still evinced little disposition to extend his passion for novelty to the Cambridge economic theory which he had learned and which he taught in turn to new generations of Cambridge pupils. Indeed, among economists the reputation of the *Tract* was highest for its subtle exposition of Cambridge monetary theory. One of Keynes's most eminent students of the mid-1920s, Professor E. A. G. Robinson, has observed that 'If Maynard Keynes had died in 1925 it would have been difficult for those who knew intimately the power and the originality of his mind to have convinced those who had never known him of the full measure of Keynes' ability'.[14] His admiring students simply judged that he applied the economics of Alfred Marshall with unusual cogency to the problems of the day. Evidently this was Keynes's opinion as well, for in the 1922 general introduction to the Cambridge Economics Handbooks, he had this to say about the condition of economic theory:

Before Adam Smith this apparatus of thought scarcely existed. Between his time and this it has been greatly enlarged and improved. Nor is there any branch of knowledge in the formation of which Englishmen can claim a more predominant part. It is not complete yet, but important improvements in its elements are becoming rare. The main task of the professional economist now consists, either in obtaining a wide knowledge of *relevant* facts and exercising skill in the application of economic principles to them or in expounding the elements of his method in a lucid, accurate, and illuminating way, so that, through his instruction, the number of those who can think for themselves may be increased.[15]

In economics such gloomy forecasts are dangerous. In 1848 J. S. Mill alleged that the theory of value was complete. In a generation the theory he had in mind was utterly displaced.

Indeed, at the very time that Keynes was expressing such unusually conventional sentiments, a new revelation was near at hand. Right in Cambridge, Keynes's valued colleague and friend, D. H. Robertson, was in the process of continuing and clarifying a train of thought which proved critically important to Keynes. Both students of Marshall and Pigou, Keynes and Robertson influenced each other in ways which enhanced the contribution of each. Robertson's austerely titled *Banking Policy and the Price Level*, his major contribution to economic analysis, focused upon a relationship between savings and investment which he had fully discussed with Keynes. Robertson's own graceful comments make the relationship clear:

I have had many discussions with Mr J. M. Keynes on the subject matter of Chapter V and VI, and have rewritten them so drastically at his suggestion, that I think neither of us now knows how much of the ideas contained is his and how much is mine. I should like to, but cannot, find a form of words which would adequately express my debt without seeming to commit him to opinions which he does not hold.[16]

In the middle of the 1920s, Keynes and Robertson were in apparent agreement upon a central issue which derived from Robertson's interest in fluctuations of output and prices. A business-cycle theorist of note, Robertson sought to grasp the monetary mechanisms which created ups and downs in economic activity. More and more he identified their essence in the savings–investment nexus. Robertson's terminology was intricate, and his argument was both complex and excessively compressed. Nevertheless, the drift of his reasoning was not hard to follow. It was a demonstration that the savings which the community voluntarily makes need not be applied by members of the community to new investment, nor need the excess savings necessarily result in increased personal consumption. Commonplace as these statements might appear, they were directly connected with the great revelation of Keynesian economics – the possibility, even the probability, that automatic mechanisms will not produce full employment, and that therefore conscious public intervention is necessary.

Robertson had broken with the old nineteenth-century generalization, Say's Law,* which alleged that increases in output (or supply) automatically generate matching increases in demand. The catchword phrase 'Supply creates its own demand' has had a long history. In twentieth-century formulations, Say's Law relied heavily upon adjustments in interest rates to produce equilibrium. Thus, if . the demand for savings by investors was vigorous, then interest rates rose, investment expanded and personal consumption declined. But if demand was languid, then savers, deprived of interest rate incentives to save, increased consumption and investment declined. By implication the argument held that upward or downward adjustments of interest rates simply shifted the distribution of total output between investment and consumption. In one fashion or another, all incomes were spent and all resources were used. If full employment did not actually characterize the economy, then the trouble was accident, monopoly interferences by business or by labour unions, immobilities of labour or capital, or inappropriate government policies.

Robertson's complicated definitions of savings and investment were analytical attempts to distinguish the situations in which new savings really were matched by new investments from other situations in which new savings resulted in either smaller or zero investment. Keynes's later emphasis upon the possibility of oversaving as a phenomenon adverse to employment and output was implicit in Robertson's apparatus.

* Named after the French economist and popularizer of Adam Smith, Jean-Baptiste Say.

If oversaving actually occurred, one remedy was public works. For his part Robertson remained a Marshallian. Although he supported public works at least as early as did Keynes, he was unwilling to cast aside the Marshallian stress upon the importance of individual prices and the central relation between wage rates and total employment. Later, sadly, Robertson and Keynes were to separate personally and professionally over the appropriate application of the insight which they shared.

Public works were not a novel proposal. Lloyd George in 1924 preached public works as the remedy for unemployment to a national audience which ignored his message. What was important in Robertson's analysis was the giant step taken towards the full-dress demonstration in *The General Theory* that economic analysis, properly understood, reinforced the common sense of the alert politician in demanding that the community undertake substantial private investment in circumstances where private investment manifestly was failing to do its job. That politicians felt the truth before economists proved it was not unique in the history of political economy. Between them Robertson and Keynes finally brought their profession up to the level of political instinct.

But the job lacked still a decade for its completion. Keynes's theoretical travels are marked by two additional milestones, his *Treatise on Money* and his pamphlet *The Means to Prosperity*. The *Treatise on Money* appeared, both substantial volumes of it, in 1930. Keynes's first major theoretical work in some five years, it was coloured equally by its author's practical involvement with Liberal Party politics and programmes and by his continuing observation of continuing English difficulties with the gold standard, high unemployment and public works remedies. An ambitious work, the *Treatise* was Keynes's bid for a central place among contemporary economics theorists. As the title implied, the two volumes treated many topics: banking, currency, index numbers, the mechanism of international exchange and the operations of the Bank of England. Fascinating historical sections traced and compared monetary disturbances of various kinds. The novel and provocative notion of profit inflation as an explanation of many historical economic booms was advanced. The effects of Spanish treasure and the course of the American boom of the 1920s were analysed in this context.

A great deal in these volumes is of permanent interest, and more still is pertinent to the evolution of Keynes's thought. But what is especially relevant to the doctrines of *The General Theory* is Keynes's discussion of savings and investment and the consequences of discrepancies between the two. He began with an appropriate acknowledgement to D. H. Robertson: 'so far as I am concerned – and I think the same is true of most other economists of the English-speaking world – my indebtedness for clues which have set my mind working in the right direction is to Mr D. H. Robertson's *Banking Policy and the Price Level* published in 1924'.[17] In truth much of Keynes's exposition took shape either in Robertson's terminology or in carefully explained departures from that terminology. 'Abortive saving' and 'abortive investment' were borrowed directly.

The central point was the same for both writers: the unequivocal conviction that saving and investment need not be equal. As Keynes put it, 'It might be supposed – and has frequently been supposed – that the amount of investment is necessarily equal to the amount of saving. But reflection will show that this is not the case.'[18] And if investment does *not* in fact increase as much as saving, then 'in Mr Robertson's language the saving has been "abortive". There is no increase of wealth in any shape or form corresponding to the increase of saving.'[19]

The point could scarcely have been either simpler or more important to the future of viable economic policy. It was this: savings were accumulated by one group of individuals while investments were made by another group entirely. Nowhere was there an automatic mechanism which rendered it inevitable that the savings which one group made were matched by the investments involuntarily undertaken by the other group. If during depressions savings exceeded investments, then the savings simply represented potential production which never materialized, goods which emerged neither as consumption nor as investment. Although only in *The General Theory* was Keynes able to explain plausibly where the unused savings 'went', he did advance sufficiently far even in the *Treatise* to cast doubt on the traditional confidence of economists that the interest rate mechanism was adequate to convert savings into investments or return them to consumption. The unpleasant third possibility was that savings might simply be wasted.

From the possibility flowed a momentous consequence. If savings might be wasted, then the conventional virtue of thrift lost much of its appeal. In circumstances where savings were excessive, it followed that thrift was a social sin. Keynes's conclusions in the

Treatise amounted to this: when employment is full and resources are completely engaged, and especially when inflation threatens, then indeed thrift is a virtue. But in any slack economy, further savings intensify the difficulty. Successful alleviation of the economy's condition demanded either increased investment or diminished saving.

Although these conclusions forecast those of *The General Theory*, Keynes's argument failed to evoke complete conviction among his peers. For one thing his language was not entirely consistent. He appeared to relapse into the old error when he alleged that 'an act of saving by an individual may result either in increased investment or in increased consumption by the individuals who make up the rest of the community'.[20] Although in the context Keynes's intention was simply to reiterate the belief that an increase of saving failed to guarantee an increase of investment, his choice of words masked the more important conclusion that saving might actually reduce total output, not simply alter its distribution between consumption and investment.

Such lapses aside, the Keynes of the *Treatise* taught another essential lesson: that investment was more important than saving, and that excessive saving might even hinder further investment by depressing the prospect for the sale of the commodities which the new investment generated. The following long passage, in its characteristic preference for the activity of the entrepreneur over the passivity of the rentier, sets the priorities straight:

It has been usual to think of the accumulated wealth of the world as having been painfully built up out of that voluntary abstinence of individuals from the immediate enjoyment of consumption which we call Thrift. But it should be obvious that mere abstinence is not enough by itself to build cities or drain fens. The abstinence of individuals need not increase accumulated wealth; — it may serve instead to increase the current consumption of other individuals. Thus the thrift of a man may lead either to an increase of capital-wealth or to consumers getting better value for their money. There is no telling which, until we have examined another economic factor.

Namely, Enterprise. It is Enterprise which builds and improves the world's possessions. Now, just as the fruits of Thrift may go to provide either capital accumulation or an enhanced value of money-income for the consumer, so the outgoings of Enterprise may be found either out of Thrift or at the expense of the average consumer. Worse still; — not only may Thrift exist without Enterprise, but as soon as Thrift gets ahead of Enterprise, it positively discourages the recovery of Enterprise and sets up a vicious circle by its adverse effects on profits. If Enterprise is afoot, wealth accumulates whatever may be happening to Thrift; and if Enterprise is asleep, wealth decays whatever Thrift may be doing.[21]

This is still not yet the Keynes of *The General Theory.*

The Keynes to come started from the assumption of unused resources and idle men, fixed his eye singly on income and employment, practically ignored price levels, looked fixedly only at deflation, and assumed without reservation that increases in investment will create the enlarged incomes out of which matching savings will be forthcoming.

Still, the distance yet to be traversed was shortening. The six-year trip between the *Treatise* and *The General Theory* was speeded by the appearance of another important intellectual helper. This was R. F. Kahn, one of the young and brilliant group who surrounded Keynes at King's College. In 1931 Kahn published an article destined for fame in the leading technical periodical, *The Economic Journal.*[22] In this brilliant article Kahn defined the concept of the multiplier – the relationship between a change in investment and the alteration in the size of national income which that change caused. The concept occupied a place of honour in *The General Theory.* However, even before 1936, Kahn's multiplier served to give Keynes the analytical notion which he needed in order to press home his case for British deficit financing. For even though Keynes had made this case frequently enough in his journalistic essays* and in his addendum to the Macmillan Committee's *Report,* convincing proof on the highest analytical level was still missing.

Keynes's first published use of Kahn's multiplier occurred in his 1933 *Means to Prosperity,* an expansion of four articles which *The Times* had printed in March of that same year. What, Keynes asked his readers, was the multiplier? Imagine, he suggested, that the government spent £500 extra and that this sum sufficed to afford employment for one man for one year in the construction of public works. Was this the end of the beneficial impact of extra government expenditure? By no means. The key passage in which Keynes explained just how much additional employment might be anticipated beyond this primary benefit went like this: 'if the new ex-

---

* See especially *Can Lloyd George Do It?* written with H. D. Henderson and reprinted in *Essays in Persuasion.* The answer was yes, but the voters could not be persuaded to install their one-time favourite in office for one more tour of duty.

penditure is additional and not merely in substitution for other expenditure, the increase of employment does not stop there. The additional wages and other incomes paid out are spent on additional purchases, which in turn lead to further employment. . . . '[23] More yet could be expected: 'The newly employed who supply the increased purchases of those employed on the new capital works will, in their turn, spend more, thus adding to the employment of others; and so on.'[24]

Did Keynes stand in danger of proving too much, of suggesting that if only somebody spent an additional pound on public works, the pound would be spent and respent forever and the increase in employment and income hence become infinite? Kahn and Keynes had the answer to the possible objection – the notion of 'leakage':

at each stage there is a certain proportion of leakage. At each stage a certain proportion of the increased income is not passed on in increased employment. Some part will be saved by the recipients; some part raises prices and so diminishes consumption elsewhere, except in so far as producers spend their increased profits; some part will be spent on imports; some part is merely a substitution for expenditure previously made out of the dole or private charity or personal savings; and some part may reach the Exchequer without relieving the taxpayer to an equal extent. Thus in order to sum the net effect on employment of the series of repercussions, it is necessary to make reasonable assumptions as to the proportion lost in each of these ways.[25]

Despite the guesswork implicit in the working out of the mechanism, the promise was plausible enough. Public works spending by government, financed by loans, was highly likely to increase employment and income by some multiple of the amounts so expended. How large was it reasonable to expect the real value of this multiplier to be? Well, answered Keynes, this depended on the size of the 'margin of unemployed resources'. If this margin was small, then the principal effect might be to raise prices or to increase imports. But given the condition of England in 1933, Keynes considered himself conservative when he estimated a multiplier of at least two. But, he continued, 'since ... I am anxious not to overstate what will be a sufficiently striking conclusion anyhow, let us take it at 1½. . . . [26] Accordingly, for every two men directly employed in consequence of increased government spending, a third man would be additionally re-employed as a result of the multiplier repercussions.

If on humanitarian grounds public works promised easement to the unemployed and their families, on fiscal grounds public works offered considerable relief to the budget. Keynes calculated that if the average public expenditure for each individual on the dole was £50 annually, then public works expenditures of £3 million which actually increased total employment by 20,000 saved about £1 million in payments on the dole – something like a third of the public works outlays. This was not the end of the budgetary benefit. Since the new capital expenditure diminished neither investment nor consumption, it necessarily expanded national income by an amount greater than itself. If the same multiplier of 1½ was applied, then national income would rise by £4·5 million. According to Keynes's estimates of applicable tax rates, approximately twenty per cent of this amount would accrue to the Treasury in the shape of tax receipts. If, he conceded, one took into account time lags in tax collection and assumed that only ten per cent was collected within the relevant time period, this approximated still an additional £450,000, and the total Treasury benefit would accordingly mount to £1·45 million – about half of the original expenditure on the new public works.

Manifestly, argued Keynes, an opportunity existed not only to relieve the plight of the unemployed but also to channel idle resources into socially useful production. Housing was a fair example. A sum of £100 million devoted to the rebuilding of the slums would not only improve the condition of life for the poor but would also return the Treasury some £50 million, computed in the fashion just described. What an inexpensive way of combining individually fruitful policies!

Keynes concluded this prescription for internal economic expansion with a word of warning. The beneficial effects of public works would be dissipated if the public works programmes were financed by reductions in other government spending, such as the salaries of schoolteachers and civil servants, who were the favourite targets of economizers in high places. Good effects were to be expected only from '*additional* expenditure made, not in substitution for other expenditure, but out of savings or out of borrowed money, either by private persons or by public authorities, whether for capital purposes or for consumption made possible by a relief of taxation or in some other way'.[27] Keynes's advocacy of deficit spending was just as unequivocal as his complementary judgement that 'the contrary policy of endeavouring to balance the Budget by impositions, restrictions, and precautions will surely fail, because it must have the effect of diminishing the national spending power, and hence the national income.'[28]

By 1933, then, Keynes had progressed a long distance from the economics which he had learned from Marshall and Pigou and which he had in his turn offered to a later generation of undergraduates. His teachers had had few doubts about the economic policies required to keep their country healthy. It was a matter of adhering to the rules of the gold standard in monetary affairs, free trade in international relations, and wage and price flexibility in business cycle policy. But it was precisely these hallowed remedies at which Keynes had been nibbling for a decade or more in his books, articles and contributions to royal commissions. He had advanced from his unsubtle, common-sense support of Lloyd George's public works proposals to the specific analysis of their cost, budgetary meaning and impact upon employment. *The Means to Prosperity* featured the multiplier process, which clinched his analysis and raised his proposals from the empiric to the theoretical level, so favoured by economists.

Much still remained to be achieved. For one thing Keynes's most heterodox proposals still addressed themselves to a multiplicity of purposes. In *The Means to Prosperity* and still more in the *Treatise on Money*, Keynes directed his readers' attention to internal price levels as well as domestic unemployment, the balance of payments as well as idle domestic resources, and inflation almost as much as deflation. He was still giving more hostages to conventional economists than the ambitious iconoclast can afford. More important still, even the multiplier analysis fell short of a complete assault upon the theoretical structure which buttressed the policy recommendations of his economic colleagues. No doubt an astute and sophisticated student of Cambridge economics who had followed Keynes's work closely would have sniffed heresy. After all, Keynes manifestly did not believe that savings flowed automatically into investment. If he departed from sound doctrine on this point, how could he defend Say's Law in any version or be confident of the powerful balancing effect of interest rate variations? If indeed he considered – heresy of heresies – that full employment was *not* the equilibrium value towards which the capitalist system moved in all circumstances (save of course when it was there), then he opened the door to all varieties of intriguing possibilities, theoretical and practical alike. For if free markets just possibly tended to produce unemployed men and idle factories, might not the case for public ownership, some form of socialism, mild or sweeping, be a good one? At the least wasn't the state entitled to intervene in order to restore desirable levels of economic activity?

In retrospect it is easy to see how much of this was implicit or even explicit in Keynes's published work before the appearance of *The General Theory*. Nevertheless, it was the opinion of economists and *a fortiori* of the general public that while Keynes was a daring chap and a thorn in the side of his fellows, he still had not produced a truly new economic revelation. This is to say that in intellectual affairs effective novelties must be recognized as innovations or they fail in their purpose.

SOURCE NOTES TO CHAPTER 3

1. Committee on Finance and Industry, *Minutes of Evidence* (London: H.M.S.O., 1931), II, 48.
2. Ibid., I, 339.
3. Ibid.
4. Ibid., II, 21.
5. J. M. Keynes, *The Economic Consequences of the Peace* (London: Macmillan, 1919).
6. J. M. Keynes, *A Tract on Monetary Reform* (London: Macmillan, 1923).
7. Ibid.
8. Ibid.
9. Ibid.
10. Ibid.
11. Ibid.
12. Ibid.
13. Sir Roy Harrod, *The Life of John Maynard Keynes* (London: Macmillan, 1951).
14. E. A. G. Robinson in Robert Lekachman (ed.), *Keynes's General Theory: Reports of Three Decades* (New York: St Martin's, 1964; London: Macmillan).
15. J. M. Keynes, Introduction in Hubert Henderson, *Supply and Demand* (New York: Harcourt, Brace, 1922).
16. D. H. Robertson, *Banking Policy and the Price Level* (Village Station, N.Y.: Kelley, 1949).
17. J. M. Keynes, *The Pure Theory of Money*, vol. I of *A Treatise on Money* (London: Macmillan, 1930).
18. Ibid.
19. Ibid.

20. Ibid.

21. J. M. Keynes, *The Means to Property*, vol. II of *A Treatise on Money* (London: Macmillan, 1930).

22. R. F. Kahn, 'The Relation of Home Investment to Unemployment', *The Economic Journal*, December 1931, pp. 173–98.

23. J. M. Keynes, *The Means to Property* (London: Macmillan, 1933).

24. Ibid.

25. Ibid.

26. Ibid.

27. Ibid.

28. Ibid.

When I first encountered economics as a college student in 1939, the textbook that my instructor asked the class to study was Garver and Hansen's *Principles of Economics*, revised edition, published in 1937. Alvin H. Hansen, now a professor emeritus of economics at Harvard, was destined to become very shortly a leading American disciple of Keynes and the independent inventor of the doctrine of secular stagnation, which interpreted the economic malaise of the 1930s as a permanent condition. In the profession he was noted at the time as a student of business cycles, and his textbook was popular in the better colleges and universities. As late as 1947 a third edition of the book was published and widely assigned.

After half a dozen years of the New Deal, unemployment was still very high in 1939. What did this guide to economics, actually one of the best textbooks of its period, contain to enlighten a young student about the causes and still more the cure of unemployment? In sad fact not very much. On page 488 there did appear a chart entitled 'Urban Unemployment in the United States', depicting the course of events between 1896 and 1936. The chart enabled the attentive reader to see that unemployment had soared to something like twenty-two per cent of the labour force in 1921, decreased later on in the decade of the 1920s, and then steadily mounted from about nine per cent in 1929 to a shade under twenty-five per cent in 1932 and 1933. What caused unemployment? The authors were not very consoling. The causes, it appeared, were 'shifts in demand and changes in technique'.[1] And 'So long as we have a dynamic society with continual change and progress,' they wrote, 'a considerable amount of unemployment will necessarily prevail'.[2]

Far from inhumane in their outlook, Garver and Hansen had a remedy to propose. 'Genuine security against unemployment,' they observed, 'makes necessary some form of unemployment insurance.'[3] Accordingly, the text devotes the whole of *two* pages to the exposition of the unemployment insurance provisions of the Social Security Act of 1935, passed just in time to be discussed in the book. This is all. At a generous estimate, these leading textbook writers and respected members of their profession scattered through a long book not more than ten pages of analysis, description and prescription regarding the dominant economic problem of the 1930s. The overwhelming bulk of their book was the standard fare of the day: pricing in individual markets, money and banking, trade unions, international trade, taxation and the economics of socialism. Eager youths who sought in the comprehension of economic principles the hope of social amelioration had a sticky time of it.

A number of years later I found myself in my turn teaching economics to college students. More years than not, the text that I have used is Paul A. Samuelson's *Economics*, an enormously popular book, now in its sixth edition. What changes has a generation wrought? Take a mechanical comparison to start with. The index to Garver and Hansen does include the word *unemployment*. Under it are references to a total of eight pages. In 1937 unemployment was well over ten per cent at the start of the year. Samuelson's sixth edition appeared in the spring of 1964, when unemployment was fluctuating within a range of five to six per cent. The index entry nevertheless refers students to a total of forty-three pages scattered through the text. Unemployment is associated with such phenomena as technology, tax burdens, deflation, protective tariffs, economic institutions and overvaluation of currency.

Other contrasts are equally startling. Garver and Hansen took no cognizance of economic growth, possibly because in 1937 the prospects for economic growth were too dismal to be lingered over. Samuelson on the other hand contains a growth entry which occupies half an index column and refers the interested to no fewer than eighty pages, or ten per cent of the entire volume. The rich menu of concepts and labels associates growth with rates, preconditions, underdeveloped economies, price stability, and an assortment of quantitative and analytical techniques.

Knowledge is not circumscribed by indexes alone. A still more remarkable contrast is visible in the two tables of contents. Part II of Samuelson has no analogue at all in Garver and Hansen. Entitled 'Determination of National Income and Its Fluctuations', this division of the book contains chapters on 'Saving, Consumption, and Investment' and, most important, 'The Theory of Income Determination'. Today's student will not suffer for want of discussion on the problems of employment and growth and on the appropriate public policies for handling these problems. For the economics of the 1960s is deeply involved in measuring the national income, identifying the forces which determine its size, assessing the relationship between employment and the total demand for goods and services, and formulating the monetary and fiscal measures which an alert government can effect.

One final comparison should suffice. Writers of textbooks usually feel an urge to justify their enterprise in the eyes of cynical or sceptical students. They tend to do so by describing the nature and stressing the importance of their subject.

The student who hearkened to Garver and Hansen in 1937 would have heard these words: 'Economics is the study of the price and value aspects of human activities and institutions. This very general definition is broad enough to cover every phase of economic life, and it is applicable to economic activity in a system of private property, state socialism, or communism.'[4]

In 1964 here is Samuelson describing the issues which he plans to emphasize: 'What kinds of jobs are there to do? What do they pay? How much in goods will a dollar of wages buy now, and how much in a time of galloping inflation? What are the chances that a time will come when a man will not be able to get any suitable work within a reasonable period?'[5] Nor was this the limit of the economist's legitimate interests, for

economics also deals with political decisions each citizen must face: Will the government add to my taxes to help unemployed miners, or are there other things it can do to help mitigate the problem of unemployment? Should I vote to build a new school and road now, or vote to put this aside until business slackens and cement prices come down and jobs are needed? Should I vote to keep married women out of public employment, so there will be more jobs for men? Will automation in factories lead to starvation wages and surplus workers? What about antitrust legislation that purports to fight monopolies?[6]

Thus, in a generation economists have learned to concentrate on different problems, redefine the scope of their principles, reinterpret public policy and transform their nomenclature. Depression, unemployment, war and the labours of many economists went into this achievement. A substantial share of the credit belongs to the Keynes who in 1936 published *The General Theory of Employment, Interest and Money*.

The first draft of *The General Theory* was completed in 1934. Written in close communion with a brilliant group of young Cambridge economists, among them R. F. Kahn, Joan Robinson and J. E. Meade, the proofs were circulated first to D. H. Robertson, then to the distinguished older economist R. G. Hawtrey, and finally to R. F. Harrod, Keynes's loyal Oxford admirer and ultimate biographer. To Keynes's distress his old friend and colleague Robertson proved unsympathetic to the strategy and the terminology alike of *The General Theory*. He was unprepared to depart as widely from the economics of Marshall and Pigou as the impatient Keynes was. Even Harrod, by his own account, endeavoured to dissuade Keynes from an all-out assault on 'classical' economics. Keynes was not to be dissuaded. When *The General Theory* officially appeared, its contents were therefore no surprise at least to the Cambridge inner circle who had participated in its production and the Cambridge students who had heard Keynes's lectures in 1934 and 1935.*

Three decades after its appearance, *The General Theory* remains a difficult, technical treatise even for specialists. It is full of subtleties of exposition, some necessary, some the consequence of obscure thought, and some apparently designed to infuriate members of his own profession. But it was also a book with a powerful central message. This was a blast at the assumption that there were mechanisms of economic adjustment in capitalist societies which automatically produced conditions of full employment of men and resources. No doubt Keynes exaggerated the uniformity of this opinion among economists, but he was broadly accurate in his judgement that most if not all economists still retained, Great Depression or no Great Depression, a sturdy confidence in the ability of competitive markets to expand employment and production if labour accepted lower wages and businessmen accepted lower prices. Flexible prices and flexible wages were still the best answer that the conventional wisdom of the profession could offer the community.

The thrust of economic analysis is towards the explanation of large numbers of events by a very few abstract principles. When the principles and the events diverge, when existing theories of market

* Keynes had the habit of making successive drafts on a series of galley proofs. He lectured directly from a set of these proofs to his students. One of them recalls that on occasion the long sheets fell from the lectern to the floor, and that when Keynes picked them up, it was not always in the appropriate sequence. True to the great tradition of university lecturing, he read on, undeterred by the break in logical sequence.

equilibrium ill accord with the persistence of unemployment and the gloomy outlook for its alleviation, economists, like labour leaders, may grow discontented. But they will cling to their existing principles until superior principles are invented, for economics is a subject in which bad theory is preferable to no theory at all. Economists like Pigou and Robertson were not blissfully happy with doctrines that preached equilibrium at full employment. In the absence of better theories, they patched up the existing doctrines. Keynes's task, then, was twofold: destruction of bad old doctrine and creation of good new doctrine.

The older theory which Keynes attacked was founded on an old generalization, the nineteenth-century French economist Jean-Baptiste Say's Law of Markets. Often summarized in the aphorism already quoted, 'Supply creates its own demand', Say's Law affirmed the impossibility of general over-production of goods, or general 'glut', in Say's word. Equally impossible therefore was general unemployment. Say's reasoning was nearly as concise and simple as his conclusion. Was it not obvious that men produced goods only in order to enjoy the consumption of other goods? Capitalists invested in order to consume their profits in the enjoyment of life. Workers laboured in order to consume their wages in acquiring the means of subsistence for themselves and their families. The more that businessmen spent on hiring labour and purchasing raw materials, the larger would be the incomes generated and the capacity of their recipients to purchase goods. Every increase in production soon justified itself by a matching increase in demand. Double production and infallibly you doubled sales. Indeed, the only limit was the amount of resources and the number of employable workers available. The version of Say's Law which Keynes quoted appeared in John Stuart Mill's 1848 *Principles of Political Economy:*

What constitutes the means of payment for commodities is simply commodities. Each person's means of paying for the productions of other people consist of those which he himself possesses. All sellers are inevitably, and by the meaning of the word, buyers. Could we suddenly double the productive powers of the country, we should double the supply of commodities in every market; but we should, by the same stroke, double the purchasing power. Everybody would bring a double demand as well as supply; everybody would be able to buy twice as much, because every one would have twice as much to offer in exchange.[7]

Did this bland and happy tale affront the common sense of the ordinary citizen, who was perfectly aware from his own behaviour and observation that no one *had* to spend all of his income, that some might be saved, and that savings seemed to reduce the demand for goods and services? Economists had an answer. The version which Keynes here quoted was the work of his old teacher Alfred Marshall:

The whole of a man's income is expended in the purchase of services and of commodities. It is indeed commonly said that a man spends some portion of his income and saves another. But it is a familiar economic axiom that a man purchases labour and commodities with that portion of his income which he saves just as much as he does with that he is said to spend. He is said to spend when he seeks to obtain present enjoyment from the services and commodities which he purchases. He is said to save when he causes the labour and the commodities which he purchases to be devoted to the production of wealth from which he expects to derive the means of enjoyment in the future.[8]

What Marshall meant was this: the wage-earner or businessman who thriftily saved a portion of his income simply either made the funds available for his own reinvestment in his own business enterprise or, using a bank as an intermediary, loaned the funds to someone who would invest them. In either event, his savings purchased goods just as surely as his expenditures on food, clothing, shelter and frivolity. Hence, in one fashion or another, the incomes which were paid out to workers, landlords, investors and lenders returned undiminished as demand for the very goods and services which workers and property owners had cooperated to generate.

Keynes conceded that few of his own contemporaries stated this doctrine as plainly as Mill and Marshall, but, said Keynes, 'Contemporary thought is still deeply steeped in the notion that if people did not spend their money in one way they will spend it in another'.[9] Although it was true that post-First World War economists were unable to express such opinions 'consistently' in the face of the 'facts of experience', these same economists failed miserably in not revising their theories and adjusting their remedies.

Such judgements dictated Keynes's initial strategy. It was to demolish the 'postulates of classical economics'. In Keynes's opinion the grand conclusion to which Say's Law led inexorably was the existence of some wage rate at which, in each circumstance, full employment was feasible. One by one Keynes identified and either accepted as harmless or rejected as mistaken the 'postulates' which supported this conclusion. It is well worth following his reasoning.

The first of the classical postulates reads in Keynes's version, 'The wage is equal to the marginal product of labour'.[10] In non-technical language this amounts to the proposition that wages tend to equal the value of the product for which the worker is responsible, after taking other costs into account.

The second postulate is somewhat more complex in statement and meaning: 'The utility of the wage when a given volume of labour is employed is equal to the marginal disutility of that amount of employment.'[11] This sentence compresses several vital assumptions, many of them with roots deep in the history of economic ideas. Five at least are important:

1. Work is painful and never undertaken for its own sake.
2. Additional work becomes more painful hour by hour.
3. Wages are pleasant because those who receive them can use them to command pleasurable objects and services.
4. Nevertheless, additional wages yield less pleasure, dollar by dollar, than their predecessors, because they gratify tastes of diminishing urgency, for individuals buy items of greater pleasure with their initial dollars of income.
5. Therefore, any worker will offer his services to an employer only in the anticipation that the pleasure he receives from the wages which are the reward of his effort exceeds the pain which the additional labour causes. Hence, in a competitive labour market, workers cease to labour just before the point where additional pleasures match additional pains.

Orthodox economic theory thus imputed to the labourer the maximizing, rational, calculating tendencies upon which economic theory has habitually based its explanations of human behaviour.

There was a most important corollary of this doctrine: the implication that any individual worker had it in his own power to find or to increase his own employment. All he needed to do was to revise his psychic computation of pleasure and pain so as to work more hours at existing wage rates, work the same number of hours at lower wages, or, if unemployed, accept a job offer at a wage rate which previously he had deemed unacceptable. The moral for individual workers and the leaders of their unions was inescapable – the partially or completely unemployed could remedy their situation at any time; all they had to do was accept lower wage rates.

From this inference flowed another. All unemployment was either frictional or voluntary. Where unemployment was frictional, workers who were seasonally idle or between jobs could confidently anticipate re-employment as the season changed or as new jobs became available. All other unemployment had to be interpreted as the voluntary preference of the unemployed. Much as an economist might justify on humane or historical grounds the refusal of a worker to accept a reduction in his standard of life, the economist could not grant him an economic justification.

This notion that unemployment for any length of time was never involuntary was deeply ingrained. Harold Wilson has recalled that the late Lord Beveridge, a pioneer student and advocate of social reform, himself failed to grasp the possibility that unemployment might really be beyond the control or influence of the unemployed. In Wilson's words, 'I remember his face, very puzzled, one day after he had visited a camp for unemployed men. He said he couldn't understand why decent, able-bodied men like the ones we had seen *could* be out of work. He didn't want to face the real problem. He wanted to think in terms of frictional unemployment.'[12]

However, in teasing and unpleasant fact, involuntary unemployment *did* exist. Any observer at all in touch with the social reality of the 1930s knew that quite frequently wages and employment had contracted simultaneously. Hence, as a theorist Keynes badly needed an appropriate definition of involuntary unemployment, one which could serve as a licence for its existence. Not the simplest grouping of words in the English language, Keynes's definition went like this: 'Men are involuntarily unemployed if, in the event of a small rise in the price of wage-goods relatively to the money-wage, both the aggregate supply of labour willing to work for the current money-wage and the aggregate demand for it at that wage would be greater than the existing volume of employment.'[13]

The definition was a summary of a mental experiment. Suppose, Keynes directed his reader, that the cost of living went up and nothing happened to the wages paid to workers. Then the average worker's *real* wage – the collection of goods he could actually purchase with his money income – must decline. Now, according to the reasoning characteristic of classical theory, the response of labourers to declines in their real income was a withholding of a portion of their labour. But was it really sensible to assume that this theoretical reaction also occurred in life? Did workers leave their jobs or work fewer hours every time the price of food and clothing went up? Of course not.

What actually happened was something quite different. Higher prices of 'wage-goods' (consumer goods) implied higher profits and a more encouraging sales outlook for the sellers of the standard items that entered into the worker's budget. These sellers tended to hire more labour as the business outlook brightened. And – this was the point of Keynes's analysis – the labourers were perfectly willing to accept new employment even though their *real wage* was lower than it would have been before the cost of living rose. Under the circumstances it could scarcely have been plainer that if ordinary workers were willing to accept jobs at wages *lower* than the previous level of remuneration, then they surely would have been willing to work at the higher real wages of the past. Hence they must have been involuntarily unemployed. If their employers had only felt it worth their while to offer additional employment at lower money and real wages, they would have found willing workers. Thus, economists who were so stubbornly confident that individual employers and individual employees between them determined the level of employment were simply completely mistaken. Often enough nothing an unemployed man or woman could do was capable of having the slightest impact on his own job prospects.

This demonstration served Keynes only as a beginning. Once the presence and theoretical possibility of involuntary unemployment were granted, the harder tasks remained. What was the explanation of the size of involuntary unemployment? What occasioned fluctuations in unemployment? It was precisely at this juncture, as Keynes argued his case, that something vital was missing from the corpus of orthodox economics – nothing less than a theory of aggregate demand. The highest distinction of *The General Theory* was not the explanation of involuntary unemployment; it was the construction of this missing piece of economic apparatus.

Once the theory is stated, the error of conventional economic policy is readily grasped. It becomes plain that the wage- and price-cutting which were approved pre-Keynesian specifics illegitimately leaped from the specific to the general. Any businessman can see that a reduction in his own costs – other things being equal – expands his profits and encourages him to increase his output. The heart of the matter is the failure of other things to remain equal when *all* businessmen reduce wages and costs. When wages in general fall, then the demand for all varieties of consumer goods and services inevitably falls in tune with the declining incomes of workers. At best, then, the demand for goods must fall in much the same proportion as wages. In the aggregate the demand for goods depends upon the incomes which, again in the aggregate, their potential purchasers earn. *One* employer can benefit from a reduction of his workers' wages. *All* employers cannot benefit by a general reduction of wages. To believe otherwise is to commit the logical fallacy of composition.

Hence the new Keynesian theory of economic activity was on the one hand an explanation of how the total *supply* of goods and services emerged from the decisions of hordes of individual businessmen, and on the other hand an account of how the total *demand* for goods and services evolved from the spending and saving choices of millions of individual consumers. As Keynes told his new story, events commence with the actions of businessmen. He assumed from the outset that it is individual businessmen or entrepreneurs who provide employment and pay incomes – wages to workers, salaries to executives, interest to bankers, rent to landlords. Entrepreneurs expect to sell the goods which result from the combination of the agents of production at prices which equal at a minimum the sums paid out in the process of producing them – including a normal profit. It follows that when the situation is stable (that is, when aggregate equilibrium is attained), the *aggregate* amount of income and employment which *all* entrepreneurs will offer just matches the volume of the sales which they anticipate making.*

When will entrepreneurs wish to expand the employment they offer, the incomes they provide, and the output they produce? The answer was related by Keynes to the notion of an aggregate *demand* function, which is the other half of the picture. Suppose that *in fact* when entrepreneurs offer a certain amount of employment and produce a certain volume of output, the *actual demand* for the goods they offer for sale exceeds their expectations. Accordingly, most businessmen discover that their stocks (or inventories) of goods are running short. At this point, if they are retailers or wholesalers, they increase their orders to manufacturers; if they are manufacturers, they increase their production. The aggregate demand function

---

* Keynes defined the aggregate supply price of the output of a given amount of employment as 'the expectation of proceeds which will just make it worth the while of the entrepreneurs to give that employment' (*The General Theory of Employment, Interest and Money*, London: Macmillan, 1936).

measures the volume of sales which corresponds to each possible level of income and output.

The actual level of employment, then, must be 'given by the point of intersection between the aggregate demand function and the aggregate supply function; for it is at this point that the entrepreneurs' expectations of profits will be maximised'.[14] The contrast with Say's Law was now complete. Say's Law blithely assumed that every time businessmen expanded supply, demand simply followed in its train. The beneficent process halted only when full employment of men and resources called a halt to expansion. Keynes's alternative doctrine contained a very different moral. In the Keynesian universe, equilibrium could be reached at *any* level of employment and income between zero and full employment. Moreover, no theoretical reason existed for saying that one level of employment was more likely to occur than any other level of employment. On the possible scale of values, full employment was simply one possibility among many. It followed that at each and every level of employment other than full employment, involuntary unemployment was more than possible; it was unavoidable. What determined the level of employment was *not* the wage bargain negotiated between labourers and their employers. No matter how humble the former were, they could not expand their own employment. What determined employment was something quite different. It was the level of aggregate demand for the goods and services of the entire economy.

What elements constituted aggregate demand? What determined its size and therefore the size of employment and income? Keynes started with the simple assumption that the government had a neutral impact upon the economy. He assumed initially that the government removed as much from the stream of national income in the shape of taxes as it placed in the income stream in the form of its own expenditures on materials and labour services. If the net effect of government operations was zero, the two remaining sources of the aggregate demand for goods and services were consumers and investors.

What factors influenced their decisions? Like Keynes we begin with the consumers. Why do individuals spend more or less? Why do all consumers increase or decrease their expenditure? Keynes classified the influences upon consumer spending under three headings: (1) the amount of income available to consumers for their own spending decisions, (2) objective factors and (3) subjective factors.

Among the major objective factors, he found, were alterations in the cost of living, unexpected capital gains or losses (windfalls, in Keynes's terminology), alterations in the rate of interest, shifts in government tax policies and revisions of judgement about the relation between present and future levels of income. In Keynes's judgement only the first of the list was quantitatively very important; the remainder either were trivial in impact, or tended to cancel each other.

Nor, in sum, were the subjective influences upon consumer behaviour quantitatively of great consequence. Here appearances were deceptive. It was true enough that in deciding between spending and saving, the individual was swayed by many possible motives. He might want to accumulate a reserve against unexpected ill fortune. Prudence might direct him to save in order to put a child through school or add to his own comfort in retirement. Again, he might plan a gradually rising standard of life, facilitated by present saving. Saving was capable of increasing the saver's 'sense of independence and the power to do things'. For the speculator saving was the means to indulging his passion. Savers with a strong sense of family continuity saved in order to bequeath a fortune to their heirs. And there were a few misers who saved just for the sheer joy of the act. These eight reasons for saving instead of spending Keynes dubbed 'Precaution, Foresight, Calculation, Improvement, Independence, Enterprise, Pride and Avarice'.[15]* It was not that these motives were individually or collectively insignificant. Keynes's point was different. In the short run, all of these motives were stable. Accordingly, it followed that since the psychology of the community altered so slowly and since *The General Theory* focused upon short-run events, Keynes could safely ignore the subjective elements in the consumer's psychology.

What was left? Only income, for if neither objective nor subjective factors were important determinants of short-run consumption, then this was the only force that remained. Keynes was convinced that he had isolated a new truth, and he stated his conviction in the form of a new 'law':

---

* For good measure Keynes added a 'corresponding list of motives to consumption, such as Enjoyment, Short-sightedness, Generosity, Miscalculation, Ostentation and Extravagance' (ibid.).

The fundamental psychological law, upon which we are entitled to depend with great confidence both *a priori* from our knowledge of human nature and from the detailed facts of experience, is that men are disposed, as a rule and on the average, to increase their consumption as their income increases but not by as much as the increase in their income.[16]

At the time Keynes had very little if any statistical support for the conclusion stated in this 'law'. Like his illustrious predecessors and colleagues in English economics, he relied confidently upon his knowledge of himself and the world in which he lived. The statistics came later as one of the many consequences of *The General Theory*. A favourite sport of economists and statisticians was 'consumption function' construction – a statistical generalization of the actual relations between income and consumption. Although later events as well as these researches demonstrated that the influences upon consumption are more numerous and more complex than Keynes assumed, these same investigations have also tended to certify the broad accuracy of Keynes's 'law'. Consumers do tend to spend most but not all of the additions to their incomes which come their way. In the United States, statisticians usually assume that consumers will spend between ninety-two and ninety-four per cent of additions to their disposable income.*

As a theoretical contribution, Keynes's definition of an aggregate consumption function was important and suggestive. Alvin Hansen was not alone among economists in assessing it as one of Keynes's major inventions. But whatever its other merits, the consumption function could not explain the *size* of national income and employment. Consumption indeed depended upon national income. What was left as an explanation of national income was necessarily the remaining constituent of aggregate demand – investment. Here at last is the key variable in the Keynesian system. Changes in investment initiate changes in the other economic magnitudes. Increases or decreases in investment generate multiplied effects upon national income and employment. Alterations in national income in their turn produce alterations in the volume of consumer spending.

It is essential, then, to be very clear on this topic. What is investment? What explains its size? In *The General Theory*, Keynes followed the general practice of economists by defining investment as a 'real' and not a financial phenomenon. Stocks and bonds are *not* invest-

---

* Disposable income equals the total amount left in the consumer's possession after the payment of personal income taxes.

ment. New factories, new tools and machines, and enlargements of business inventories *are* investment. Hence what differentiates investment from consumption is not an item's material qualities but the use that is made of it. A salesman's Chevrolet is an item of investment and so esteemed by the salesman's employer and the employer's accountant. A consumer's Chevrolet is rightly perceived by its owner as a portion of his consumption. Similarly, a case of beer in a grocer's basement is a portion of his inventory, and inventories are a part of investment. Transferred to the home of an imbiber, the same beer is a part of consumption. *All* investment goods are instrumental: they facilitate the production of final products which are consumer goods. Hence *all* consumer goods, serving the end of personal satisfaction only, reach their ultimate destination when they reach the hands of individual purchasers. Properly understood, the destination of a machine tool is different; it is the consumer goods produced with the tool's aid.

Such a definition isolates three other investment characteristics. First of all, investments are made by businessmen, not consumers, with the general objective of profitable production and sale. Second, all investments are risky. The businessman who uses his own money or borrowed funds to buy a machine places a bet in effect that he will be able to sell the commodities which the machine produces during its lifetime – two, five, ten or more years – at profitable prices. Implicit in such bets are the confidence that consumer tastes are either stable or foreseeable and the faith that competitors will not undercut markets by introducing superior products or more efficient techniques. The durability of machines and the riskiness of their purchase imply a third characteristic of the investment process: that investment is postponable.* As a general matter, businessmen need not expand their operations, at least not immediately. Usually, a businessman can even postpone replacing obsolescent equipment with improved models. Consumers can similarly drive an old car a year longer, but they can scarcely put off eating, and they can delay expenditure on clothing, medical and dental care, and rent and household expenses only for relatively short periods.

In spite of these uncertainties, investment does occur. Even in depressions investors are prepared to take gambles on the future.

* Among conservative British businessmen, it is said, the climate is cool to investment because when business is bad money is too scarce to a low investment, and when business is good there is no need to invest.

What enters into their decisions? Keynes's answer focused upon a comparison between the *profits* which a prospective investor expected over the lifetime of the machine* and the interest charges which he incurred when he borrowed the money to buy the machine.†

In an uncertain world, the key word in this analysis was *expectation*. Expectation is the strategic factor in the investment decision. In the asterisk footnote at the bottom of the page, the illustrative numbers refer to *expected* profits from the use of a new machine. Because these and all other expectations are extremely volatile, the marginal efficiency of capital must also be subject to rapid and substantial change. If the marginal efficiency of capital fluctuates, so also must the level of investment. A powerful theory of investment, accordingly, must elucidate the forces which enter into the long-run expectations of prospective investors, and explain more generally the 'state of confidence ... to which practical men always pay the closest and most anxious attention'.[17]

The difficulties in the path of understanding are grave. If, said Keynes, we are honest with ourselves, we will at once admit just how little we know about the probable profits of a given investment: 'If we speak frankly, we have to admit that our basis of knowledge

* Keynes called these expected profits the 'marginal efficiency of capital'. He defined the concept in these words: 'I define the marginal efficiency of capital as being equal to that rate of discount which would make the present value of the series of annuities given by the returns expected from the capital-asset during its life just equal to its supply price' (op. cit.). A simple arithmetic example might clarify the notion. Suppose that a machine has a life of just two years and that the investor expects to earn from its use $1,100 during the first year and $2,420 during its second and last year of life. Stipulate further that the price of the machine is $3,000. Then the marginal efficiency of capital is that rate of discount which makes $1,000 received the first year and $2,420 the second just equal to $3,000. It can be computed as follows:

$$\$3,000 = \frac{\$1,100}{(1+r)} + \frac{\$2,420}{(1+r)^2}$$
$$= \frac{\$1,100}{(1.10)} + \frac{\$2,420}{(1.21)}$$
$$= \$1,000 + \$2,000$$

In the denominators of the fractions, each r stands for the estimated marginal efficiency of a particular investment. Thus, 1 added to .10 amounts to 1.10. The squaring of 1.10 to derive 1.21 simply reflects the fact that profits deferred longer (two years instead of one) must be more sharply reduced in present value.

† If the investor uses his own money instead of borrowed money, then he loses the opportunity to earn a return from this money in an alternative use, such as the purchase of a fixed income security – a bond. Hence, analytically, the two cases amount to the same thing.

for estimating the yield ten years hence of a railway, a copper mine, a textile factory, the goodwill of a patent medicine, an Atlantic liner, a building in the City of London amounts to little and sometimes to nothing; or even five years hence.'[18] Although, Keynes granted, this condition is occasionally mitigated by the ability of some long-term investors to diminish their risks, as the builder does by selling on mortgage to occupiers and the public utility does by virtue of its monopoly position, the bulk of investment is extraordinarily chancy. Its risks are all the greater because stock market speculation intensifies the psychological uncertainties of genuine investment.

Keynes judged that even apart from the influence of stock markets, organized more like gambling casinos than like investment markets, there was an element of instability which was 'due to the characteristic of human nature that a large proportion of our positive activities depend on spontaneous optimism. ... Most, probably, of our decisions to do something positive, the full consequences of which will be drawn out over many days to come, can only be taken as a result of animal spirits.'[19] As a man of wide practical experience in financial markets, as journalist and speculator, Keynes knew how important the tides of irrational optimism and pessimism were in the decisions of businessmen to invest or to hesitate in the hope of better days. One of the corollaries to Keynes's attitude was an awareness that reforming governments have the usual effect of upsetting the animal spirits of the financial community. 'If,' remarked Keynes, 'the fear of a Labour Government or a New Deal depresses enterprise, this need not be the result either of a reasonable calculation or of a plot with political intent; – it is the mere consequence of upsetting the delicate balance of spontaneous optimism.'[20]

Keynes's analysis of investment motivation led him to a still more constricting conclusion. Since the swings of opinion were so frequent and so violent, Keynes questioned the efficacy of interest rate policy. After all, if investors swung in mood between a pessimism which saw profit nowhere and a euphoria which envisaged riches in every financial commitment, small changes of the order of one or two per cent in rates of interest were unlikely to cause substantial effects upon the volume of investment. What remained if one adopted Keynes's scepticism about interest rate tinkering? It seemed apparent that we needed to grant the state 'an ever greater responsibility for directly organizing investment'. The state, unlike the individual businessman, was in a position to 'calculate the marginal efficiency of capital-goods on long views and on the basis of the general social advantage'.[21]

Taken literally, this position made a substantial increase in state activity inescapable. In fact, the complementary portion of Keynes's theory of investment, his theory of the rate of interest, did provide a possible loophole, given somewhat different assumptions about interest rates and marginal efficiencies of capital. This theory of the rate of interest quickly became and remained one of the most controversial portions of *The General Theory*.

To make plain the novelty of Keynes's position, it is necessary to explain classical doctrine on interest rates. Most simply, the doctrine went like this. The supply of savings is determined by the time preferences of those who receive incomes and contemplate savings. On the premise that most people prefer present satisfactions from spending money to satisfactions in the future, then the interest rate evokes the savings of those who regard it as a sufficient payment for the postponement of immediate gratification from present spending. Thus, a man who postpones the expenditure of $1,000 of his income for a full year in order to collect $42.50 of interest in effect decides that $1,042.50 one year from today is worth something more to him than $1,000 today. He responds to a $4\frac{1}{4}$ per cent interest rate by this quantity of saving. To say that he or any other person becomes thriftier is to say that he will save money more than $1,000 at the same rate of interest or the same $1,000 at a rate lower than $4\frac{1}{4}$ per cent. By extension, a thriftier community must be one whose aggregate savings increase despite constant interest rates or remain the same even in the face of falling interest rates.

Classical theory explained the demand for savings by reference to a complementary marginal principle, that of the marginal productivity of capital. Why would a businessman willingly pay 5 per cent or more as the price of borrowed funds? It would be worth his while if he believed that the profits he might derive from the machines he purchased with his loan would exceed 5 per cent. The marginal productivity in question was that of the new equipment. In equilibrium the rate of interest settled at that value where the amounts voluntarily saved and the amounts willingly borrowed were identical. In the real world, interest rates rose or fell as thrift waxed or waned and as the productivity of capital increased or decreased. The indispensable role of the rate of interest was that of allocating the community's resources between individual consumption and business investment.

Compared to this tidy doctrine, Keynes's explanation of interest rate determination was decidedly heterodox. By his account the rate of interest depended neither on the time preferences of savers nor on the marginal productivities of capital assumed by investors. For Keynes the rate of interest was a purely monetary phenomenon intimately associated with the preferences of the holders of money, *not* for present over future gratifications, but rather for perfectly liquid assets over less liquid assets. As Keynes saw the issue, some people held money for reasons which had more to do with the level of their incomes than with time preferences of any variety. Businessmen maintained deposit accounts to facilitate their current payments to employees and suppliers. Individuals carried loose cash in order to buy lunches, newspapers and daily transportation from home to job and back. In such circumstances unspent income had nothing to do with interest rates. What was related to interest rates was yet a third set of activities.

These activities all came under the heading of the speculative motive for holding instead of spending income. What is the nature of the speculator? He is a person engaged in the purchase and sale of securities in accordance with his own estimate of the imminent course of security prices. That speculator who believes stock prices will rise in the near future is a speculator impelled to buy more stock and accordingly hold less money. Very probably he will borrow on margin the better to profit from his judgement. Now, a prediction about stock prices, Keynes pointed out, is inevitably a prediction also about interest rates, since a stock yield – the relationship between stock prices and dividends disbursed – *is* an interest rate. It follows that when stock prices rise, interest rates *must fall*, for a dollar dividend of a certain amount is a smaller percentage of a higher-priced security.

This is far from the end of the matter. If most speculators are convinced that stock prices are fated to rise and interest rates to fall, they will bid actively for the securities controlled by the minority of pessimists who hold the opposite opinion. But the very attempts of the bulls among the speculators to expand their security holdings will produce the results which caused the actions. To some extent this is another instance of the self-fulfilling prophecy. Stock prices truly rise and yields accordingly do drop. In short, interest rates shift because speculators expect them to shift and act in such a fashion as to validate their own predictions.

The situation is symmetrical. If speculators anticipate a decline in the market and rising yields, logic directs them to dispose of their securities and to sell short into the bargain. They attempt to increase their stock of money in order to purchase securities at a later date and lower prices. However, their effort to sell securities *before* they decline in value has the effect immediately of depressing the stock market, lowering average stock prices, and raising average stock yields. Once more today's rate of interest is the consequence of speculators' expectations about tomorrow's rate of interest. In sum, the rate of interest is indeed a premium, but a premium paid for surrendering cash, the perfectly liquid asset, for securities, imperfectly liquid assets.

Upon this proposition Keynes constructed some substantial conclusions. The most provocative concerned public policy. If the speculators behaved as Keynes insisted they did, the monetary authorities, in America the Board of Governors of the Federal Reserve System and in England the Directors of the Court of the Bank of England, had strong weapons of reaction in their hands. Thus, if the authorities believed it inadvisable for interest rates to rise even though speculators put selling pressure on the stock market in anticipation of falling security prices and rising stock yields, then they could simply purchase on behalf of the central bank the securities which the speculators unloaded – at unchanged prices and yields. This is the most potent of monetary weapons, open market operations.

Open market operations are perfectly capable of actually lowering interest rates. When the Open Market Committee of the Federal Reserve System begins to purchase securities, its action raises stock prices and lowers security yields. Central banks conventionally buy and sell only government securities, but what happens in this segment of the market quickly spreads to corporate securities, bank loans and mortgage rates. Thus it is that the rate of interest is within the control of public policy. In effect if not in law, any country's financial authorities can supply speculators with all the money or all the securities they wish. Public authority, after all, prints both the money and the government securities.

This theory of interest completes the Keynesian account of the investment process. Keynesian investors compare marginal efficiencies of capital with rates of interest. A given speculator contemplating a specific purchase will ask himself whether the expected profit (the marginal efficiency of capital) exceeds the cost of the funds he needs to buy the machine (the rate of interest). If the marginal efficiency of capital exceeds the rate of interest, the investor makes his commitment. If the rate of interest is higher than the marginal efficiency of capital, he will refrain. When other elements of the problem are constant, investment increases when either interest rates fall or expected profits rise, and of the two interest rates are firmly within the power of public agencies.

What happens when a favourable conjuncture of marginal efficiencies and rates of interest causes investors to expand their expenditures? The Keynesian theory sketches a multiplier process. The first impact upon national income is equal to the size of the new investment. New investment orders become income to machine-builders and their employees. This is the first step in a sequence. Kahn's multiplier measures the complete change in national income by focusing upon the marginal propensity to consume – the proportion of *additional* income that individuals spend. When the marginal propensity to consume is one-half, the multiplier is two. An extra million dollars of investment accordingly increases national income *first* by a full million, *then* by the half-million which consumers spend out of their increased incomes, *then* by the quarter-million which the next group of income recipients devotes to consumer purchases, and so on. The sum of the increments to national income is two million dollars. In exactly the same fashion, any decrease in investment must diminish national income and employment by amounts greater than the size of the initial decline in investment.

It is plain just how heavily the Keynesian theory of income determination depends upon the behaviour of investors and the quantity of investment. The skeleton of the theory is simple enough. Investment is determined by the marginal efficiency of capital and the rate of interest. The marginal efficiency of capital in turn is jointly influenced by the profits expectations of investors and the prices of the machines which they contemplate buying. The rate of interest emerges partly from the liquidity preferences of speculators and partly from the open market decisions made by the monetary authorities. It is within the discretion of these authorities to lower interest rates. If the investment community is receptive, lower rates of interest stimulate investment. If the marginal propensity to consume is high, the investment multiplier will also be large. A huge multiplier implies a very sizeable change in national income in response to a comparatively small change in investment. Under ideal conditions, interest rate (or monetary) policy can shift the economy from an unsatisfactory equilibrium level marked by high unemployment to a full-employment equilibrium level.

*

Ever since the appearance of *The General Theory*, conservative Keynesians have been inclined to rely heavily upon the efficacy of monetary policy. Monetary policy's virtues are substantial. Of all tools of economic policy, interest rate manipulation requires the smallest bureaucracy, the least interference by politicians and the most expertise. A Montagu Norman could manipulate the levers of the Bank of England over a generation partly because of the jealously guarded independence of the venerable institution whose affairs he controlled, but partly also because it was conceded even by Labour Party critics of his policies that only central bankers really grasped the esoteric mysteries of the bank rate. Monetary policy has other merits. It is rapidly implemented, and it is readily reversible when circumstances alter. The crown of its merits is good manners. Coercing interest rates is a quiet and discreet matter, scarcely felt even by those whom interest rates influence.

For such reasons as these, monetary policy has been enjoying a revival among economists and public officials. Although nothing in the Keynesian system contradicts the virtues of monetary policy, Keynes himself often doubted that it would suffice to resuscitate a depressed economy, particularly when business confidence had really waned.

Nor was it necessary to rely on monetary policy to do the whole job of economic rescue. Keynes's theoretical construction now at last provided a powerful justification for his old favourite among practical anti-depression weapons – public works financed by government deficits. With Keynesian assumptions given, the point was plain enough. Unemployment and depression were the consequences of a deficiency of aggregate demand for goods and services. If investment flagged, one way to stimulate it was variation of interest rates. Granted. But a surer and a quicker policy was increased government expenditure. All the favourable multiplier effects of expanded private investment could be as reasonably anticipated from an increase in the government's deficit. Analytically, in fact, an increase in government spending, unaccompanied by an increase in taxes, was identical in meaning with an autonomous expansion of private investment.

Naturally, Keynes preferred that kind of public spending which supported projects of social utility – housing, schools, hospitals, parks, and the like. But at worst 'pyramid-building, earthquakes, even wars may serve to increase wealth, if the education of our statesmen on the principles of the classical economics stands in the way of anything better'. Keynes made his central point – what counts is extra spending regardless of its form – still more strikingly in this bravura passage:

If the Treasury were to fill old bottles with banknotes, bury them at suitable depths in disused coal-mines which are then filled up to the surface with town rubbish, and leave it to private enterprise on well-tried principles of *laissez-faire* to dig the notes up again ... there need be no more unemployment and, with the help of the repercussions, the real income of the community, and its capital wealth also, would probably become a good deal greater than it actually is. It would indeed be more sensible to build houses and the like; but if there are political and practical difficulties in the way of this, the above would be better than nothing.[22]

After all, the marginal product of unemployed men is zero. If the community puts the unemployed to work at totally useless jobs, such as the leaf-raking and ditch-digging which were the derided activities under the W.P.A. in New Deal America, their marginal product will be zero still. But the incomes from this fruitless labour will be expended on food, clothing, shelter, medical care and recreation. The incomes of the producers of these commodities and services will grow and so will their own spending. Thus, even totally *wasteful* employment has the result of increasing *useful* output and *useful* labour.

In Keynes's somewhat selective reading of history, he did identify a disposition on the part of political leaders to prefer the foolish to the sensible in public projects. He could not help laughing at the obtuseness of some of these choices:

Ancient Egypt was doubly fortunate, and doubtless owed to this its fabled wealth, in that it possessed *two* activities, namely, pyramid-building as well as the search for the precious metals, the fruits of which, since they could not serve the needs of man by being consumed, did not stale with abundance. The Middle Ages built cathedrals and sang dirges. Two pyramids, two masses for the dead, are twice as good as one; but not so two railways from London to York. Thus we are so sensible, have schooled ourselves to so close a semblance of prudent financiers, taking careful thought before we add to the 'financial' burdens of posterity by building them houses to live in, that we have no such easy escape from the sufferings of unemployment. We have to accept them as an inevitable result of applying to the conduct of the State the maxims which are best calculated to 'enrich' an individual by enabling him to pile up claims to enjoyment which he does not intend to exercise at any definite time.[23]

Didn't common sense suggest that when willing workers are idle and unfilled social needs are numerous, there ought to be some device for using the first to alleviate the second? How could the consequences be anything except beneficial to the community?

In his discussion of fiscal policy, Keynes emphasized the public works route to economic expansion. However, the same or substantially the same impact upon national income and employment can be produced by an alternative fiscal technique – tax reduction accompanied by an unchanged level of public expenditure. The 1964 American tax reduction measure, more fully discussed in Chapter 11, was an experiment with this fiscal device.

However, even though the impact upon national income of a $14 billion reduction in federal taxes may approximate the impact of a $14 billion expansion of public programmes, in one important respect the two policies imply different social meanings. Reducing taxes enlarges the sphere of private control over spending, but expansion of public spending widens the sphere of the socially determined allocation of the community's resources. The two routes to prosperity have two different emphases, one on the private economy and one on the public sector. Preference for one rather than the other is likely to be based less on the comparative impact upon national income and more on personal valuations of the importance of outstanding social needs and the merits of the consumer's freedom to allocate the maximum proportion of his own income.

Inevitably, Keynes understated the difficulties in the path of public works as a major administrative device. These, a generation of experience has demonstrated, are not conceptual or theoretical. They are administrative, technical and political. Particularly in the United States, it is hard to persuade democratic legislatures to take prompt and appropriate action. It is not easy to define the types of public works appropriate to various economic contingencies, nor can the flow of expenditure be readily turned off when the need has passed. The larger the scale of the public work, the more it displays the embarrassing tendency to reach maximum impact on national income and employment after the depression has vanished, when a prudent administration might prefer to curtail rather than enlarge its spending.

Keynes himself envisaged three additional complications. Unless the financing of public works was carefully managed, an additional government demand for funds might have the adverse effects of raising interest rates and discouraging private investment. All the more was it necessary, therefore, to coordinate monetary and fiscal policy. Again, because of the 'confused psychology' of investors,[24] public works might have an adverse effect upon their confidence, the marginal efficiency of capital, and the level of private investment. Finally, under conditions where foreign trade is important to the economy – England's constant situation – a portion of the employment benefits from public works flows to other countries, which enjoy the chance to enlarge their exports. Less firmly Keynes suggested a fourth point, that the marginal propensity to consume might decline as the income of the community expanded.

It is worth emphasizing that Keynes's original reservations and those which are derived from American and British experimenting with public works do not invalidate the theoretical case for public works. What they do suggest is rather greater complexities in the public administration of the policy than Keynes's jovial remarks about buried bottles, Egyptian pyramids and medieval masses for the dead might suggest to the unwary. Put to the choice, no modern government would care to restrict its tools against depression to monetary policy. All sophisticated administrators strive for the appropriate, efficacious mixture of monetary and fiscal measures. The last presidential candidate who believed otherwise finished an extraordinarily bad second in 1964.

In this altered Keynesian universe, what would become of the classical remedy for economic depression – a general reduction in wages? The outcome had its points of paradox. In the end Keynes did not deny that a 'reduction of money-wages is quite capable in certain circumstances of affording a stimulus to output, as the classical theory supposes'.[25] But as Keynes demonstrated, the manner in which the stimulus operated would be quite different in the Keynesian and the classical systems. Keynes was prepared to claim that even where reductions in money wages might fairly be assumed to increase employment, it was possible to produce the same effects much less painfully by manipulating interest rates instead of wages.

The tale as Keynes told it went like this. To begin with, a general wage reduction was incapable of expanding employment simply because producers' costs were thereby reduced. As incomes dropped because of wage reduction, demand inevitably fell. At best the two movements would offset each other, and real wages and real output would be unaffected. But this was only the preliminary to the argument proper. The appropriate way to identify the impact of wage cuts was to examine their influence upon the key variables of the Keynesian system: the marginal efficiency of capital, the rate of interest, and the propensity to consume.

Keynes commenced with the last of the three. If wages fall, so will prices. Some redistribution of real income will also occur, essentially away from wage-earners, whose compensation is flexible, to lenders and landlords, whose compensation is fixed for substantial periods by contracts and leases. On balance this redistribution is unfavourable to spending and employment, for it takes income away from the poor, whose marginal propensity to consume is high, and awards it to the prosperous, whose marginal propensity to consume is taken to be lower. In the circumstances total consumption is likely to be reduced.

What will happen to investment? If money wages at home fall and abroad remain stable, then exports in the wage-reducing country should rise and imports fall. A favourable balance of payments should emerge. Since this is defined as a portion of total investment, total investment accordingly appears to be stimulated. There is a second favourable possibility. The business community may expect the wage reduction to be temporary. If they are convinced that wages will soon recover, investors will find it advantageous to invest now and steal a march on competitors who will be compelled later on to pay higher prices for equipment, since it will be produced by better-paid labour. The third favourable effect of wage reduction is psychological. Businessmen may simply feel more cheerful each time wages drop. As a result, their animal spirits will rise, the marginal efficiency of capital will ascend and investment will soar.

This is to put the issue in its best light. It is at least equally possible for the consequences of wage reduction to be unfavourable to investment. For one thing debt becomes more burdensome to entrepreneurs when prices sag. For another entrepreneurs are quite likely to interpret a general wage reduction as evidence that wages will continue to decline. Such an expectation is as hostile to further investment as its opposite is favourable. What the psychological and economic sum of these possibilities is, no one can say *a priori*.

Indeed, there is only one variable which is unequivocally moved in the right direction by wage reduction; the rate of interest. The reasons are these. When wages and prices fall, the amount of money needed by businessmen and consumers simply to finance their current transactions also declines. The funds released from the pockets of consumers and the checking accounts of businessmen become available as speculative balances. These expanded balances permit speculators to bid more vigorously for the available supply of securities. Accordingly, the prices of stocks and bonds rise, their yields decline, and other interest rates follow this downward course. Thus, *if* the influence of wage reduction upon the marginal efficiency of capital and the propensity to consume is no worse than neutral, *then* the decrease in interest rates can be counted upon to stimulate investment, set the multiplier in motion, and enlarge income and employment.

So much, in appearance, Keynes conceded to his antagonists. An Indian-giver, he quickly withdrew his temporary concession. For if in this roundabout way the single favourable result of wage reduction was a lower interest rate, was it not possible to achieve the identical effect in a simpler, quicker and more equitable fashion? Of course it was. All the monetary authorities needed to do was purchase securities on the open market, enlarge the supply of money, bid up the prices of stocks and bonds, and thus achieve an appropriate reduction in interest rates.

Reducing wages was the royal road to trouble with the trade unions. Its effects were inequitable. Inactive lenders and landlords were favoured, and active workers and businessmen suffered. Wage reduction caused general uncertainty and gloom. A simple increase in the supply of money by the central banking authorities was accompanied by none of these drawbacks. Its effects were soothing and inspiriting. The active were encouraged. Investment was stimulated. The burden of debt diminished. All the social classes were more justly handled. By the time he had finished, Keynes had reduced wage policy to the status of an inefficient and unjust sub-stitute for monetary policy. Trade-union leaders had been right all along in their reluctance to accept the arguments in favour of money-wage reductions. It was their betters, the economists and the finan-ciers, who were in the wrong.

Such is the story of *The General Theory*'s triumphs. Keynes had simultaneously assaulted orthodoxy, substituted a dazzlingly novel theory of employment and income, and supplemented that doc-trine with a whole series of public policies. In the course of his opera-tions, he attacked many of the shibboleths which economists vener-ated in common with ordinary citizens. As Adam Smith had asked long ago, was the prudence of the careful head of a family an ade-quate or even an acceptable model for the conduct of a great nation? Not at all. In time of depression, governments which raised taxes or reduced public spending simply threw their constituents out of work and failed even to balance the government's own budget. The reduced income of ordinary citizens infallibly diminished the tax collections of the governments which had mistakenly initiated the train of events.

Was the rate of interest the reward of the thrifty and the measure of the efficiency of the entrepreneur? No, it was not. Fundamentally, it was a price paid to speculators in exchange for the surrender of their command over cash, the most liquid of all resources. Interest rates fluctuated according to the liquidity preferences of this morally neutral group. The thrifty and the enterprising had little to do with the matter.

Was individual thrift at least still a virtue? Not during times of economic adversity. At such times the citizen who indulged himself by spending his income also benefited his fellows in society by in-creasing aggregate demand and employment. Blessed are the extravagant, for theirs shall be full employment. Thrift was a virtue only in time of economic boom.

Were not the debts incurred in the course of financing public works a 'burden' upon future generations, as General Eisenhower has always believed? How could houses, schools and roads be a burden on the very people who benefited from them? And even if the public funds were used frivolously, public debt was as much an asset to those who held it as a liability to the taxpayers who con-tributed to the interest payments.

The dragon Keynes rode out to slay was the formidable Puritan ethic which has always condemned spending, applauded savings, and considered the accumulation of riches as the occasion for stewardship, not luxurious expenditure. No doubt the ethic had its uses when capital was scarce, saving vital to economic expansion, and employment full. Elsewhere Keynes himself had eloquently sketched the benefits of high saving in a period like 1870–1914. During a war saving became virtuous indeed. But in advanced economies afflicted with persistent tendencies towards economic sluggishness and high unemployment, thrift impeded economic growth. Not the least of Keynes's successes was the weakening of the identification between virtue and thrift.

SOURCE NOTES TO CHAPTER 4

1. F. B. Garver and A. H. Hansen, *Principles of Economics*, rev. edn (Boston: Ginn, 1937).
2. Ibid.
3. Ibid.
4. Ibid.
5. Paul A. Samuelson, *Economics*, 6th edn (New York: McGraw-Hill, 1964).
6. Ibid.
7. Quoted in J. M. Keynes, *The General Theory of Employment, Interest and Money* (London: Macmillan, 1936).
8. Ibid.
9. Ibid.
10. Ibid.
11. Ibid.
12. Interview with Harold Wilson, *The Observer*, 9 June 1963.
13. Keynes, op. cit.
14. Ibid.
15. Ibid.
16. Ibid.
17. Ibid.
18. Ibid.
19. Ibid.
20. Ibid.
21. Ibid.
22. Ibid.
23. Ibid.
24. Ibid.
25. Ibid.

What everybody knows is frequently not so. Thus it has been with the public reputation of the first two Roosevelt administrations. As time has passed, prejudice become rooted and memory faded, the economic policies of the New Deal have been almost routinely linked with the monetary and fiscal recommendations of *The General Theory*. Remembering the early Roosevelt years as a time of massive federal deficit, many conservative citizens draw from inaccurate recollection the mistaken conclusion that the failure of unemployment to respond adequately to the deficit spending represented the failure of Keynesian public finance in actual application. More than one anti-Keynesian must have taken comfort from George Humphrey's declaration during his service as Secretary of the Treasury in the Eisenhower years that we cannot spend ourselves rich.

What the 1930s demonstrated is something quite different. A majority of economists would now in all probability agree on these four propositions.

First: Not until 1938 were Roosevelt's major advisers strongly influenced by Keynes. Moreover, no evidence exists that Roosevelt himself ever fully comprehended or completely sympathized with unbalanced budgets, deficit spending or a larger national debt. The 'great spender' was in his heart a true descendant of thrifty Dutch Calvinist forebears.

Second: From a Keynesian standpoint, the 1930s simply proved that fiscal policies which are too timid, too wavering, and too often contradicted by other measures with quite different tendencies will not expand employment and income by the amounts requisite to restore prosperity. Oscillating between reform and recovery, the New Deal achieved less than it wished of each.

Third: The laboratory demonstration of the efficacy of Keynesian remedies occurred not in the 1930s but during the enormous wartime surge in national output and the post-war boom in consumer goods which ensued. These two episodes finally proved that a government which spends enough and borrows enough can eliminate unemployment. As Keynes himself had noted in *The General Theory*, military expenditure was one of the few respectable ways of increasing aggregate demand by government action.

Fourth: In the end Keynesian doctrine did have an explicit effect upon public policy, but this effect was postponed until the end of the Second World War. In the 1930s the Keynesian influence was more considerable among economists and relatively junior public officials than it was among politicians and the heads of the important public agencies.

What in fact was the economic policy of the first two Roosevelt terms of office? It is hard not to derive a certain wry amusement from the first portion of the record. As Chapter 4 noted, Roosevelt's platform and still more his campaign speeches castigated Hoover for his deficits and for his extravagance with public funds which had caused the deficits. Indeed, if there is any clear doctrine at all which emerged from Roosevelt's campaign utterances, it is an echo of that English Treasury preference for public economy in time of depression upon which Keynes lavished much of his best invective. The historian William Leuchtenburg quotes Roosevelt at Sioux City in September, 1932, as saying, 'I accuse the present Administration of being the greatest spending Administration in peace time in all our history. It is an Administration that has piled bureau on bureau, commission on commission, and has failed to anticipate the dire needs and the reduced earning power of the people.' This was not an isolated statement. In Pittsburgh a few weeks later, Roosevelt returned to the charge: 'I regard reduction in Federal spending as one of the most important issues of this campaign. In my opinion, it is the most direct and effective contribution that Government can make to business.'[1] It is no wonder that one of Roosevelt's admirers commented later, 'Given later developments, the campaign speeches often read like a giant misprint, in which Roosevelt and Hoover speak each other's lines'.[2]

In his campaign speeches, Roosevelt never got around to deficit spending, public works, public housing, slum clearance, the National Industrial Recovery Administration, the Tennessee Valley Authority, progressive taxation, liberalized treatment of trade unions or massive relief programmes. Whatever Roosevelt offered a bewildered electorate in the summer and autumn of 1932, it was not the agenda of the New Deal. The explanation was quite possibly Roosevelt's own uncertainty about the items which ultimately constituted that agenda.

Nor were the statements simply campaign rhetoric. Once in office, Roosevelt genuinely endeavoured to honour his public pledges by reducing federal salaries and laying off government employees. More expansive and more appropriate policies soon superseded this misguided piece of statecraft. It is easily possible to exaggerate the size of the deficits which the New Deal incurred and apparently almost impossible to avoid misinterpreting the motives of the policies which resulted in the deficits. One useful benchmark to the scale of these deficits is the size of the largest peacetime deficit of our experience – the $12·4 billion unexpectedly incurred by the Eisenhower administration during the fiscal year 1959. By comparison, the 1929–41 record is one of modest deficit. Here is the evidence.

RECEIPTS AND EXPENDITURES BY THE FEDERAL
GOVERNMENT: 1929–41* (IN BILLIONS OF DOLLARS)

Year	Receipts	Expenditures	Surplus or Deficit
1929	3·8	2·6	1·2
1930	3·0	2·8	0·3
1931	2·0	4·2	– 2·1
1932	1·7	3·2	– 1·5
1933	2·7	4·0	– 1·3
1934	3·5	6·4	– 2·9
1935	4·0	6·5	– 2·6
1936	5·0	8·5	– 3·5
1937	7·0	7·2	– 0·2
1938	6·5	8·5	– 2·0
1939	6·7	9·0	– 2·2
1940	8·6	10·1	– 1·4
1941	15·4	20·5	– 5·1

SOURCE: Derived from Norman F. Keiser, *Macroeconomics, Fiscal Policy and Economic Growth* (New York: Wiley, 1964). Rounding approximations explain the apparent inconsistencies between the items in the last column and the differences derived from the second and third columns.

* The dollar values are those of each year, unadjusted for subsequent price changes in current prices. The budget concept employed is the national income and product account variant, preferred by students of public finance to the more familiar administrative budget. Unlike the latter, the national income and product account budget reflects accrual accounting of taxes and profits as well as disbursements and collections flowing out of or into the important trust funds: social security, government employees' retirement and highway construction. It is a much better index of the impact upon the economy of government operations than the more publicized administrative budget. President Kennedy considered budget concepts sufficiently important to devote a portion of his Yale commencement speech in 1962 to clarifying the different implications of various methods of presenting the federal government's fiscal operations.

Even taking into account the very much lower price levels of the 1930s, these were not sums which by themselves could conceivably have elevated to prosperity as large and as depressed an economy as the United States's in the 1930s. However, even these modest amounts overestimate the actual size of government stimulus. During much of the decade, state and local governments were pursuing quite different financial policies, usually out of absolute necessity. At the same time that the federal government was running its deficits, after 1933 these lesser units were actually piling up aggregate surpluses of anywhere between $100 million and $700 million. Thus, in 1936, when the federal deficit reached its 1930s peak of $3·5 billion, states and localities actually achieved, if that is the proper word, a surplus of $500 million. Hence the *net* stimulating effect of the deficits of all government units combined was only $3 billion. The point deserves additional emphasis. In only two years, 1931 and 1936, when Congress enacted special veterans' bonuses,* did the net stimulus to aggregate demand exceed the amount provided by all government units *in* 1929.

All the same, for whatever reasons, unemployment *did* contract. From the disastrous twenty-five per cent of 1933 it declined to twenty-two per cent in 1934, to twenty per cent in 1935, to seventeen per cent in 1936, and to fourteen per cent in 1937. This slow but apparently dependable progress persuaded a still thrifty President to yield to the financial puritans in his own administration, curtail spending, and bring the budget practically into balance. The effort had two momentous consequences – the sharp recession of 1938, and Roosevelt's belated and incomplete conversion to the Keynesian doctrine of beneficent deficit. Of this more later.

Roosevelt's actual policies were responses to immediately menacing emergencies. Of the immediate crises the most ominous concerned credit and banking. In 1932 over 1,400 banks had failed, and early in 1933 the stability of the remainder was so uncertain that, commencing with Detroit and Michigan, no fewer than twenty-one states declared banking moratoria or operated their banks under special state supervision. On the very day of the President's inauguration, New York's and Illinois's proclamation of bank holidays had the immediate effect of shutting the doors of their stock and commodity exchanges as well. Roosevelt was doing no more than

* Roosevelt, as well as Hoover, opposed the bonuses, vetoed the original bills and suffered the indignity of congressional passage over the vetoes.

completing a process when almost immediately he declared a nation-wide bank moratorium and imposed an embargo on gold movements. A Congress frightened into quick responsiveness speedily passed the emergency legislation which permitted the President to reorganize and reopen the closed banks on a presumably sounder basis.

The country craved action. The New Deal answered the craving with a series of improvisations which embodied the advice of ideologues devoted to varied panaceas, administrators granted a hearing at last, and practical men willing to try anything. One tactic widely popular within and outside the administration was inflation, or as the semantic innovation of the time had it, 'reflation'. Higher prices are immediately popular with any group which has something to sell, and the members of such groups seldom are given pause by the prospect of paying more for the things that they buy. When the United States went off the gold standard on 19 April 1933, and simultaneously raised the price at which the Treasury was willing to buy gold from $20.67 to $34.45 an ounce, the thought within the administration was that the resulting flow of gold into the country would have the effect of raising the domestic price level. In May, 1933, the first Agricultural Adjustment Act conveyed to the President the power to coin silver and to issue greenbacks in an amount up to $3 billion without the formality of metal backing of any kind. The Silver Purchase Act of 1934, primarily designed to subsidize the silver-miners of six Western states, also aimed at currency inflation.

Experiment was the response to the needs of other economic groups. Of all the sectors of the economy, farming had been depressed longest and had sunk to the lowest depths. Farm prices had been falling ever since the brief post-First World War boom had collapsed. Mortgage interest and property taxes constituted ever-rising percentages of steadily dropping farm incomes. The reactions of farmers to prospects of foreclosure grew increasingly ugly in the 1930s. On more than one occasion, lawyers or sheriffs who endeavoured to conduct auctions of foreclosed properties were threatened with lynching. Milo Reno's Farmers' Holiday Association urged farmers to withhold shipments until they were assured of fair prices. Next to the shaky financial structure of the country, the nation's farmers demanded quickest attention and promptest relief.

The administration's remedy was the enactment into law of the pastoral myth of the golden age. Justice for the farmer, declared the Agricultural Adjustment Act, consisted in a return to those happy years of 1909–14 when farmers received high prices for their crops and paid low prices for their tools, supplies and hired hands. Since there was no wish on the part of the administration to lower industrial prices (quite the contrary), the remaining way to help the farmers was by raising the prices of farm produce. The technique chosen to accomplish this end was the restriction of production – an odd enough aim in a needy world, but the best that the experts could devise. The programme was designed to cost the administration nothing, for processing taxes levied on flour mills, meat packers and other food technologists were intended to finance the subsidies to farmers. In no sense therefore was the first A.A.A. a deficit financing measure. When the Supreme Court invalidated the 1933 Act in 1936, the 1938 replacement did establish, through the device of a parity payment plan, an apparently permanent federal expenditure out of general revenue, but this result flowed from judicial vagary rather than from conscious policy.

Industrial prices were also depressed. The alphabetical agency which supervised industry was the National Recovery Administration (N.R.A.), guided by one of the more colourful characters of the day, General Hugh (Ironpants) Johnson. Like most other significant New Deal recovery legislation, the National Industrial Recovery Act was a hodgepodge bathed in hoopla. By the summer of 1933, the large Blue Eagle which was the symbol of compliance with the code of one's industry was prominently displayed in many thousands of businessmen's windows. By legislative directive each industry had written its own set of rules for good economic behaviour, generally after only the most perfunctory consultation with consumer and labour representatives. Once sanctified by General Johnson, the codes had the force of law. Since generally speaking the largest corporations dominated the code proceedings, the codes tended to incorporate strong provisions against 'chiselling' (a synonym for price competition), price-fixing at profitable levels, and, as a sop to the administration and the unions, slight wage increases and reductions in maximum work weeks. Although the code device was the central feature of the N.R.A. as well as the element in the statute which the Supreme Court ultimately declared unconstitutional, Congress wrote into the legislation an authorization for $3·3 billion in public works as well as the famous Section 7a, which declared as a new government policy that collective bargaining between unions and managements should be encouraged.

The N.R.A. was not the last price-raising measure the New Deal offered industry. The 1936 Robinson–Patman Act, prohibiting price discrimination by sellers among their customers, was aimed at the quantity discounts which large retailers were in the habit of extorting from manufacturers. Two years later the Miller–Tydings Act authorized manufacturers to set retail prices on the items they produced. The intention of the Act was to protect small retailers against the discounting and loss-leader tactics of the department stores.

There were not only bankers, farmers and industrialists clamouring for aid. There was also the 'forgotten man', so frequently recalled in the 1932 campaign, the ordinary unemployed citizen who long since had exhausted his savings and lost his home. There was the forgotten man's son, who had never lost a job because he had never been lucky enough to find one. And there were the forgotten man's brothers, the homeless tramps who in their many thousands rode the rails in search of jobs which were nowhere to be found. The relief and security measures which administration policy designed did indeed enlarge government outlays and add to the deficit, not because the deficit was good but because every man deserved assistance. The Civilian Conservation Corps, of which the Johnson Job Corps is an echo, supplied jobs in the woods to unemployed youths. The Public Works Administration spent over $7 billion during Harold Ickes's scrupulous overseeing of its affairs, although it did comparatively little to alleviate unemployment. Under Harry Hopkins's guidance, the Works Progress Administration, the often praised and often derided W.P.A., did rather better. Between 1935 and 1942 it expended $10·5 billion and employed millions of people.

The Great Depression had made it plain that even the prudent man could not protect himself against indigent old age, lengthy unemployment, and other vicissitudes of an unstable economy. Germany had recognized as much in the age of Bismarck and England during the first Lloyd George government. The Social Security Act of 1935 was America's belated attempt to protect the elderly, the unemployed and needy dependent children. In the eyes of Franklin Roosevelt, the deficits which initially emerged from the operation of the Social Security Act and other welfare devices were inescapable corollaries of genuine attempts to help whole categories of citizens who could not help themselves. But it was the *help*, not the *deficits*, which pleased the President. When the W.P.A. was savagely criticized by the anti-administration Press as a leaf-raking boondoggle, the administration's defence was the denial of the charge, not a Keynesian declaration, that even useless labour enlarged employment, income and the production of useful goods and services.

To inflation and relief the New Dealers joined a third set of policies, reforms of many kinds. Was it not self-evident, after all, that something was wrong with American business and American finance? How else could so grave an economic disaster have occurred? Since the great industrialists and financiers had been delighted to take credit for the prosperity of the 1920s, what could be fairer than to debit them with the failures of the ensuing decade? A veritable flood of legislation testified to the power of such insights. The Banking Acts of 1933 and 1935 separated security affiliates from their parent banks, established the Federal Deposit Insurance Corporation, and so reorganized the Federal Reserve Board as to give this semi-public agency more power over the private banking system. The Sale of Securities Act of 1933 protected gullible investors almost in spite of themselves by compelling companies which desired to list their securities on public exchanges to file detailed information with the Securities and Exchange Commission, which a companion act set up in 1934.

Still more to the alarm of the business community, the administration began to intervene actively on the side of the unions. Section 7a was bad enough, but it was only a declaration of intention. Far more menacing to the open shop and the American Way was the National Labor Relations Act of 1935 (the Wagner Act), which created the National Labor Relations Board, made collective bargaining the law of the land, and frankly stated a need to increase the strength of unions in their dealings with employers. The businessmen who were infuriated by such heresy were not soothed by the Walsh–Healy Act of 1956, which initiated a government policy to enter into contracts only with businessmen who paid union wages, or by the Fair Labor Standards Act of 1938, which established as law the minimum wages and maximum hours of labour that had briefly been embodied in the abortive, unconstitutional N.R.A.

As these examples imply, it was never very clear whether the primary purpose of the New Deal was simply to raise prices and promote recovery, create deficits which would 'prime the pump', or remove the chronic inequities of American life. It was this uncertainty of aim which caused Keynes on one occasion to advise the President either to nationalize the public utilities (as Keynes himself wished) or, in default of this clear-cut tactic, simply to leave them alone.[3] Such measures as the Tennessee Valley Authority and the Public Utility Holding Company Act, whatever their merits, nibbled at private ownership and interfered with some of the more fanciful devices favoured by public utility promoters, but they followed neither of Keynes's prescriptions. Favouring recovery over reform as a first American priority, Keynes saw the issue in this way:

Businessmen have a different set of delusions from politicians; and need, therefore, different handling. They are, however, much milder than politicians, at the same time allured and terrified by the glare of publicity, easily persuaded to be 'patriots', perplexed, bemused, indeed terrified, yet only too anxious to take a cheerful view, vain perhaps but very unsure of themselves, pathetically responsive to a kind word. You could do anything you liked with them, if you would treat them (even the big ones) not as wolves and tigers, but as domestic animals by nature, even though they have been badly brought up and not trained as you would wish. It is a mistake to think that they are more *immoral* than politicians. If you work them into the surly, obstinate, terrified mood, of which domestic animals, wrongly handled, are so capable, the nation's burdens will not get carried to market; and in the end public opinion will veer their way.[4]

In the generation that has elapsed since this 1938 communiqué, American businessmen, once again lords of much that they survey, have become no doubt a trifle less timid and possibly a touch more greedy. Still, Keynes's simple point had a lasting merit. If a government is resolved to operate through the mechanisms of private capitalism, that government should refrain from upsetting the delicate state of confidence of businessmen, large and small. On the business state of confidence depends the marginal efficiency of capital, the level of investment and the direction of change of national income and employment. If an administration wishes to substitute state for private direction of investment, the case is very different, but such was never the intention of the Roosevelt administration.

Thus, it is plain that despite some contact between Roosevelt and Keynes, and rather more between Keynes and a number of New Deal officials, the first five years of the New Deal were Keynesian only by occasional coincidence. One can only speculate how much difference would have been made by a personal rapport between Keynes and the President. No such rapport existed. As Frances Perkins, Secretary of Labor during the Roosevelt years, recalled the relation of the two giants, 'Roosevelt himself was unfamiliar with the economics of Keynes'. When Keynes visited Washington in June of 1934, 'He was liberally consulted, not, I think, by Hugh Johnson, but by a number of other people in the government who were anxious to have his comment'. Again, 'When we began to draw in our horns on public works and relief expenditures in 1937, he predicted what turned out to be true, that we would have another decline'.[5] However, the valued consultant and accurate prophet was welcome in neither role at the White House. When Roosevelt and Keynes actually talked in 1934, Roosevelt's comment to Miss Perkins was, 'I saw your friend Keynes. He left a whole rigamarole of figures. He must be a mathematician rather than a political economist.'[6] For his part Keynes confided to the same Miss Perkins that he had 'supposed the President was more literate, economically speaking'.[7] So much for the impact of the great upon the great.

Of course, there is more to the tale than a personal failure of communication. Keynes's influence in time did spread among New Dealers. In 1935 Harry Dexter White, one of Secretary Morgenthau's important aides at the Treasury, listened closely to Keynes's suggestion that currency stabilization be promoted by arrangements among the American, British and French Treasuries in preference either to action by private banks or to international treaties.[8] There was also an interesting coincidence. That appealing Far Western financial maverick, Marriner Eccles, Roosevelt's Chairman of the Board of Governors of the Federal Reserve System, continued in 1937 to advocate, as he had for years, a programme of deficit spending which, though totally innocent of Keynesian influence, nevertheless accorded well with the views of Keynesian advocates within the administration. Eccles's memorandum of December, 1937, attacked the analogy between private and public debt, argued that it was the size of the national income and not of the deficit that mattered, and judged that the reduction of public expenditure was unsafe until something like full recovery had occurred.[9]

When on 19 October 1937, the stock market cracked disastrously, ominously on another Black Tuesday, and the signals flashed red for the sharp recession that marked the end of 1937 and the first portion of 1938, the Keynesian influence on people like Herman Oliphant,

Harry Dexter White and Roswell Magill within the Treasury and on other officials outside it, among them Leon Henderson, Harry Hopkins and Lauchlin Currie, was sufficiently powerful to overcome Henry Morgenthau's stubborn adherence to balanced budgets. It could not have helped Morgenthau in the administration that as early as 1936 he had argued strenuously for a return to a balanced budget on the ground that even though 'the patient might scream a bit when taken off narcotics', it was high time to 'strip off the bandages, throw away the crutches', and discover whether the economy 'could stand on its own feet'.[10]

Although Roosevelt frequently thwarted his Secretary of the Treasury, Morgenthau's opinions prevailed in the formulation of the calamitous 1937 budget. Now that the recession had come just as the critics predicted and the relief lines had once more begun to lengthen in the industrial cities of the East and the Middle West; now that the Federal Reserve Board Index of Industrial Production had fallen to seventy-nine, a mere ten points higher than it had stood in 1932, Morgenthau encountered unavoidable defeat. Though Roosevelt had wound up Harold Ickes's Public Works Administration only a few months earlier, the President now sought renewed public works funds as well as additional appropriations for a number of other programmes. In an election year, in the midst of a recession obviously triggered by a shift to fiscal orthodoxy, a Congress which had been so recently restive at relief scandals and 'huge' deficits voted in June, 1938, a $3·75 billion omnibus measure. Harold Ickes's reactivated P.W.A. got nearly a billion to expend and authority to make loans aggregating another billion. Harry Hopkins secured for his W.P.A. over $1·4 billion, and smaller sums were directed to public housing, agricultural parity payments, the Farm Security Administration and the National Youth Administration.

Indeed, the Roosevelt administration finally accepted the key public policy conclusion of Keynesian economics: deficits in time of unemployment are fine because they stimulate national income and employment. If deficits are beneficial, it follows that they should be large enough to do their job. Yet the episode was not so educative as it might have been. The President continued to deplore deficits publicly, to yearn privately for balanced budgets, and to promise his constituents that just as soon as possible, fiscal orthodoxy would be restored.

The relationship between the Roosevelt administration and Keynesian doctrine, then, was at best one of tepid affection. In the longer run, what counted more than the 1937–8 fiscal episode was the growth to academic power, even to academic dominance, of an indigenous Keynesian school. The conversion of Keynesian public policy into administrative routine which has been an achievement of the Kennedy–Johnson years was based upon the training of a generation of economists and students in a new set of techniques and a new set of practical consequences.

When Paul A. Samuelson exclaimed that 'To have been born as an economist before 1936 was a boon – yes. But not to have been born too long before,'[11] he was faithfully recalling the emotions of graduate students of his own vintage at Harvard, the centre of the New Economics. Theirs was a typical young scholar's reaction to novelty – discomfiture and criticism on one side and curiosity and challenge on the other. In Samuelson's words, it did not matter that 'My rebellion against its [Keynesian economics'] pretensions would have been complete, except for an uneasy realization that I did not at all understand what it was all about'.[12] It is undeniably exciting suddenly to perceive a solution to analytical difficulties which impede action. All the better that the solution is difficult to the very brink of incomprehensibility. Young intellectuals enjoy puzzles.*

The leader of American Keynesianism was Harvard's Alvin H. Hansen, the same Hansen whose textbook entered the discussion some pages earlier. Hansen became the most influential expositor of Keynesian doctrine both to fellow professionals and to a wider public, the inventor of an American version of Keynes's prediction of capitalism's long-run future, and inevitably the target of the ill-informed and the prejudiced in and out of public life.

Hansen's own career is an example of the power of the Keynesian analysis. A specialist in business cycles, Hansen had come to the conclusion that the cycle was an exceedingly complex phenomenon, affected by the degree of inequality in the distribution of income, uncertainties of investors, fluctuations of inventories and poor co-ordination of the parts of the economy. In his early writings, this

---

* I can recall the same excitement as an undergraduate at Columbia College. There one of Keynes's own pupils, migrated to the United States, taught us the way income was determined and employment manipulated. We were especially fascinated by the multiplier doctrine, which at the first telling always seems to imply one of life's dreams, getting something for nothing, or at least a great deal for very little.

conception of the business cycle had been paralleled by a cautious even conservative estimate of the potentialities of public intervention. There was little evidence in these works of sympathy with Keynes's activist preferences.

The opposite was more nearly the case. Hansen had been a severe critic on theoretical grounds of the *Treatise on Money*. On economic policy his own 1932 volume, *Economic Stabilization in an Unbalanced World*, refused to concede that government intervention was a valid specific remedy for depression. Like such devoted friends of free market adjustment as Harvard's Joseph Schumpeter and the London School of Economics' Lionel Robbins, the Hansen of the early 1930s expected that natural price and wage changes would in time relieve the malady of depression. Along with the mandarins of the British Treasury, Hansen was maintaining in 1933 that government deficits and spending were simply subtractions from private spending and investment. Within this context there is nothing astonishing in the cool, almost hostile tone of Hansen's review of *The General Theory*. He said of it:

The book under review is not a landmark in the sense that it lays a foundation for a 'new economics'. It warns us once again, in a provocative manner, of the danger of reasoning based on assumptions which no longer fit the facts of economic life.... The book is more a symptom of economic trends than a foundation stone upon which a science can be built.[13]

According to Hansen's Harvard colleague of long standing, Seymour Harris, at the time Hansen wrote the review, he had not evolved the economic maturity doctrine, which is discussed later in this chapter; he still questioned the reality of under-employment equilibrium, and continued to oppose the use of public mechanisms to transfer private savings into public investments.[14] But as a result of his own reconsiderations and discussions with colleagues and students, Hansen rapidly shifted his ground. His 1938 collection of essays, *Full Recovery or Stagnation*, contained an old and a new Hansen. If the critical review of *The General Theory* represented the older Hansen, a concluding group of essays devoted to the 1937 recession, the concept of pump-priming, and the doctrine of secular stagnation clearly represented an endorsement of a larger role of government in general and of Keynesian public finance policy in particular.

Once begun, the evolution of Hansen's opinions continued undeviatingly. His 1941 *Fiscal Policy and Business Cycles* completed his shift towards Keynesian attitudes and Keynesian analysis. In Hansen's formulation Keynes became both more concrete and more comprehensible, for it was the strength of *Fiscal Policy and Business Cycles* that its author gave the flesh of American statistics to the bones of abstract theory. Thus, Hansen's concluding remarks on the meaning of federal borrowing followed a long historical and analytical account of how borrowing works. By the time he came to it, even the sceptic might readily have accepted Hansen's firm definition of the distinction between public and private debt:

A public debt, internally held, is not like a private debt. It has none of the essential earmarks of a private debt. The public debt is an instrument of public policy. It is a means to control the national income and, in conjunction with the tax structure, to regulate the distribution of income.[15]

The advantages, especially in the United States, of Hansen's careful, detailed approach appeared particularly in the handling of the consumption function. Keynes's treatment had been *a priori*, abstract, and unadorned by example. In contrast, Hansen, who had come to value highly the income–consumption relation, first looked at the consumption function from a cyclical standpoint and illustrated his argument with some genuine statistics of family income. Then he applied a long-run secular analysis to the data, computing lines of relationship between recorded income and consumption data. He rounded out his case for the concept with a statistical appendix prepared by Paul Samuelson which dealt closely with the major data on incomes and expenditures collected by Simon Kuznets, the pioneer investigator of the national income magnitudes.

Hansen was equally persuasive in his exposition on public spending and taxing. His long chapter on Keynesian fiscal policy, 'Pump-Priming and Compensatory Fiscal Policy', centred upon the distinction between the two concepts of deficit finance.

As Hansen defined pump-priming, it 'carries with it the implication that a certain volume of public spending ... will have the effect of setting the economy going on the way toward full realization of resources on its own power without further aid from government'.[16] Within the Roosevelt administration, there were some optimists who were convinced that a short period of government deficit would rapidly stimulate business confidence, increase private investment and eliminate the need for further deficits.

Compensatory spending implied a less euphoric outlook, 'merely that public expenditures may be used to compensate for the decline in private investment'.[17] By this time Hansen was convinced that the prime reason for economic depression was inadequate private investment. Compensatory expenditure simply supplemented private investment. As businessmen raised their investment expenditures of their own accord, compensatory spending could decline. It was a short step from the identification of this role for government to the notion of a federal budget balanced not each year but over the entire business cycle. As the economy contracted, compensatory spending would generate deficits. The deficits, according to the value of the multiplier, would raise the national income by amounts larger than themselves. Symmetrically, during expansion, surpluses would accrue as the usual consequence of rising tax receipts and constant or declining public expenditures. In a typical business cycle, the algebraic sum of the deficits and the surpluses would total zero.

The power of compensatory spending depended upon the size of the multiplier. What was a sensible value in the United States? Hansen accepted the estimate of the Columbia economist John Maurice Clark, that the leakages* were in the order of one third. Thus, it followed that $1 billion of new investment or $1 billion of additional public spending, financed by debt or created credit, would produce an increase in consumer spending initially of $667 million, then of two-thirds of $667 million, and so on in a diminishing progression. Including the initial $1 billion added to national income, the total effect of the government's action or of a private increase in investment would equal $3 billion. The multiplier, three, was as always the reciprocal of the leakages. With great care and the aid of a series of vivid charts, Hansen made this multiplier process as concrete and plausible as it had been abstract and confusing in Keynes's version.

Hansen completed his exposition with a piece of synthesis. Borrowing from his brilliant student Paul Samuelson's investigations, Hansen demonstrated that the older principle of acceleration† could

---

* Leakage, as noted earlier, is the portion of income which is saved, devoted to the payment of debts and taxes, or expended on imported goods. Keynes's guess at a higher percentage of leakage for England was associated with the much greater importance of imported goods in England than in the United States.

† The acceleration principle is symmetrical to the multiplier. It assumes that there is a definable relation between increases in consumption and increases in investment. At some point in the expansion of income, an increase in consumer

be combined with the multiplier to generate a model of cyclical fluctuation.

What Hansen had written was a teachable version of Keynesian economics, applied in some statistical detail to the American economy. If he had done no more, his leading position among American Keynesians would have been secure. In fact he enunciated the only truly original American extension of Keynesian economics until at least the 1950s. This was the notion of secular stagnation, a sufficiently plausible and persistent vision of the American situation as to deserve a section of its own.

In 1938 Alvin Hansen was president of the American Economic Association. This is an honour which the profession delights in conferring upon eminent and active economists who, it is judged, still have something significant to say to their fellows. By custom the outgoing president rounds off his one-year term of office with an address at a dinner meeting of the Association's December convention. Few presidential addresses can have been more influential than the speech which Alvin Hansen delivered in Detroit on 28 December 1938. Entitled, 'Economic Progress and Declining Population', it amounted to the bold statement that not even compensatory spending, much less pump-priming, could lift the American economy to satisfactory levels of economic activity.

Why was this so? As the answer went, 'We are passing, so to speak, over a divide which separates the great era of growth and expansion of the nineteenth century from an era which no man, unwilling to embark on pure conjecture, can as yet characterize with clarity or precision'.[18] How had the American economy so altered as to pass from growth in the nineteenth century to somnolence in

demand will strain the productive facilities of suppliers. They will then invest in new machines. If the technical relation between the finished goods and the machines which produce them is typical, an increase in consumer demand of a given magnitude will result in still larger increases in investment, thus:

If ten shoe machines, priced at $100,000 each, produce $200,000 of shoes each year;

If consumer demand rises by $20,000; and

If a shoe manufacturer purchases a new machine to fill that demand and pays $100,000 for the machine,

Then the acceleration coefficient must be five. This is to say that each dollar of additional demand has resulted in $5 of additional investment.

In general the acceleration principle is significant during cyclical upswings when existing plant capacity begins to be strained.

the twentieth? Hansen's answer was composed of three elements. Most important was the rate of population growth. Second, American dynamism in the nineteenth century had been stimulated also by the opening of successive continental frontiers and the exploitation of the natural resources of the West. And there was a third major source of economic energy: new inventions and their application. These were the three pillars of investment, and investment, earlier as later, was the source of rapid growth and satisfactory employment.

A mature economy was that of a nation no longer spurred by high investment. Such was the condition of the American economy. Consider first the overriding role of population change. From the *Wealth of Nations* onward, economists had recognized the importance of a rapid increase in population as a stimulus to high investment. As Hansen reminded his audience, Adam Smith had demonstrated that growing populations facilitated a finer division of labour and higher *per capita* productivity. More than that, larger populations facilitated the extension of the market for finished goods. The broader this market, the more encouragement it offered to still further division of labour.

We had come a long way from 1776. Could Smith's vision be adapted to American circumstances? Hansen's effort required two novel concepts, the 'widening' and the 'deepening' of capital.

As he put it, the distinction was this: 'The widening of capital is a function of an increase in final output, which in turn is due partly to an increase in population and partly to an increase in *per capita* productivity, arising from causes other than a larger use of capital per unit of output.' Or, as a paraphrase might go, capital widens when the national output of consumer goods, housing, factories and the like creates a demand for more machines and equipment to meet market demand. Widening of capital assumes stable technique. By contrast, 'The deepening of capital results partly from cost-reducing changes in techniques, partly (though this is probably a much less significant factor) from a reduction in the rate of interest, and partly from changes in the character of the output as a whole, with special reference to the amount of capital required to produce it'.[19] In short, capital is said to be deepened whenever machinery is substituted for labour in the productive process and the amount of capital required to produce a given quantity of goods is expanded. Thus, the contemporary argument over the incidence of automation (see Chapter 11) is concerned with a problem of deepening of this kind: has capital been substituted for labour at an unusually rapid rate or in a significantly different manner?

As Hansen advanced his argument, population growth has a connection with both the widening and the deepening process. Even if nothing else of economic significance occurs, a rapidly expanding population will demand a widening of capital. But it is plain that a rapidly expanding population will call not only for more goods than will a stationary population but also for a drastically different assortment of goods. A growing population implies rapid family formation, which in turn causes a buoyant demand for new housing and household furnishings. A stationary population requires only replacement of that portion of the housing stock which becomes unusable. Moreover, since it contains a higher proportion of the elderly, the demand for personal services – medical, domestic, even custodial – increases. Housing involves large capital expenditure; personal service does not. Hence any shift from a rapidly increasing population to a slowly increasing or stationary population must imply a declining ratio of capital to output as a whole – the reverse of the deepening situation.

How much of the American investment boom of the nineteenth century was the consequence of the vigorous population increase? Hansen's examination of the record began with the notation that up to the First World War, total output in the United States rose at the rate of nearly four per cent each year. More than half of the annual increment was attributable to the expansion of the labour force. Now, if it is assumed that capital formation proceeded at about the same rate as the rise in aggregate output, then 'We may say that the growth of population in the last half of the nineteenth century was responsible for... about sixty per cent of the capital formation in the United States'.[20] To say the least, then, any substantial decline in the rate of population growth must have had seriously adverse effects upon investment incentives.

In fact, the population rate of growth had slowed. In a central passage, Hansen summarized the American experience:

In the decade of the nineteen-twenties the population of the United States increased by 16,000,000 – an absolute growth equal to that of the prewar decade and in excess of any other decade in our history. In the current decade we are adding only half this number to our population, and the best forecasts indicate a decline to a third in the decade which we are about to enter.[21]

Hansen's predictions stood or fell upon this demographic projection – one which he shared with most students of population at the time.*

What accounted for the remainder of the nineteenth-century growth in capital investment were Hansen's second and third influences, the exploitation of new frontiers and resources and the stimulus of technical invention. The atmosphere of the twentieth century was less propitious to these varieties of investment as well. As far as frontiers were concerned, 'These outlets for new investment are rapidly being closed'.[22] This was not only a matter of the completion of settlement in the American West; it was the result also of the narrowing of opportunities for foreign investment. Foreign investment had served France and England during the nineteenth century as a substitute for an open land frontier. But, said Hansen ominously, 'No one is likely to challenge the statement that foreign investment will in the next fifty years play an incomparably smaller role than was the case in the nineteenth century'.[23]

If population growth was slowing to a halt, if frontiers were closing, and if foreign investment was shrinking, what was left as a last hope was a 'world in which we must fall back upon a more rapid advance of technology than in the past if we are to find private investment opportunities adequate to maintain full employment'.[24] Under the circumstances everything possible must be done to encourage the emergence of new industries. In the past spectacular novelties like railroads, electricity and automobiles had created massive investment booms. In the future we would be compelled to rely still more heavily upon the important innovation.

Nevertheless, the outlook was scarcely brighter here than elsewhere, for a whole array of 'institutional developments' restricted initiative and damped opportunity. Among the impediments to investment in new industries and processes were 'the growing power of trade unions and trade associations, the development of monopolistic competition, of rivalry for the market through expensive persuasion and advertising, instead of through price competition'.[25] Price competition compelled even reluctant businessmen to acquire

* As a science demography is as precarious as meteorology. The actual increase in the population of the United States between 1940 and 1950 was 19,008,086, substantially more than the 16,000,000 of the 1920s and over double the 8,894,229 increase of the 1930s. Moreover, in the 1950s population expanded by 27,766,875 persons. See *Statistical Abstract of the United States, 1962* (Washington, D.C.: U.S. Bureau of the Census, 1963).

cost-cutting new techniques even if the price was the scrapping of old equipment which was still physically usable. The price of delay was speedy elimination by rivals of superior alertness. But where monopoly, oligopoly or monopolistic competition* characterized the market, patents might be suppressed, old equipment used until it wore out, and investment and innovation alike held to a minimum.

Thus, at the end of his exploration, Hansen concluded that 'The main problem of our times, and particularly in the United States, is the problem of full employment'. It was an era marked by weak business recoveries and protracted depressions: 'This is the essence of secular stagnation – sick recoveries which die in their infancy and depressions which feed on themselves and leave a hard and seemingly immovable core of unemployment.'26

A grim enough problem. In his speculations about the presence of a similar economic condition in England, Keynes had contemplated the extreme remedy of comprehensive nationalization of investment. In the 1930s no one in a position of genuine power or influence in the United States dared or possibly cared to go as far.† For his part Hansen was far from sanguine. Although he had a good word to say for the stimulation of consumption through tax reductions and for public investment 'in human and natural resources and in consumers' capital goods of a collective character designed to serve the physical, recreational and cultural needs of the community as a whole', he feared for the 'economic workability' of some of these devices, and he even wondered how much public spending could be done 'without adversely affecting the system of free enterprise'.27 There might be adverse effects from a rising public debt. Worse still, very substantial public spending might indeed shift the

---

* Monopoly is the domination of an industry in a substantial geographic area by a single firm, oligopoly is the domination by a small number of very large firms, and monopolistic competition is a rivalry among relatively large numbers of sellers confined to advertising, packaging and display. Thus, in New York City, Consolidated Edison is a monopoly. The automobile industry, like most other major manufacturing industries in America, is a good illustration of oligopoly.

† William E. Leuchtenburg quotes Adolf Berle in 1938 to the effect that 'unless the government nationalizes great blocks of industry, reliance must be had on at least seven times as much private activity as government activity' (*Franklin D. Roosevelt and the New Deal, 1932–1940* (New York: Harper & Row, 1963)). However, Berle's moral was not the desirability of nationalization but the inapplicability of old panaceas like anti-trust crusades.

economy towards full employment but only at the price of a
damaging inflation.

The United States was in a dilemma. On the one hand, 'Continued
unemployment on a vast scale, resulting from inadequate private
investment outlets, could be expected sooner or later to lead straight
into an all-round regimented economy'. On the other, 'So also, by
an indirect route and a slower process, might a greatly extended
program of public expenditure'.[28] Not a happy outlook in either
direction. The best policy was a programme of 'net income-creating
governmental expenditures' which were prudently 'tapered off
as we approach a full-employment income level'. Even here the
pitfalls were treacherous: production bottlenecks, rising costs,
aggressive wage demands and the 'familiar vicious spiral of
rising costs and rising prices with growing inefficiency'.[29] As
Hansen confessed, the complete solution was not in his hands:
'The problems which I have raised offer a challenge to our profession.'[30]

The late 1930s were not a happy time. Keynesians like Hansen
might properly point out that full-scale compensatory finance had
not been ventured, but Hansen had his own doubts and reservations
about the policy's efficacy. These were related both to his doctrine
of secular stagnation and to his shorter-term fears of inflation. All the
experiments, all the hopes of talented New Dealers who surrounded
an imaginative and compassionate President had neither created a
satisfactory national policy nor, much more importantly, restored
anything like prosperity. As one of Roosevelt's biographers has
speculated, 'If Roosevelt had urged spending programs on Congress
rather than the court plan and certain reform measures in 1937, he
probably could have both met his commitments to the one-third ill-
housed, ill-fed, and ill-clothed and achieved substantial re-employment'.[31] In actual fact Roosevelt wanted to balance his budget and
confound his conservative critics. Although Roosevelt and his
advisers were jolted by the consequences of their aspiration, they
were highly reluctant Keynesians. As Harrod has said, 'It is not clear
that he [Roosevelt] acted on the principle that it was the deficit,
rather than the public works themselves, that was the potent agency
in reducing unemployment'.[32]

It is not hard in retrospect to identify the weakness of Rooseveltian fiscal policy. Spending had been much too timid and cautious

to achieve a return to prosperity. At the same time, enough *had* been spent, a sufficient number of spending agencies had been created, to alarm the business community, which by now had taken up arms against the Democratic administration. Accentuated by the colourful political rhetoric of the New Deal, this alarm probably did diminish private investment. After all, when the acknowledged leader of Keynesian thought could enquire whether 'the government intervention [has] created a hybrid society, half-free and half-regimented, which cannot operate at full employment',[33] ordinary businessmen might be forgiven a qualm or two about the economic prospects before them.

The tragi-comedy of economic policy during the 1937–8 recession was entirely consistent with the empiricism which Roosevelt applied to all domestic issues. After his initial flirtation with reducing government salaries and employment, Roosevelt shifted to heavy expenditure. As a spender he fluctuated between direct relief to the needy and the Ickes emphasis on substantial public works. On the international scene, one of the President's first acts had been to torpedo the London Economic Conference. No sooner had he offered this evidence of economic nationalism than he allowed his Secretary of State to undertake a crusade for reciprocal trade agreements and lower tariffs. Thus it had gone.

The double shift in 1937–8, first towards a balanced budget and then once more towards deficit-financed public works, was therefore not the failure of Keynesian doctrine but another sign of the inadequacy of an eclectic method of public management. It was typical that even when Roosevelt reverted to spending, he hedged his bet by requesting authorization from Congress of an investigation into the concentration of economic power in the United States. Congress cheerfully established the Temporary National Economic Committee, under the chairmanship of a distinguished Far Western trust-buster, Senator Joseph C. O'Mahoney. On the one hand the New Deal stimulated, on the other it alarmed the business community.

At the end of this depressing tale of bungled policy and missed opportunity, there is a question. What stopped Roosevelt from adopting a single massive policy of public spending as the release from the unremitted burden of unemployment which the country bore until Pearl Harbor? James MacGregor Burns has posed the issue in this way:

Deficit spending was ideally suited to Roosevelt's ideology and program. He was no doctrinaire capitalist; twenty years before his presidency he was a New Deal state senator favoring a host of government controls and reforms, and he had stood for progressivism as a Wilson lieutenant and as governor. He was no doctrinaire socialist; he had never embraced the idea of central state ownership of the means of production. Rejecting both doctrinaire solutions, Keynesian economics was a true middle way – at a time when New Dealers were groping for a middle way that worked.[34]

The explanation of Roosevelt's failure of commitment is complex, but part of the answer is located in the nature of Roosevelt's official family. The President's advisers and intimates were perennially disunited on the causes and the cures of depression. Occupying the central economic post in any administration was Henry Morgenthau, an undeviating enemy of deficit spending, whose consent to public expenditure usually testified to humanitarian sympathy for the victims of economic hardship rather than reasoned comprehension of the virtues of deficits. A budget balancer like Morgenthau was the exception in the New Deal, but among the remainder of Roosevelt's aides there were more opinions than was helpful to a perplexed chief executive.

At the least five rival theories contended for the President's favour. There were those, most prominently Gardiner Means and Senator Joseph O'Mahoney, who maintained that the depression persisted because of the failure of big corporations to lower their prices. These price rigidities were caused by a concentration of economic power in too few hands. Hence the remedies were congressional exposure and much more active anti-trust enforcement. This argument derived some of its inspiration from Justice Brandeis's powerful arguments for small units and decentralization of economic decision as necessary protections for political freedom. Even in the 1930s, there was a second group of experts, headed by Secretary Henry Morgenthau, who worried more about inflation than depression. Some of Roosevelt's advisers, among them Lauchlin Currie, were convinced that if business could be persuaded or coerced into paying out more of its earnings as dividends, purchasing power would grow. The legislative monument to this sentiment was a tax on undistributed profits, which was soon to be repealed. The moderate Keynesians, influenced by Hansen, argued initially for pump-priming and then for compensatory finance as the sovereign remedies. As evidence they used the precedents of 1935 and 1936, years when deficits did coincide with economic expansion. And finally there were men like Paul Sweezy, left-wing Keynesians more single-mindedly devoted to the reality of secular stagnation than the inventor of the hypothesis himself, who had lost faith in American capitalism and opted for modes of intervention far beyond mere compensatory spending. No wonder Franklin Roosevelt, blown about by the winds of doctrine, hesitated, wavered and often pursued more than one policy at the same time.

But the chances are that even if the President's confidants had spoken in a single voice, crying, 'Spend, spend, spend', Roosevelt would have hesitated. The master's temperament, his intellectual habits, even his scepticism, were hostile to that full-scale commitment which alone is capable of making fiscal policy work during a really deep depression. By nature Roosevelt distrusted single remedies, enjoyed experiment and rejoiced in the combination of the apparently irreconcilable, in doctrine as in people. '"Lock yourselves in a room, and don't come out until you agree," he would say blithely to people who differed hopelessly in their economic premises – to free traders and nationalists, to deflationists and inflationists, to trust-busters and collectivists, to spenders and economizers.'[35] Roosevelt's instincts as a politician reinforced his temperamental preferences. Why not heed each group of his intimates, on occasion, and in moderate degree?

For politics and for human relations, this programme was impeccable. Unfortunately, a combination of measures which gratified simultaneously the spenders and the trust–busters substantially diminished the stimulus of the spending by adversely affecting the marginal efficiency of capital and the resulting level of investment. This was the point of Keynes's 1938 letter to Roosevelt in which he advised the President to treat businessmen carefully and gently. A full-scale investigation of monopoly practices in American industry and finance was scarcely the appropriate complement to a fiscal policy aimed at encouraging more investment by the very people whom the Temporary National Economic Committee was grilling.

In the midst of these cross-currents of ideology and political compromise, there was a certain irony. Even the relatively modest reversion to deficit spending in 1938 had a favourable influence upon employment and national income. The sequence of events tells an uncomplicated story. In the fiscal year 1938 (ending 30 June 1938), federal tax collections slightly exceeded $7 billion and federal expenditures were slightly under $7·2 billion. The deficit in the administrative budget was an inconsequential $100 million. The more realistic cash budget produced an actual surplus. The depressing effect of this surplus was aggravated by substantial increases in state and local taxes. Altogether the three levels of government were removing larger sums in taxes from the community than they were returning to the community in the shape of public expenditure. This perverse public finance in a year whose unemployment averaged fourteen per cent had predictable effects. The gross national product fell from a 1937 value of $91 billion to a 1938 value of $85 billion. Private investment plummeted by a full fifty per cent, from $10 billion in 1937 to $5 billion in 1938.

The 1938 resort to deficit finance created a gap of $2·9 billion between federal receipts and expenditures during the fiscal year 1939 as federal spending rose to $9·4 billion and federal revenues contracted to $6·6 billion. A grateful economy responded appropriately: G.N.P. in 1939 returned to its 1937 level and investment partially recovered, to $7 billion. The effect on employment was less gratifying. Reaching nineteen per cent in 1938, unemployment was still 17·2 per cent in 1939 and 14·6 per cent in 1940 – slightly higher in the last years than the 1937 figure. It symbolizes the failure of Rooseveltian policies that 1937's employment figure was the peak achievement of the pre-war years.[36]

In other words, Roosevelt's critics who charged him with failing to resolve the dominant domestic problem of his administration were unquestionably in the right. In many instances, however, they were mistaken about the reasons for the failure. Conservatives who maintained then and later that deficit finance had not worked, and that the only sensible recourse was the tested orthodoxies of cost and wage reduction, small government and balanced budgets, were simply mistaken. Equally in error were Marxist economists like Paul Sweezy, who contended (in 1946) that the disasters of the 1930s 'are not simply a "frightful muddle" but are the direct and inevitable product of a social system which has exhausted its power, but whose beneficiaries are determined to hang on regardless of cost'.[37]

The lessons of the 1930s were less sensational. The new Keynesian economics had accomplished only half its mission by converting Hansen and other economists and by infecting the lower echelons of the federal bureaucracy. There were still the politicians and the public.

As for the first, neither the President nor his major advisers had completely grasped the intellectual content of Keynes's message. As for the public and the Congress which represented it, the intellectual distance was still greater between the dominant traditional opinion and the newer revelations of modern economics.

Thus it was that the administration's actions consisted almost entirely of *ad hoc* responses to economic emergencies and compassionate attempts to alleviate the hardships of afflicted farmers, home-owners, unemployed workers and poverty-stricken pensioners. Hansen's 1941 judgement was accurate in its perception that 'For the most part, the federal government engaged in a salvaging program and not in a program of positive expansion'.[38] So it occurred also that federal, state and local policies stimulated the economy more substantially in the early 1930s than in the later years of the decade. In those years tax collections rose more rapidly than government expenditures, and it is evident that if the economy had approached anything like full employment, very substantial surpluses would have been generated.

The last word on the influence of Keynesian fiscal policy properly belongs to one of the leading students of the 1930s: 'Fiscal policy, then, seems to have been an unsuccessful recovery device in the 'thirties – not because it did not work, but because it was not tried.'[39] Of course, the same has been said about Christianity. However, the full-scale trial of Keynesian public finance had a shorter postponement. The Second World War was an incomparable laboratory demonstration that deficits do cause prosperity. As Keynes had said, 'It would indeed be more sensible to build houses and the like,' but there were (and are) still 'political and practical difficulties in the way of this. ...'[40]

SOURCE NOTES TO CHAPTER 5

1. Quoted in William E. Leuchtenburg, *Franklin D. Roosevelt and the New Deal, 1932–1940* (New York: Harper & Row, 1963).
2. Marriner Eccles in Sidney Hyman (ed.), *Beckoning Frontiers: Public and Personal Recollections* (New York: Knopf, 1951).
3. See John M. Blum, *Years of Crisis, 1921–1938,* vol. l of *From the Morgenthau Diaries* (Boston: Houghton Mifflin, 1959).
4. Quoted in ibid.
5. Frances Perkins, *The Roosevelt I Knew* (New York: Harper & Row, 1964).
6. Quoted in ibid.

7. Quoted in ibid.

8. Blum, op. cit.

9. Ibid.

10. Quoted in Leuchtenburg, op. cit.

11. Paul A. Samuelson, 'The "General Theory"', in Robert Lekachman (ed.) *Keynes's General Theory: Reports of Three Decades* (New York: St Martin's, 1964; London: Macmillan).

12. Ibid.

13. Alvin H. Hansen, review of J. M. Keynes's *The General Theory of Employment, Interest and Money* in *The Journal of Political Economy*, October 1936; reprinted in Seymour Harris (ed.) *The New Economics* (New York: Knopf, 1947). The review was one of the earliest to appear in the United States.

14. Ibid.

15. Alvin M. Hansen, *Fiscal Policy and Business Cycles* (New York: Norton, 1941; London: Allen & Unwin).

16. Ibid.

17. Ibid.

18. Alvin M. Hansen, 'Economic Progress and Declining Population', in American Economic Association, *Readings in Business Cycle Theory* (Philadelphia: Blakiston, 1944).

19–30. Ibid.

31. James MacGregor Burns, *Roosevelt: The Lion and the Fox* (New York: Harcourt Brace, 1956).

32. Sir Roy Harrod, *The Life of John Maynard Keynes* (London: Macmillan, 1951).

33. Alvin H. Hansen, *Full Recovery or Stagnation* (New York: Norton, 1938).

34. Burns, op. cit.

35. Ibid.

36. See Norman F. Keiser, *Macroeconomics, Fiscal Policy, and Economic Growth* (New York: Wiley, 1964).

37. Paul M. Sweezy, 'John Maynard Keynes', in Lekachman, op. cit.

38. Hansen, *Fiscal Policy and Business Cycles*.

39. E. C. Brown, 'Fiscal Policy in the Thirties: A Reappraisal', *American Economic Review*, December 1956.

40. J. M. Keynes, *The General Theory of Employment, Interest and Money* (London: Macmillan, 1936).

In 1939 John Maynard Keynes was fifty-six. By now world-renowned, he commanded in private audience and journalistic utterance the immediate attention of the influential and the powerful, especially in his own country and the United States. The contrast could scarcely have been sharper between the brash, rising young don of 1914 and the theoretical innovator of 1939, a mature man of affairs and a seasoned veteran of countless polemical encounters. There was a less fortunate physical contrast between 1914 and 1939. In 1937 Keynes had suffered a severe heart attack which had incapacitated him for some months. Even in 1939 he was incompletely recovered, under orders from his doctors to maintain a reduced schedule of activity and subject to the nursing regimen of his devoted wife. As a Cambridge friend and colleague recalls, 'None of us imagined it possible that he should play a part in this war comparable to the part that he had played in 1914–18'.[1]

Keynes's friends were mistaken. Their colleague's role in this conflict was much more important than his part in the First World War. Very quickly Keynes took hold, characteristically in the public Press. In three November, 1939, articles printed in *The Times*, Keynes outlined the organizing economic ideas which guided the deployment of British resources and the shape of British public finance during the six years of the Second World War. Rapidly reprinted as the pamphlet *How to Pay for the War*, these three articles were typical Keynes. They started with the insistence that 'More lucidity ... is our first need'.[2] The principal barrier to lucidity was the failure to perceive that 'all aspects of the economic problem are interconnected. Nothing can be settled in isolation. Every use of our resources is at the expense of an alternative use.'[3]

The war economy could not be separated from the civilian economy, but there was a central difference between peace and war. During peace, when the labour force expanded, the extra workers used their additional income to purchase the very goods which they had helped to produce. During a war, by contrast, any enlargement of total output appropriately went into the war effort, which consumed absolutely everything not essential to the minimum civilian standard tolerable to the labouring population. It followed that the central task of war finance was the transfer of extra income from workers to government. Although immediate necessity was the controlling consideration, Keynes saw no good reason that a good system of wartime finance should prevent future social improvement. With this objective in mind, many of the details of *How to Pay for the War* were designed to promote wartime equity and peacetime social justice.

Technically, Keynes's contribution was an extension of the doctrines of *The General Theory* to an economy threatened by inflation instead of depression. He substituted for the orthodox budgetary approach to the financing of war* the national income and employment framework upon which the analysis and the policies of his economics hung. The merit of the substitution was its realism. Officials were enabled to concentrate on the fundamental truth that in the end wars are supported not by money and taxes but by the physical resources which are susceptible of rapid conversion into ships, artillery, ammunition, tanks, aircraft and uniforms. The quantity of these resources is in principle readily measured: it is the sum of the capital equipment, raw materials and labour which the community controls, less those essential to the health and efficiency of the civilian population. Properly defined, then, the problems of war finance are problems of real aggregate demand and real aggregate supply. And the most influential customer was the military establishment.

Keynes's government was ready to listen. Already some of his pupils were in the Treasury, and within weeks of the appearance early in 1940 of *How to Pay for the War*, Keynes's disciples had convinced Treasury officials that it was necessary to establish an economic section of the Cabinet Office, primarily devoted to the improvement of national income statistics. James Meade and Richard Stone, two Cambridge Keynesians, were put in charge of the work, and as early as the 1941 budget their labours began to have their effects. Moreover, Keynes himself soon entered government service. After

* In 1914 Keynes's concentration upon the limits of taxation had caused him to predict a short war on the ground that no government could 'afford' a long one.

Winston Churchill's assumption of control, he appointed Lord Catto and his old critic Keynes as his principal economic advisers. Intervening wherever he chose, Keynes seems to have moved from his emphasis on internal finance in the early years of the war to an increasing preoccupation with the shape of the post-war world.

In the evocative passages which follow, one of Keynes's Treasury colleagues recalled Keynes's mode of operation:

Despite the physical frailty from which Keynes was still suffering as a result of his illness, he characteristically took all of the Treasury's financial and economic activities as his province. He sat in daily at the Treasury for long hours. He saw every important paper that the Treasury produced or that was wandering through the Treasury. Many he put away for reference, and out of any heap of papers in one of his locked drawers Keynes could unerringly pull out the one he wanted. He irrupted frequently and unexpectedly into major questions such as the use of man-power, the necessity for allowing no waste of resources, the problems of taxation, such as 'pay-as-you-earn', the income-tax credits, and the work on the statistics and presentation of the national income. In his last years, he paid particular attention to the balance of payments.

He read official papers voraciously and always remembered what he wanted to remember, though he was not incapable of inventing what he asserted to be a fact. He accepted all these burdens not only as a good and unselfish colleague, but for deeper reasons. As is said at an earlier stage of this essay, Keynes was specially interested in the application of economic theory to the practical problems of government. He was increasingly impressed with the necessity for allowing the whole stream of official work to flow through his consciousness if he wanted to produce any economic plan whose structure would resist informed criticism. Although he had been thinking and writing about schemes like the Clearing Union as far back as 1938 the plan that he produced for public discussion was reinforced by his knowledge of the actual situation confronting the United Kingdom. Similarly, his more tentative proposals for international commodity policy derived much from the experience of bulk purchases during the war and from the anxieties created by the often uncontrolled rise in commodity prices in many of the supplying countries.

But it was in his presentation of the case for the American Loan that his journeyman's work at the Treasury showed its full achievement. There was no figure that Keynes used at Washington whose application to the present and future life of the English people he could not illustrate from his knowledge of the practical details of government and administration. Conferences in Keynes' room at the Treasury were seminar classes in adult education and his new, but middle-aged, pupils at the Treasury experienced something of the same sense of excitement as the younger men who had worked with Keynes when he was a teacher at Cambridge.

Even on the many journeys he made abroad he took care to receive and read regularly the most important of the current papers reaching the Treasury. The feel and touch of things was to him a large part of the area of government.[4]

In the eyes of his old friends, Keynes had become almost ridiculously respectable. The former heretic of the financial world was in 1940 raised to the eminence of a position on the Court of the Bank of England. He commented wryly in the tradition of the old Bloomsbury, 'I am not sure which of us is being made an honest woman – the Old Lady or me'.[5] Keynes's worry was groundless: he hadn't softened his principles; his old antagonists had capitulated to reason. Then in June 1942, Keynes became Lord Keynes of Tilton. Unsuccessful in defeating Keynes, the official world had embraced him.

Keynes seized his position to promote the goals of his programme. Although his largest immediate service to the orderly conduct of the war was no doubt the conversion of Treasury calculation into the national income framework of accounting, the portion of his blueprint which attracted the most public attention was the sketch of means to social equity. Since a just war was not the occasion for the enrichment of any segment of the community, much less for the imposition of unnecessary sacrifices upon the poor, Keynes offered an ingenious package of proposals which simultaneously controlled inflation and promoted justice. Keynes's measures, 'universal family allowances in cash, the accumulation of working-class wealth under working-class control, a cheap ration of necessaries, and a capital levy (tax) after the war',[6] sopped up excess purchasing power immediately, imposed a heavier ultimate burden upon the rich than the poor, and projected a release of purchasing power from compulsory savings which might in the post-war world head off renewed depression.

By no means did all of these proposals become law, although the compulsory saving plan, the subject of much controversy, was adopted in limited form in 1941. If the national government had accepted the entire programme, England would have used the Second World War to redistribute income and wealth in the direction of much greater equality. Even the forced saving plan by itself removed a larger share of earned income from the temptations of immediate expenditure than purely voluntary saving could have done. Moreover, forced saving (with a promise of future consumption) damped work incentives far less than an increase in taxation designed to siphon off similar amounts would have. Forced savings during a war could be presented as a future title to the good things of a peacetime society.

In the British Treasury, the Second World War was fought according to Keynesian principles of finance and the Keynesian analysis of aggregate demand and supply. All the same Keynes was disappointed in the failure to follow his proposals all the way. He had hoped to raise £550 million each year by deferred savings. Actually the average for the war years was only £121 million. As a result the rationing and the price-fixing which Keynes had hoped to minimize by a large-scale combination of taxes, voluntary saving and forced saving became necessary. Nor was the British government, a coalition in which the Conservatives were the senior partners, willing to redistribute income and wealth so substantially as Keynes considered desirable.

How Keynesian was the American conduct of the war? How willing were Americans to accept doctrines in war that they had resisted in peace? How much of American planning for the post-war era bore the marks of Keynes's ideas? A good place to begin consideration of such questions is with the spectacular transformation of the American economy from depression and under-employment to overfull employment and massive output of every kind of good and service.

Between 1939 and 1944, the peak of the war effort, the real value of the nation's output rose over seventy per cent. Still more remarkably, private product expanded by over half at the same time that the value of the government's output more than trebled and its share of total output rose from slightly more than ten per cent in 1939 to between a fifth and a quarter in 1944.

Accompanying these shifts in the national product was a nationwide redeployment of the labour force. In 1939 the total membership of the armed forces was a meagre 370,000. At the cessation of hostilities in 1945, some 11,410,000 men and women were in uniform. Nevertheless, the total civilian labour force numbering 55,230,000 individuals in 1939 dropped only to 53,860,000 in 1945. The numbers contain no mystery. The elderly, the maimed and the drunken, housewives, pensioners and students turned out in the missions at the call of patriotism and high wages. And suddenly there was no unemployment problem. By 1942 the rate was 4·7 per cent, but in 1943 it was 1·9 per cent and in the succeeding year a wartime low of 1·2 per cent. The miracles of war production were a tribute to the energies and the organizational talents of millions of Americans. But they were made possible by the tremendous slack which existed in the 1939 economy.

As that slack was taken up, the same problems of resource allocation and price restraint concerned American administrators as had earlier challenged their British colleagues. In a liberal democracy, the minimum objectives of wartime finance are the efficient allocation of resources to the military, the avoidance of economic scandal, and the uncoerced movement of workers into the right jobs and capital into the appropriate industries. In the management of economic resources, patriotism must be supplemented with more tangible rewards. At least the appearance if not the reality of equality of sacrifice is essential.

No more than England was the United States able to finance wartime expenditure out of wartime taxation. This inability can be traced in the upward movement of the national debt from $40·4 billion in 1939 to $258·7 billion by the end of 1945, a more than sixfold increase. Taxes were nevertheless an indispensable supplement to borrowing. Taxes diminished the purchasing power which the expansion of the economy generated. And taxes were deployed as a technique of social equity. The record of taxes, expenditures, deficits and federal debt during the years 1939–45 makes plain the decision of American leaders to tax equitably and heavily. An almost tenfold increase in tax receipts between 1939 and 1945 measures the impact of this decision.

FEDERAL TAXES, EXPENDITURES, DEFICITS, AND
NATIONAL DEBT: 1939–45 (IN MILLIONS OF DOLLARS)

Year	Taxes	Expenditures	Deficit	National Debt
1939	$ 4,979	$ 8,841	$ 3,862	$ 40,440
1940	5,137	9,055	3,918	42,968
1941	7,096	13,255	6,159	48,961
1942	12,547	34,037	21,490	72,422
1943	21,948	79,368	57,420	136,696
1944	43,563	94,986	51,423	201,003
1945	44,362	98,303	53,941	258,682

SOURCE: Adapted from *The Economic Report of the President* (Washington, D.C.: U.S. Government Printing Office, January, 1964).

Taxes rose because the economy expanded, but they rose also because in 1942 an excess profits tax was enacted and because each year the rates applied to personal income were elevated. In 1939 the income tax was paid by only four million prosperous Americans, but in 1942 no fewer than forty-two million Americans filed returns.[7] The bulk of the increases in personal and corporate income–tax rates occurred in the later years of the Second World War, after idle men and resources had been absorbed. Nevertheless, with the single exception of 1944, the tax increases failed to keep pace with mounting government spending on the war. In consequence both deficits and the national debt made spectacular leaps.

Quite possibly tax rates could have been increased more sharply, although no one can be certain that adverse effects upon incentives to labour and investment might not have followed. It is conceivable that some version of forced saving might have been installed. This is conjecture. The fact is the failure of taxes to remove enough of the extra spending power generated by wartime production to obviate the need for rationing and price controls. It quickly became essential to supplement these with wage and salary restraints.

In these events and decisions, what was the Keynesian influence? Keynes himself was pleased with the extent to which his ideas had spread among the younger officials of the administration. On his 1941 visit to the United States, Keynes addressed a National Press Club dinner which had been arranged so that he could meet Leon Henderson and Henderson's principal associates in the Office of Price Administration. In his talk Keynes urged higher taxes as an anti-inflation device. One of the dinner's sequels was a correspondence with Walter S. Salant in which Salant explained that American economists were taking into account both the multiplier and the acceleration impact upon the economy of defence spending. 'It was satisfactory to Keynes to find that his own tools of analysis were being used by those responsible for framing policy with characteristic American statistical thoroughness.'[8] As Keynes's comment in a letter to Salant noted, it was the young who were the most receptive:

There is too wide a gap between the intellectual outlook of the older people and that of the younger. I have been greatly struck during my visit by the quality of the younger economists and civil servants in the Administration. I am sure that the best hope for good government of America is to be found there. The war will be a great sifter and will bring the right people to the top. We have a few good people in London, but nothing like the *numbers* you can produce here.[9]

Although Morgenthau remained as untouched by the New Economics as ever, young Keynesians were fairly numerous in the Treasury, especially in Harry Dexter White's division. And they were scattered through other agencies, including the special agencies of wartime control – the Office of Price Administration and the War Production Board. These economists routinely applied income analysis to wartime problems. According to an observer of later eminence, the quality of wartime economics in Washington was high, significantly superior to the German level of economic analysis.[10] Like their confrères in England, the American economists conducted their investigations in terms of the real raw materials, labour and capital available to the community. The aggregative technique was a truer guide for resource allocation than purely financial measures.

The war pointed a sharp Keynesian moral. As a public works project, all wars (before the nuclear era) are ideal. Since all war production is sheer economic waste, there is never a danger of producing too much. Even an enlightened nation might build enough schools, roads, houses, parks and hospitals to meet its own standards. What happens when the demand for perfectly useless objects is multiplied almost without limit? What happens when this demand is financed in reality if not in appearance by the printing of new money? In the world of 1941–5, what occurred was full employment, bustling factories and an increase in the production of useful as well as useless things. In real life these were the consequences of waste. They were also the consequences predicted by Keynes. In the Second World War the equivalent of the Egyptian pyramids, the medieval cathedrals, and the buried bottles full of money were the tanks, the bombers and the aircraft carriers.

Both by their numbers and by their influence, American Keynesians did much in Washington to enhance the reputation of American economics. Samuelson conjectures (plausibly for other economists at least) that the nature of their graduate training prepares economists to cope effectively with the issues of choice and allocation which are at the centre of wartime economic decision. In the early war years, these indeed were practically the only problems on which economists worked. There was a war to be won. However, by 1944 when victory was over the horizon, their focus of interest shifted increasingly to the planning of the post-war world.

It was probably inevitable that the renewed concern for a peacetime economy took its point of departure from the immediate prewar discussions on the apparently intractable 'normal' dilemmas of deficient private investment, inadequate rates of economic expansion and persistent unemployment. Alvin Hansen's doctrine of secular stagnation had been accorded its boldest and most radical amplification in a polemic by a group of Harvard and Tufts economists writing in the gloom of the 1937-8 recession.[11] These seven young Keynesians took it for granted that 'The economic development of America may be divided into two periods. The first, beginning when the earliest colonists set foot on our shores, was the period of economic expansion. It came to a dramatic close with the collapse of 1929. The second period has so far been one of economic stagnation.'[12]

Obviously, the New Deal had not defeated stagnation, but as far as it had gone, it had found the right track in expanded deficit spending: 'One of the lessons of the past five years has been the striking demonstration of the efficacy of public spending in promoting national well-being.'[13] If the New Deal had spent more, the results undoubtedly would have been more satisfactory. However, the 1937-8 recession implied the need for a more substantial change in the American economy than deficit spending by itself. Resumption of public spending as a temporary measure was not enough. Since 'Today the country is faced with a long-run change in trend',[14] what was required was a coordinated government attempt to repair the institutional arrangements which had caused the deficiencies of aggregate demand that in turn generated high unemployment.

Such a programme divided itself into two major sections. The first featured a drastic redistribution of national income. The seven authors argued less from attachment to social justice and more from Keynesian principle. Since the wealthy saved relatively large proportions of their incomes and spent relatively small proportions, funds taken away from them and transferred to the bulk of the population, whose marginal propensity to consume was much higher and whose marginal propensity to save was accordingly much lower, would have the desirable effect of raising consumer expenditure on goods and services and diminishing aggregate saving. If saving was smaller, then full employment was consistent with a lower level of private investment than was necessary before the income redistribution. Since the crux of the problem of stagnation was deficient private investment, income redistribution was a large portion of the effective treatment. And if only the few suffered while the many benefited, surely this was no argument against the proposal.

The poor would gain still more from the complementary proposal of public investment which the Harvard–Tufts group advanced. The principal argument for public investment was the failure of private markets to satisfy urgent public demands. In the words of the manifesto,

Since private enterprise has been unsuccessful in the provision of new housing for the lower-income families, public agencies must themselves undertake extensive housing construction if the dwelling standards of these families are to be raised. Large public investment in building schools and hospitals will be similarly necessary if the country is to provide itself with more adequate education and health services.[15]

Possibly as a prudential afterthought, the seven economists finally got around to reassuring their readers that their programme was not red socialism, but indeed was designed to 'protect private enterprise in the traditional private sector of the economy'.[16] Nevertheless, businessmen and other naturally conservative types were unlikely to rejoice at the list of necessities for the preservation of private enterprise. These included a vigorous expansion of the public sector of the economy, sharp increases in the progression of the tax system, indefinite increases in the public debt, enlargement of old-age benefits, assistance programmes for health and education, and massive commitments to housing and urban development.

All the same the Harvard–Tufts group had done no more than emphasize clearly and firmly the implications of the stagnation doctrine, and economists of their general habit of thought were scattered through the wartime agencies as well as the old-line departments. It was natural for them to become increasingly apprehensive about the future as the war neared its end, since the dangers of stagnation had been postponed and not diminished by the war.

For a time it seemed that every articulate soul in the United States had something to say about the shape of the post-war era and the policies required to make it attractive. When the Pabst Brewing Company organized an essay contest on the topic of post-war employment, it was inundated by 36,000 entries, including contributions from leading economists and social thinkers. The Legislative Reference Service's annotated bibliography of *important* books and articles on employment written between 1943 and 1945 covers fifty-six closely printed pages. Within the government post-war planning was the rage. Projects were undertaken by the Department of Commerce, the Department of Agriculture, the War Production Board, the Public Works Administration, the Maritime Commission, the Defense Plant Corporation, the Bureau of the Budget, the Rural Electrification Administration, the National Housing Agency, the Treasury Department and the State Department – among others. This was a sample, not the complete list. [17]

The agency which had made the most persistent attempt to prepare for the peace was the National Resources Planning Board, which even possessed the temerity to include the word *planning* blatantly in its name. Completely an idea agency, the N.R.P.B. had neither administrative responsibility nor control over the direction of public funds. Possibly for these reasons, it was somewhat freer in its speculations than the more conventional government departments. The price of its freedom was to be high, for in 1943 Congress effectively silenced it by denying it further appropriations.

But not before it produced in March of that year its *magnum opus*, a 400,000-word report on *Security, Work and Relief Policies*. This report was Keynesian in its reasoning, not very distant in its initial assumptions from the Harvard–Tufts group. Like the seven economists, the N.R.P.B. favoured redistributive tax policies, continuing programmes of public works, broadened social security and assault upon monopolies. Their argument bore the marks of Keynesian preferences for the manipulation of aggregate demand, Wisconsin's experiment in the preceding decade with welfare legislation, a Brandeisian suspicion of giant corporations and Harvard fears of stagnation. The most striking bit of rhetoric in the long document was a New Bill of Rights, whose nine points made inspiring reading:

1. The right to work, usefully and creatively through the productive years.
2. The right to fair play, adequate to command the necessities and amenities of life in exchange for work, ideas, thrift and other socially valuable service.
3. The right to adequate food, clothing, shelter and medical care.
4. The right to security, with freedom from fear of old age, want, dependency, sickness, unemployment and accident.

5. The right to live in a system of free enterprise, free from compulsory labour, irresponsible private power, arbitrary public authority and unregulated monopolies.
6. The right to come and go, to speak and to be silent, free from the spying of secret police.
7. The right to equality before the law, with equal access to justice in fact.
8. The right to education for work, for citizenship and for personal growth and happiness.
9. The right to rest, recreation and adventure, the opportunity to enjoy and take part in an advancing civilization.[18]

The brew contained echoes of the Rooseveltian Four Freedoms, but the economic ingredients were sufficiently prominent and far-reaching to imply a considerable departure from prior government attitudes.

Liberal reaction was joyous. *The New Republic*'s editors, Bruce Bliven, Max Lerner and George Soule, celebrated the New Bill of Rights in a special eighteen-page section entitled 'Charter for America'. Emphasizing and reiterating the major propositions of *Security, Work and Relief Policies*, *The New Republic* started from the premise that 'No action likely to be taken in the United States in the visible future will do away with long-range unemployment, which will be particularly acute after the war'.[19] It adopted a Keynesian analysis of the triumphs and the failures of economic policy during the 1930s:

During the last depression, the incurring of a public deficit to pay relief was accompanied by a steady increase in the national income from 1933 to 1937. Then social security taxes began, while deficit-financed relief payments fell, so that in 1938 the federal budget was practically in balance. Result – a halt in the growth of the national income; indeed a drop for 1938 and 1939.[20]

In *The New Republic*'s judgement, what was now required included 'a permanent policy of large-scale public works', 'comparatively heavy taxation emphasizing individual incomes and inheritance', and 'effective measures against monopoly'.[21] The major belief which permeated *The New Republic*'s reasoning was in a continuity between pre-war and post-war experience. The same trends, especially declining population growth and stronger institutional obstacles to innovation, must be expected to intensify the same problems: inadequate investment, deficient aggregate demand

and unbearable rates of unemployment. Therefore, it was none too soon to sketch an American programme far more ambitious than the Beveridge proposals for 'cradle to grave' social security which had just emerged in England. Although the editors of *The New Republic*, like the N.R.P.B. in its report, conceded a substantial role to private business, they firmly declared that 'It had better be recognized at the very start that the old ideal of laissez-faire is no longer possible. ... Some sort of planning and control there will have to be, *to an increasing degree.*'[22] According to the editors, American choices lay among a corporate economy run by business, full-scale government planning as in the Soviet Union, and cooperation between business and government. On the public's terms the third was infinitely the preferable outcome.

As the prospect of victory brightened, *The New Republic*'s editors and the Keynesians who were its contributors, among them Seymour Harris, Alvin Hansen, Paul Samuelson and Oscar Gass, became increasingly worried about post-war unemployment, the equities of demobilization, the quality of post-war planning and the danger that business could appropriate a disproportionate share of the good things of the peacetime world. Business intentions were much on *The New Republic*'s mind in 1944 and 1945.

Initially, the journal had welcomed a new, liberal business group, the Committee for Economic Development, which had been chartered within ten days of the congressional extermination of the National Resources Planning Board. The magazine applauded the C.E.D.'s promise 'to promote and aid planning for high level employment and production by commerce and industry in the post-war period'.[23] *The New Republic* also found itself impressed by the C.E.D.'s able research group, which included Theodore Yntema, then of the University of Chicago; Gardiner C. Means, the foe of monopoly; and Howard Myers, formerly of the W.P.A. staff. Suspicion soon replaced approval. Oscar Gass said of the C.E.D.'s 1944 tax programme that 'they have written a "Postwar federal tax program for high employment" that is, in fact, an Intelligent Rich Man's Guide to Profits and Prosperity'.[24] Gass found more to approve in the C.E.D.'s willingness to contemplate peacetime federal spending of between $16 and $18 billion annually. Although this was 'refreshing', he himself estimated that $25 to $30 billion was a true measure of national need.

The New Republic did not entirely lose hope in the enlightenment of business opinion. It gave space to Macy's ingenious Beardsley Ruml, who went a good distance for a businessman in declaring that 'We require for success in the attack by business and government on the danger of mass unemployment a commitment on the part of government that, through an explicit fiscal and monetary policy, it will act when business, as business, cannot act to sustain employment and effective demand'.[25] *The New Republic* was happy that a leading businessman had accepted the government's necessary role as an agent of full employment. It was much less pleased with Ruml's more conventional business pleas for lower taxes and his wish to limit public works to the stabilization not of the entire economy but of the construction industry only.

Liberal opinion grew increasingly alarmed that the pace of reconversion might cause unemployment to soar once more. Paul Samuelson, in 1944 a Washington official on leave from M.I.T., wrote gloomily about the production slashes which were planned for the final three months of the year. As Samuelson described the prospect, with V-E Day and the reduction of the war to a single front, this country should 'anticipate unemployment or underemployment of around five million men'.[26] His Washington colleagues were amazingly complacent: 'The experts have not perceived the magnitude of the storm ahead. The executive branch of the government does not have even a normal year's amount of public works in a processed form ready to go into quick operation.' This was all the more a pity because up to this time the economists' role in the national effort had been so valuable: 'It has been said that the last war was the chemist's war and that this one is the physicist's. It might equally be said that this is an economist's war.'[27] But unless the peace also was directed by sound economic principles, the nation was in for troubled times. Samuelson's concluding summary contained a stern warning:

Every month, every day, every hour the federal government is pumping millions and billions of dollars into the bloodstream of the American economy. . . . We have reached the present high levels of output and employment only by means of $100 billion of government expenditures, of which $50 billion represents deficits. . . . Any simple statistical calculation will show that the automobile, aircraft, shipbuilding and electronics industries combined, comprising the fields with the rosiest postwar prospects, cannot possibly maintain their present level of employment or one-half, or one-third of it.[28]

Samuelson properly ranked as only a moderate pessimist. James G. Patton of the liberal National Farmers Union predicted nineteen million unemployed unless a bill that he had drawn up was enacted by Congress. Patton's plan directed the government to increase its own spending by amounts equal to any decreases in private investment: 'The bill I have proposed would call for quarterly adjustment, up or down, of the rate of government investment so that, as private investment decreased, that of the national government would move in the opposite direction.'[29] *The New Republic*'s own programme took serious note of such cries of alarm. Its five points were unusually concrete in presentation:

1. Avoid postwar inflation essentially by retaining price controls and rationing, and, if necessary, by extending rationing to additional commodities;
2. Minimize and compensate postwar unemployment by offering more generous unemployment insurance and social security, making retraining programs available, and filling any remaining gaps with construction expenditures;
3. Adopt a compensatory fiscal policy for the long term as an anti-stagnationist measure;
4. See that big business does not throttle production;
5. Back an expanding economy on a worldwide scale.[30]

To *The New Republic*'s Keynesians, the 1945 outlook had in no way improved. At the beginning of the year Seymour Harris wondered, 'Are we likely to find profitable investments at the rate of $30 billion (say) a year?' Were consumers dependable? Possibly not: 'Consumption expenditures of $115-135 billion which are required at a full-employment income may not be attained.' The moral was easy to draw: 'Many in Washington will concur that the prospects for a high level of employment are not too bright unless the government is prepared to step in. To many it appears that an investment program of $10-15 billion annually is inevitable.'[31] So spoke most liberal economists, social reformers and New Deal Democrats.

As always liberal sentiment was a mixture of attitude, social valuation, political affiliation and legislative proposal. In 1945 liberal opinions of American business were shaped by the disasters of 1929-33, whose causes, in the liberal judgement, were the financial immorality and social irresponsibility of stockbrokers, industrialists and plain millionaires. These opinions were solidified by the scurrility of the conservative assault on Franklin Roosevelt, after New Deal policies had checked economic disaster and initiated recovery in sales and profits. Liberal hostility to business was reinforced by the resistance of some industrialists to wartime arrangements and the desire of some business leaders to reap rapid profits from reconversion. Liberals invariably favoured the 'victims' of business selfishness – factory workers and their unions, the indigent elderly, small farmers, and racial minorities denied equal access to jobs by their employers. Within this context of opinion, the Keynesian mechanisms were perceived as the means to income redistribution, larger public investment and public control of private enterprise. In the 1940s Keynesianism and liberalism were very nearly symbiotic. The 1960s were to give a surprising twist to this relationship.

What liberals wanted and needed in 1944 and 1945 was a cause, a legislative embodiment of the apprehensions and the hopes which spurred their discussions. In particular they needed reassurance that the aftermath of the Second World War would be less disruptive than the sharp recession which followed the First World War. As the forecasts came flooding in, predicting anywhere from five million to eleven million unemployed in the spring that followed peace, preventive government action appeared more and more urgent.

An honourable exception to the general pessimism was the late W. S. Woytinsky, who in July, 1944, concluded that the aftermath of the Second World War would differ substantially from its predecessor. The central differences, as Woytinsky accurately foresaw them, were the existence of $250 billion in savings and liquid consumer reserve and a very large volume of long-deferred demand for consumer goods of every variety.[32]

But in general the same economists who had done a competent job of forecasting under controlled wartime conditions did much less well in their sketches of the immediate post-war picture. Indeed, if economic policy had been based literally upon some of the more pessimistic forecasts, the consequence would have been a major post-war inflation.

Why the prognosticators went so badly wrong is a long story, not without a touch of *hubris* in its ramifications. There were, to begin with, far too many uncertainties in the period between V-E Day in May, 1945, and V-J Day in August, 1945 (when many of the forecasts were made), to permit as much dogmatism as the rasher fore-casters expressed. No one knew how rapidly military expenditures would be cut back, how many soldiers and sailors would be brought home in what length of time, how tax policy would be revised and how effectively industry could reconvert its machines and factories from wartime production to peacetime output of automobiles, appliances and civilian amenities. And there was only the dimmest awareness of the scale of immediate assistance that our allies and our defeated enemies would require.

Many of the forecasts suffered from significant errors of analysis. These centred upon the consumption function. Before and during the war, Keynesians had been accustomed to relating the consumer spending of a particular period to the disposable income paid out to consumers in that same period. If this rule was extended to the post-war era, it was very natural to argue that incomes would drop because of sharp curtailments of war production, and that when incomes did drop, consumer expenditure would decline in the per-centage determined by the pre-war value of the marginal propensity to consume. If the M.P.C. was two thirds – a common pre-war estimate – then a $30 billion drop in income would produce a $20 billion drop in consumption.

Woytinsky was almost alone in perceiving that there were at least two other major influences working on consumer behaviour. The first was the tremendous expansion of liquid wealth in the hands of a very large proportion of the community. This was wealth accumu-lated by workers labouring long hours at overtime rates, soldiers unable to spend their pay on the barren islands of the Pacific, wives and mothers who had saved the allotments which their husbands and sons had directed to them, and citizens of every category who had responded to patriotic appeals by purchasing over $65 billion of readily negotiable war bonds.

Here was approximately $250 billion readily available, if ordinary Americans wanted to spend it. Why should they not have wanted to spend it? The 1930s had been a decade of uncertainty and despair. Many families had run their cars to the last wheeze, worn their clothes to the last thread, and lived among increasingly rickety bits and pieces of household furnishings. During the war they had acquired the means to buy what they had so long deferred, but the means had been useless. Steel had gone into cannons, not auto-mobiles and electrical appliances. Cloth had gone into uniforms, not civilian clothing. When the war at last ended, most Americans were eager to gratify the thwarted tastes of fifteen years.

All that was needed was the goods. And American manufactures poured out of the factories more rapidly than the wildest optimism had ever contemplated. Reconversion was a matter of months, not of years. The economists could console themselves later that after a wild buying spree, consumers did return to a normal relation between income and consumption. Under the circumstances the consolation was slender compensation for massive error.

The error had at least one additional root. This was the stagnationist orientation of too many of the analysts. Stagnation had been on their minds, and no present evidence served to remove it. If disaster is an axiom, it can scarcely help becoming part of a forecast.* It was an axiom reinforced by historical analogy: if a recession had followed the smaller conflict of the First World War, a still larger recession ought to succeed the Second World War – larger in every dimension.

In due time the mistakes of the forecasters became public property and the occasion for that special glee which accompanies the public discomfiture of any variety of expert. In 1945 these forecasts were taken seriously, for they expressed in deceptively exact terms the post-war economic fears of a good many Americans. Liberals naturally used the forecasts to bolster programmes of public works and social amelioration which they supported on ethical and humanitarian grounds. As for businessmen, many perceived in the cheerless predictions an excellent argument for greater official understanding of the special problems of industry, more favourable tax treatment, generous terms of sale to private buyers of government plants, and elimination of price and rationing controls.

The quest for a legislative cause on the part of liberals and the divided opinions of the business community came to focus on the Full Employment Bill of 1945 as it began its legislative history, and on the Employment Act of 1946 as it terminated that history. The stormy congressional course of this measure accurately measured the powerful economic and ideological interests which clashed over the

* Sir Roy Harrod has observed that economists are born little inflationists or little deflationists, and go through their lives fearing the onset of inflation or deflation respectively. For the most part, the Washington forecasters belonged in the second category.

government's future role in the economy.[33] The record begins on 22 January, 1945, when Senator James E. Murray introduced the full employment measure in the names of Senators Robert Wagner of New York, Elbert Thomas of Utah and Joseph O'Mahoney of Wyoming, as well as his own. The four were possibly the Senate's most effective liberal voices and the sponsors of some of the most significant of the New Deal's legislative projects. From the outset the sponsors endeavoured to broaden support for their project beyond the liberal periodicals and organizations which had long busied themselves with post-war employment. Stephen K. Bailey analyses the bill's friends in these words:

The proponents of S. 380 were from the beginning conscious of the fact that they had an uphill fight on their hands. The war was still on and public attention was riveted to military news. Labor and liberal organizations, although interested in full employment as a goal, were split on methods and divided among themselves institutionally and power-politically. Opposition to S. 380 was to be expected from a large part of business, conservative farm organizations, to a lesser extent from the old-line veterans' organizations, and strangely enough from an influential left-wing group in the C.I.O. Strategically, therefore, the proponents of the Full Employment Bill had three major jobs on their hands outside of Congress: (1) to arouse public interest, (2) to mobilize and unify the friends of the Full Employment Bill and (3) to split the opposition.[34]

The contrast between the original and the final measure will be made later in some detail. Here it is enough to state the conclusion of the comparison: S. 380 became law only at the price of much of its substance.

How this occurred is a case study in political warfare. Realizing just how hard the fight was, advocates of the bill began to arouse public interest with a barrage of speeches, articles and letter campaigns. They enlisted the Press and radio, and encouraged state legislators to formulate miniature full employment measures of their own. There was also the touchy job of holding liberals in line. Liberal groups tend to be quarrelsome. Their strength is in their capacity to generate fruitful ideas as the basis of public action, but their corresponding weakness is excessive attachment to these same ideas and extreme reluctance to compromise or surrender them in a common effort. Liberals, like the college faculties of which they are often members, too readily translate matters of tactics or detail into issues of principle. A Continuations Group was organized by Senators

Murray and Wagner in an attempt to coordinate liberal pressure. The Continuations Group met regularly from June to December, 1945.

Its activities were reasonably successful. The liberals infrequently strayed from the reservation. Even the two quarrelsome organizations of labour unions were persuaded to support the bill instead of automatically choosing opposite sides after their usual fashion. The attempt to split the enemies of the legislation was less effective. The liberal National Farmers Union did indeed militantly favour full employment, a cause that its president had been preaching for years. But the old-line farm organizations were disappointing. The National Grange issued a statement and offered testimony so ambiguous that Congressmen were uncertain whether the organization favoured or opposed the legislation. However, there was no doubt about the powerful American Farm Bureau Federation's stand. From first to last, its representatives opposed the bill.

Business was still more hostile. Although two small groups of businessmen, several individuals and the Committee for Economic Development favoured some sort of legislation, the most powerful business groups, led by the National Association of Manufacturers and the Chamber of Commerce, mounted a militant campaign soon after the Senate passed a version of the bill and the House of Representatives in the autumn of 1945 began its debates. The quality of the business arguments appears in the section headings of a major piece of N.A.M. literature called *A Compilation in Excerpt Form of Statements and Expressions of Views Exposing Inherent Fallacies and Contradictions of the So-called 'Full Employment Bill', S. 380*, a descriptive title but surely not one that will live in the annals of literature. The eight section headings were:

Section 1: The Full Employment Bill (S. 380) Means Government Controls.

Section 2: The Full Employment Bill (S. 380) Destroys Private Enterprise.

Section 3: The Full Employment Bill (S. 380) Will Increase the Powers of the Executive.

Section 4: 'Full' Employment Guaranteed – Criticisms – Terms.

Section 5: The Full Employment Bill (S. 380) Legalizes a Compensatory Fiscal Policy – Federal Spending and Pump Priming.

Section 6: The Full Employment Bill (S. 380) Leads to Socialism.

Section 7: The Full Employment Bill (S. 380) Is Unworkable, Impractical, and Promises Too Much.

Section 8: The Full Employment Bill (S. 380) – Items for Ridicule.

The faithful reader of this piece of literature would end at least by knowing the bill's legislative number. A sample of 'ridicule' can complete the illustration of the business contribution to the public discussion:

RIDICULE AND LAUGH AT THEM

The Majority Report Observes:

'Witnesses before the subcommittees and correspondents whose letters are in the Record emphasized that the present postwar outlook is *as unstable as our past experience*' (Senate Report on S. 380, p. 2).

What! In the face of the abundant life brought in by the New Deal?

What! After fifteen years of super-efforts of the New Deal for 're-covery and reform'?

What! After spending $23 billions of government money in peacetime and over $250 billions in war?[35]

While less ludicrous and virulent in its opposition, the Chamber of Commerce may have been more effective. Its 1,700 local organizations represented a larger number and wider variety of businessmen than the relatively small number of very big industrialists banded together in the N.A.M.'s crusade against the twentieth century.

Although business maintained a very nearly united front, there is question whether business opposition alone could have emasculated the bill. Fighting on business's side was the continuing lack of public interest. The excitement at the termination of the Pacific war took precedence over anything that Congress was doing, certainly including this measure. American support for some legislative action was at best wide but not deep. In 1944, for example, a *Fortune* poll reported that 67·7 per cent of the respondents believed that the federal government should take up the job slack when necessary. Moreover, both political parties, Thomas Dewey's Republicans and Franklin Roosevelt's Democrats, had pledged themselves during the 1944 campaign to all the government action that might be needed to stimulate full employment. Evidently, however, the supporters of S. 380 had not succeeded in making the link between such sentiments and the actual legislation which sought to give them meaning. Public apathy was great. An Illinois poll taken in July of 1945 found that sixty-nine per cent of the voters had never heard of the bill; of those who had heard of it, nineteen per cent hadn't the slightest idea what it contained, and four per cent had a seriously erroneous opinion of its contents; and only eight per cent both had heard of the measure and held accurate information on its contents.[36] Ignorance and misinformation offered a clear field to business propaganda and the obstructionist talents of conservative members of the House of Representatives.

Even so, this ignorance might have been dispelled as the emotions of V-J Day waned had it not been for the embarrassing buoyancy of the economy. The dire projections of massive unemployment were fulfilled neither after V-E Day nor after V-J Day. Civilian industry proved unexpectedly capable of absorbing hordes of returning veterans and legions of discharged war workers. Given these circumstances, the public, rejoicing at the unexpectedly abrupt conclusion to a long war, might have been forgiven a certain indifference to the fate of a technical piece of legislation on a difficult and complex subject. Possibly the sponsors and the supporters of S. 380 were fortunate to push any bill at all through an increasingly reluctant Congress.

What finally emerged was a very different animal from the depression-eater of 1945. The initial bill boldly used the fearsome words 'full employment' in its statement of purpose:

A BILL to establish a national policy and program for assuring continuing full employment in a free competitive economy, through the concerted efforts of industry, agriculture, labor, State and local governments, and the Federal Government.[37]

In title and underlying thrust, the Murray measure, despite pleasant verbal assurances of devotion to free enterprise, accorded well with the international discussions of full employment, exemplified in England by the Conservative government's White Paper of 1944 and Lord Beveridge's *Full Employment in a Free Society*.

By contrast, consider the Employment Act of 1946's 'Declaration of Policy':

The Congress hereby declares that it is the continuing policy and responsibility of the Federal Government to use all practicable means consistent with its needs and obligations and other essential considerations of national policy with the assistance and cooperation of industry, agriculture labor, and State and local governments, to coordinate and utilize all its plans, functions, and resources for the purpose of creating and maintaining, in a manner calculated to foster and promote free competitive enterprise and the general welfare, conditions under which there will be afforded useful employment, for those able, willing, and seeking work, and to promote maximum employment, production, and purchasing power.[38]

The non-stop sentence pursued a tortuous path to an ambiguous conclusion, that other things equal, the federal government really ought to assist the industrious poor to find jobs, if other national objectives did not interfere. 'Full Employment', that phrase of semantic charm, vanished entirely from the title and the declaration of purpose. Also sunk without trace was the notion of right to employment, which in the original draft maintained that 'all Americans able to work and seeking work have the right to useful, remunerative, regular and full-time employment, and it is the policy of the United States to assure the existence at all times of sufficient employment opportunities to enable all Americans who have finished schooling and who do not have full-time housekeeping responsibilities freely to exercise this right'.[39]

These were only the preliminaries. The original and final drafts differed still more dramatically in their substantive clauses. The framers of S. 380 intended to make the federal government responsible for the preservation of full employment, and if federal spending was needed to fulfil that responsibility, the bill directed federal funds to be spent. Section 2(d) declared it 'the responsibility of the Federal Government to pursue such consistent and openly arrived at economic policies and programs as will stimulate and encourage the highest feasible levels of employment opportunities through private and other non-Federal investment and expenditure'; and Section 2(e), hard upon its heels, made it plain that 'to the extent that continuing full employment cannot otherwise be achieved, it is the further responsibility of the Federal Government to provide such volume of Federal investment and expenditure as may be needed to assure continuing full employment'.[40]

The bill's authors stopped just short of openly accepting deficit spending and deliberately unbalanced budgets, but they deceived no one. Still, such statements might have been discounted as nine parts rhetoric and one part action had it not been for the next major section, entitled 'The National Production and Employment Budget'. This was the heart of S. 380. This section prescribed a procedure and imposed a new responsibility upon both the President and the Congress.

As usual the section pursued the soothing strategy of starting with the stimulation of increased private investment and employment. But the pieties disposed of, the drafters' attachment to public spending was unmistakable. The section first directed the President to submit a national production and employment budget at the beginning of each congressional session. For the ensuing fiscal year at least, this budget was to be a forecast of the size of the labour force, private investment, government spending and consumer expenditure. From these forecasts the President was supposed to infer a policy on which he was to base appropriate legislative proposals. In guarded but explicit language, the framers of the bill ordered that

To the extent, if any, that such increased non-Federal investment and expenditures as may be expected to result from actions taken under the program set forth ... are deemed insufficient to provide a full employment volume of production, the President shall transmit a general program for such Federal investment and expenditure as will be sufficient to bring the aggregate volume of investment and expenditure by private business, consumers, State and local governments, and the Federal Government, up to the level required to assure a full employment volume of production.[41]

The words were unlikely to cause riots in the streets, but the bill meant business nevertheless. A timetable was set for congressional action whenever the President's national production and employment budget contained a deficit. A new high-level Joint Committee on the National Production and Employment Budget was instructed to report not only its observations on the President's budget but also a general policy which was to guide other congressional committees in their preparation of legislation to ensure full employment.

Whether this mechanism could ever have worked is an open question. Political responsibility was shared between a President responsible for the forecasts and programme and a Congress charged with making its own analyses and legislative proposals. Nor did any possible sanction ensure congressional adherence to the timetable written into the measure. However, at the very least, S. 380's friends were offering the voters the right to hold their President and their Congress responsible for unemployment, lagging economic growth and the general malfunction of the economy.

Nothing was plainer than the commitment to Keynesian national income accounting, a Keynesian emphasis upon aggregate demand and Keynesian fiscal policy. Indeed, the commitment was probably excessive. As soon became evident, forecasting in the 1945 state of the art failed to project the movement of the economy with enough precision to define appropriate compensatory action. As far as the legislative prospects of the measure were concerned, it was a misfortune that the doleful predictions of early and mid-1945 were already being disproved by the strength of the economy in the autumn and early winter of the same year. It is even conceivable that Congress did an unwitting service to the reputation of economists by its refusal to retain this key section of the bill.

Whatever Congress's intentions, its surgery was radical. The new law dropped overboard the entire national production and employment budget. The responsibilities of the President and Congress alike were made much less burdensome. The President was directed to favour Congress within sixty days of its convening with an economic report designed to carry out the extraordinarily vague 'Declaration of Policy' (see p. 144) and to provide a general review of economic conditions. Congress graciously extended permission to the President, at his own discretion, to convey to Congress any supplementary reports which he cared to make. All that the law retained of the stellar Joint Committee on the National Production and Employment Budget was the pale shadow of a Joint Committee on the Economic Report. And all that this Committee was enjoined to do was study and assess, not prepare new legislation.

The act also established a new executive instrument, the Council of Economic Advisers, whose 'duty' and 'function' included advising the President on the preparation of an economic report, collecting current business and economic information, appraising the employment and income activities of other federal agencies, and preparing 'national economic policies to foster and promote free competitive enterprise, to avoid economic fluctuations, or to diminish the effects thereof, and to maintain employment, production and purchasing power'.[42] Congress had carefully removed the political sting from S. 380's tail. A President was asked only to prepare one more report. Congress was directed to do no more than study it. Neither was compelled to do more than implement a policy so vague that it could be construed to mean almost anything at all.

Who had won? The valiant liberals, who had fought long and hard for full employment legislation and ended with an Employment Act which nowhere used the words 'full employment'? Or the National Association of Manufacturers, which had opposed legislation of any kind on this topic?

Senator Taft, among other intelligent conservatives, was able to vote for the final measure because the teeth and claws of S. 380 had been removed; Congress's practice of considering economic legislation in its own way and its own time was unimpaired. The national budget and the awesome Joint Committee which was to evaluate it were guillotined. Nobody really had to do much more than he was currently doing. Any rational opponent of S. 380 would have been fully entitled to conclude that he had helped defeat the compensatory spending devices of Keynesians in and out of the administration.

The other side of the case depends upon the importance one gives to symbols and beginnings. However reluctantly and even ambiguously, Congress for the first time had accepted some responsibility for maintaining, if not full employment, at least 'high levels of employment'. Moreover, the Council of Economic Advisers and *The Economic Report of the President* were instruments which in the hands of a determined chief executive could be turned into powerful agents of public action. Although S. 380's explicit commitment to public spending and expansionary deficits was sheared away, at the least the President and his Council were not debarred from recommending a compensatory tax or expenditure policy in the name of 'high levels of employment'. The influence of Arthur F. Burns in the councils of the Eisenhower administration and the role played by Walter W. Heller in the education of President Kennedy both attest to the opportunities that the act opened to astute Chairmen of the Council of Economic Advisers. And at a minimum the existence of the Council hastened the introduction of the Tax Reduction Act of 1964 and facilitated the open declarations of both Presidents Kennedy and Johnson to the principle of deficit financing.

There is a more subtle point. Each national administration since the end of the Second World War has tacitly accepted a vital political proposition: the public will not maintain in office a President and a Congress who permit unemployment to rise very high and last very long. This recognition is far more significant than any possible piece of legislation, for it converts into activists even conservative Presidents and old-fashioned Congressmen. The debate over S. 380 and the Employment Act of 1946 which resulted from it in their way helped to create this political fact of life. In the end it is the electorate and their expectations of action, more than the theories of economists or the personal prejudices of politicians, which determine the shape of national economic policy.

SOURCE NOTES TO CHAPTER 6

1. E. A. G. Robinson, 'John Maynard Keynes', in Robert Lekachman (ed.) *Keynes's General Theory: Reports of Three Decades* (New York: St Martin's, 1964; London: Macmillan).

2. J. M. Keynes, *How to Pay for the War* (London: Macmillan, 1940).

3. Ibid.

4. Quoted in Robinson, op. cit.

5. Quoted in ibid.

6. Keynes, op. cit.

7. Norman F. Keiser, *Macroeconomics, Fiscal Policy, and Economic Growth* (New York: Wiley, 1964).

8. Sir Roy Harrod, *The Life of John Maynard Keynes*, (London: Macmillan, 1951).

9. Quoted in ibid.

10. See Paul A. Samuelson, 'The Modern Scene', in Ralph E. Freeman (ed.) *Postwar Economic Trends in the United States* (New York: Harper & Row, 1960).

11. Richard Gilbert, *et al.*, *An Economic Program for American Democracy* (New York: Vanguard, 1938).

12–16. Ibid.

17. On this topic see Stephen Kemp Bailey, *Congress Makes a Law* (New York: Columbia University Press, 1964).

18. Quoted in ibid.

19. 'Charter for America', supplement, *The New Republic*, 19 April 1943.

20. Ibid.

21. Ibid.

22. Ibid. The italic is added.

23. *The New Republic*, 26 July 1943.

24. Oscar Gans, *The New Republic*, 16 October 1944.

25. Beardsley Ruml, *The New Republic*, 28 February 1944.

26. Paul Samuelson, *The New Republic*, 11 September 1944.

27. Ibid.

28. Paul Samuelson, *The New Republic*, 18 September 1944.

29. *The New Republic*, 6 November 1944.

30. 'A Program in Brief', *The New Republic*, 27 November 1944.

31. Seymour Harris, *The New Republic*, 15 January 1945.

32. W. S. Woytinsky, *The New Republic*, 31 July 1944.

33. Stephen Kemp Bailey's *Congress Makes a Law* is an extremely useful history of the antecedents and History of the Employment Act of 1946. In the pages that follow I have drawn upon it substantially.

34. Ibid.

35. Quoted in ibid.

36–42. Ibid.

V-J Day had ended the first war conducted on Keynesian principles. The evidence was plentiful for the claim. The war agencies analysed needs and resources within the national income framework constructed by Keynes and accorded statistical serviceability by our own Department of Commerce. It became routine for economists to calculate inflationary gaps by comparing consumer incomes with the sum of the price tags on consumer goods, or noting that the sum of private investment and public deficit was smaller than the sum of private saving and tax receipts. From these calculations they derived the case for the price and rationing controls which were successful features of wartime planning. As in Britain prices, wages, budgets, taxes and controls were instruments for the physical deployment of men and resources, not gauges of financial viability or national solvency.

By the war's end the habit of Keynesian thinking and the public expectation of continuing prosperity led to action in many places. A Conservative-dominated English coalition, a Democratic American government and administrations of various political complexions in Canada, New Zealand, Australia, Sweden and the Union of South Africa all proclaimed a national responsibility for the preservation of high levels of employment. The British White Paper of 1944 was typical in its opening declaration that 'the government accepts as one of their primary aims and responsibilities the maintenance of a high and stable level of employment after the war'.[1] A year later a Canadian statement stressed the necessity of 'levels of employment and income greatly above those ruling before the war',[2] and apparently refrained from an explicit promise of full employment only out of apprehension about foreign trade and seasonal fluctuations. The Australians were less guarded. In 1945 the Australian document *Some Problems of Economic Policy* not only flatly stated that 'governments should accept the responsibility for stimulating spending on goods and services to the extent necessary to sustain full employment', but in explicitly Keynesian tones insisted that economic activity 'depends on the demand for goods and services – that is, on expenditure by individuals, firms, public authorities and overseas buyers'.[3] For its part, Sweden constituted a post-war Economic Planning Commission in February, 1944, headed by Gunnar Myrdal, best known in this country as the author of *An American Dilemma* but also one of his country's eminent economists.

In the main, governments other than the American were prepared to contemplate concrete policies as well as new administrative structures. Sweden's Public Works Planning Board was charged with drawing up programmes of public investment suitable to counteract swings in private investment. Australia prepared to enlarge public expenditure on schools, libraries, medical services and assistance to the ill and the elderly. Canada's 1944 Family Allowance Act increased the incomes of poor families, where numerous children were most frequently to be found. Thus, on now conventional Keynesian lines, the governments of three continents prepared to influence aggregate demand by stimulating consumption, private investment, public investment, or all three. Whether or not they understood the faith that they professed, the statesmen of the West had converted to the notion of the primary importance of adequate levels of aggregate demand.

In this way did Keynesian economics as a planning tool win public vindication in peace and war. As a person, Keynes had still other roles to play in the last years of his life. One was in international affairs. *The General Theory*, among its other heroic simplifications, had described a closed economy in which neither exports nor imports were of any consequence. Keynes's fiscal remedies were designed for societies which had complete internal discretion over their own affairs. His simplification was no more than heuristic; he was always aware of the importance to Britain of a flourishing foreign trade. In the 1940s it was equally apparent to him that England's hope for post-war prosperity was intimately connected with the reformation of the gold standard and the international mechanisms of trade. Britain was fated to enter the peace a debtor nation, burdened with an industrial plant which was elderly before 1939 and which had deteriorated further because equipment had not been replaced during the war. Something had to be done to make it possible for debtor nations like Britain as well as the single giant creditor, the United States, to conduct trade while reconstruction was carried forward.

The conference at Bretton Woods – an enchanting locale for a technical discussion – was the Allied attempt in the summer of 1944 to plan in good time for exigencies such as these. The two major post-war international economic organizations which were the children of this conference aimed to stabilize currency values, avert a repetition of the chaotic competitive currency devaluations of the 1930s and increase the flow of international investment from the rich to the poor. Though never by itself an adequate source of international lending, the International Bank for Reconstruction and Development (the World Bank) has played an honourable role in the support of sound projects in the underdeveloped as well as the Western European countries. The second institution, the International Monetary Fund, is displaying inadequacies two decades after its birth. On these inadequacies two comments are in order. Any international institution which operates reasonably well for twenty years must be doing something right, and what it has been doing wrong is attributable not to Keynes's lack of vision but to the dilution of his proposals, primarily by American negotiators.

Keynes's central role in the Bretton Woods negotiations was an astonishing extension of a persistent intellectual interest. Starting with his initial writings on Indian currency before the First World War, Keynes had been closely and ingeniously concerned with the international gold standard and the flow of international investment and trade. His *Tract on Monetary Reform* of the early 1920s centred upon a series of measures aimed at loosening the strait jacket of gold which encircled domestic policies. During the Second World War, Keynes saw this range of issues as demanding for their solution an amendment of world currency arrangements so as to combine short-term stability in the value of each nation's currency with long-term flexibility. The latter implied national freedom to alter currency ratios without the danger of prompt retaliation from other nations. It permitted freedom to plan for full employment at home without fear that gold losses would enforce a deflationary policy. It was insupportable to Keynes that the world should return to a condition in which governments automatically raised interest rates, contracted bank credit, and created unemployment every time an adverse balance of payments appeared.

Keynes's solution was an International Clearing Union, an

approach to an international currency and an international bank. Keynes's statement of the Union's purposes ran like this:

We need an instrument of international currency having general acceptability between nations, so that blocked balances and bilateral clearings are unnecessary....

We need an orderly and agreed method of determining the relative exchange values of national currency units, so that unilateral action and competitive exchange depreciations are prevented.

We need a *quantum* of international currency, which is neither determined in an unpredictable and irrelevant manner as, for example, by the technical progress of the gold industry, nor subject to large variations depending on the gold reserve policies of individual countries; but is governed by the actual current requirements of world commerce, and is also capable of deliberate expansion and contraction to offset deflationary and inflationary tendencies in effective world demand.

We need a system possessed of an internal stabilizing mechanism, by which pressure is exercised on any country whose balance of payments with the rest of the world is departing from equilibrium *in either direction,* so as to prevent movements which must create for its neighbours an equal but opposite want of balance.

We need an agreed plan for starting off every country after the war with a stock of reserves appropriate to its importance in world commerce, so that without undue anxiety it can set its house in order during the transitional period to full peacetime conditions.

We need a central institution, of a purely technical and non-political character, to aid and support other international institutions concerned with the planning and regulation of the world's economic life.

More generally, we need a means of reassurance to a troubled world, by which any country whose own affairs are conducted with due prudence is relieved of anxiety for causes which are not of its own making, concerning its ability to meet its international liabilities; and which will, therefore, make unnecessary those methods of restriction and discrimination which countries have adopted hitherto, not on their merits, but as measures of self-protection from disruptive outside forces.[4]

In this pregnant statement appeared Keynes's lifelong preoccupations with a world in which free international trade and free domestic policy coincided instead of conflicting. Keynes made it equally plain that he detested the limitations of free choice which barter arrangements between pairs of nations entailed and feared a renewal of life's vagaries under the gold standard. The third paragraph in particular expressed Keynes's strong desire to make world currency arrangements serve the purposes of high domestic demand and employment rather than the other way round. In a world in which Britain owed the debts and the United States owned most of the gold, Keynes was understandably eager to hold the balance fairly between creditors and debtors. Thus, the fourth paragraph contains the argument that when world trade is disturbed, the burden of adjustment properly falls not only upon those nations which are running unfavourable balances of payments but also upon the nations which are enjoying surpluses. It was almost as plain to the American negotiators as to representatives of the debtors that something had to be done to allow the debtors to rearrange their affairs before they were exposed to the full blast of international competition.

Although the details of Keynes's specific proposals inevitably were highly technical, they focused upon the creation of a new international bank money to supplement gold. Called *bancor* by Keynes, the value of this new international money was to be 'fixed (but not unalterably) in terms of gold and accepted as the equivalent of gold by the British Commonwealth and the United States and all the other members of the Union for the purposes of settling international balances'.[5] Countries which ran favourable international balances would pile up credit balances of bancor units with the International Clearing Union. On the other side, countries incurring deficits in their international account would run debit bancor balances. In effect the Union would extend short-term loans to the debtor countries, financed from the surpluses accumulated by those countries whose balance of payments was favourable.

Naturally, there would be boundaries which would check the tendencies of debtors to enlarge instead of paying their debts. The Union would assign each country a drawing quota, defined by the volume of its trade. Moreover, a country which persisted in imprudent financial practices might have its account suspended, just as a private banker might terminate arrangements with a careless borrower. But the point of Keynes's proposal was this: trading nations which happened to be in deficit would be accorded enough financial leeway so that temporary balance of payments difficulties would not compel them to turn to domestic deflation. There was no doubt that the Union would favour prospective debtor countries like Great Britain rather than certain creditor countries like the United States. Even though no nation would be free to accumulate debits beyond its quota, the quotas themselves were sufficiently generous to cause American apprehension that the United States would incur a vast liability to finance the deficits of most of the rest of the world.

Hence Keynes's scheme encountered something less than full acceptance by American officials. Their counterproposal was the brain child of Harry Dexter White and his Treasury associates. The White plan coincided with Keynes's Union in some important features. Most important, it accepted the necessity of an international agency to regulate trade and currency. Moreover, by proposing a scarce currency clause, White did accept the principle that creditors as well as debtors had their responsibilities in the restoration of international trading equilibrium.*

However, the contrasts between the White and Keynes plans were more striking than the similarities. Keynes's proposals in effect established an international central bank (a vast expansion of the Bank of England or the Federal Reserve System) which was to possess its own currency and its own authorizations to make loans. The American plan was more conventional. It started with the notion of a fixed fund based on amounts initially voted by participating governments. Unlike Keynes's Union, the fund would not expand automatically as international trade itself recovered and expanded. Other differences were also significant. Keynes's plan based drawing or overdraft privileges upon the volume of foreign trade. This criterion would have given England rights roughly equivalent to those of the United States, a much larger economy in which foreign trade was relatively much less important. By contrast, the American proposal measured borrowing privileges according to the criteria of initial gold contribution and size of national income. By no special accident, these criteria as substantially favoured the American position as Keynes's standards would have strengthened the British situation.

In the 1943 and early 1944 discussions which preceded the convening of the Bretton Woods Conference, a compromise was negotiated. On behalf of Britain, Keynes was persuaded (or compelled) to surrender the principle of the Clearing Union and accept

---

* The scarce currency clause permitted a nation in serious deficit to a trading partner to discriminate against imports from that partner. Thus, if England was badly short of dollars because of inadequate sales of her exports to the United States, this clause permitted her to impose controls on tobacco, movies, automobiles, appliances and other merchandise exported to England by American suppliers. This represented a very considerable concession by a country which had every reason to believe that the clause would be applied only to herself.

the American-sponsored International Monetary Fund. The Fund, moreover, was to hold on deposit a mixed assortment of gold and the currencies of its members rather than a single new international currency. In return, the Americans definitely accepted a scarce currency clause. As one British economist assessed its importance, it placed 'the onus of relative adjustment on creditor as well as debtor'.[6]

Keynes was not delighted with the outcome. The Fund was an inferior instrument, less flexible, less novel and less helpful to debtors than his own International Clearing Union. Nevertheless, as a practical man well aware that the Fund was the best that the Americans were going to offer, he was prepared to defend the plan against those who argued that he had wrongly consented to the re-establishment in concealed form of the old gold standard. In a powerful speech delivered before the House of Lords in May, 1944, Keynes asserted that the new arrangement preserved three central principles intact:

The external value of sterling shall conform to its internal value as set by our own domestic policies, and not the other way round. Secondly, we intend to retain control of our domestic rate of interest, so that we can keep it as low as suits our own purposes, without interference from the ebb and flow of international capital movements or flights of hot money. Thirdly, whilst we intend to prevent inflation at home, we will not accept deflation at the dictates of influences from outside. In other words, we abjure the instruments of bank rate and credit contraction operating through the increase of unemployment as a means of forcing our domestic economy into line with external factors.*

Did his critics dare to believe, asked Keynes, that after he had struggled for so many years to achieve these goals, he had then casually surrendered them? His answer rang:

I hope your Lordships will trust me not to have turned my back on all I have fought for. To establish these three principles has been my main task for the last twenty years. Sometimes almost alone, in popular articles in the press, in pamphlets, in dozens of letters to *The Times*, in text books, in enormous and obscure treatises I have spent my strength to persuade my countrymen and the world at large to change their traditional doctrines and, by taking better thought, to remove the curse of unemployment. Was

* One wonders how many members of Harold Wilson's government, several of them, including the Prime Minister, economists, recalled this passage in October, 1964, when a sterling crisis compelled the government to raise the bank rate to the crisis level of seven per cent.

it not I, when many of to-day's iconoclasts were still worshippers of the Calf, who wrote that 'Gold is a barbarous relic'? Am I so faithless, so forgetful, so senile that, at the very moment of the triumph of these ideas when, with gathering momentum, governments, parliaments, banks, the press, the public, and even economists, have at last accepted the new doctrines, I go off to help forge new chains to hold us fast in the old dungeon? I trust, my Lords, that you will not believe it.[7]

In 1944 Winston Churchill was not the only Englishman capable of noble rhetorical flight.

When Keynes got down to particulars, he enumerated five very substantial benefits to Great Britain. The first was recognition that 'During the post-war transitional period of uncertain duration, we are entitled to retain any of those wartime restrictions, and special arrangements with the sterling area and others which are helpful to us'. On this point neither the original Keynes nor the first White plan had been so explicit. The second benefit promised was a return to a world in which national currencies were fully convertible. In Keynes's judgement, 'For a great commercial nation like ourselves, this is indispensable for full prosperity'.[8] The fact was that if currencies were not freely exchanged, then London would lose its place as an international financial centre, the sterling bloc would disintegrate, and Britain would descend as a world power.

The plan's third merit was 'what is, in effect, a great addition to the world's stock of monetary reserves'. Of course, conceded Keynes, his own Clearing Union proposal would have enlarged reserves still more, but even the present plan contemplated an expansion of £2·5 billion, out of which Britain was to be entitled to draw at least £325 million – 'a sum which may easily double, or more than double, the reserves which we shall otherwise hold at the end of the transitional period'. No one argued that the British quota was large enough to subsist on. But this was never the intention of what was designed as 'an iron ration to tide over temporary emergencies of one kind or another'.[9]

There was still a fourth benefit to Britain. It engaged any creditor country 'to release other countries from any obligations to take its exports, or, if taken, to pay for them'. And the final advantage of the plan was institutional, for it 'sets up an international institution with substantial rights and duties to preserve orderly arrangements in matters such as exchange rates which are two-ended and affect both parties alike, which can also serve as a place of regular discussion between responsible authorities to find ways to escape those many unforeseeable dangers which the future holds'.[10]

Thus did Keynes argue powerfully a not entirely congenial brief. Once committed, however, he fought hard for the Fund at Bretton Woods in July, 1944. There he headed a British negotiating team which included Professor Lionel Robbins and his old friend, former colleague and more recent critic D. H. Robertson. Some 750 persons attended the huge conference in the magical White Mountains. The complexities of the negotiations and the feats of diplomacy essential to progress were such as to leave Keynes, never fully recovered from his illness of 1937, prostrated after each day's work, and he was restored for the next day's labours only by the devoted nursing of Lady Keynes. Of Keynes's final speech which moved the plan's acceptance, E. A. G. Robinson had this to say: 'Conscious of his share and of the way that, despite fatigue and weakness, he had dominated the conference, the delegates paid their tribute by rising and applauding again and again.'[11]

Keynes had not succeeded in freeing British domestic policy completely from the influences of international vicissitude; Britain was politically too weak for that. But at a minimum, he had separated British home programmes from the automatic adjustment once forced upon debtor nations by the rationale of the gold standard and the expectations of creditors. He had persuaded other nations to extend central banking into international exchanges. And the International Monetary Fund was the financial world's public recognition that the old gold standard was gone.

After slaying this ancient dragon, Keynes faced a last labour. During the Second World War Britain had been supported substantially by massive lend-lease allocations from the United States. Partly out of necessity and partly by design, she had allowed her exports to other countries in Latin America and elsewhere to shrink to near invisibility. Although lend-lease amounted to a free gift, Britain had incurred substantial debts in her dealings with the Dominions. In large part these debts took the shape of blocked sterling balances – balances held in London banks to the credit of Egyptians, Indians, Canadians, South Africans and Australians but not convertible into other currencies. These vast balances hung over the British economy as a contingent liability that had to be discharged honourably for the sake of her commercial reputation.

This was common knowledge. What aggravated Britain's immediate situation in 1945 was the unexpectedly sudden close of the war against Japan and the equally unexpected announcement by President Truman in September, 1945, that all lend-lease allocations, save the amounts in transit or pipeline, were to be terminated. Britain lacked the reserves, the export capacity, and perhaps most important the immediate will to make up the deficit which suddenly gaped in her import accounts. Whether President Truman was legally compelled to issue his proclamation at the time that he did is open to dispute. There was no question that Britain had an immediate need for some form of financial assistance.

Once more Keynes made the familiar trip to Washington, this time as a suppliant. Or so it rapidly became clear. For Keynes had not concealed his hope that the Americans would make an unqualified gift, in recognition of the fact that in the advancement of the common war objectives, Britain had borne more than her share of sacrifice and loss. In Robinson's words, 'This case was argued in full, and listened to with patience and sympathy. But it was very soon apparent (to quote Keynes' own words to the House of Lords) "that primary emphasis on past services and past sacrifices would not be fruitful".'[12]

What the United States offered, what Keynes accepted, and what many Englishmen judged an ungenerous act was a loan of $3·75 billion designed to tide Britain over the next three or four years of difficult readjustment. Interest payments were set at two per cent, to begin in 1951, and these could be postponed should Britain be unable in any year to meet them. The greater portion of the lend-lease account was cancelled. One clause was to cause future trouble. This was Britain's commitment to return quickly to free conversion of the pound sterling into other currencies, for practical purposes the dollar. Britain grumbled, but Britain in the end agreed. The only alternative was such a sharp curtailment in British dollar imports as seriously to diminish the British standard of life and retard her effort to restore her competitive position in world markets.

For Keynes it was nearly the end. Returning to England in December, 1945, he encountered much criticism. He met it staunchly, saw the relevant legislation through Parliament, and, fatigued from the labours of years and the illness of nearly a decade, began to think of rest. One last trip intervened, to Savannah, Georgia, where the inaugural meetings of the Bretton Woods institutions were held. Back from Savannah, he returned to Tilton. There, on

Easter Sunday, 21 April 1946, he suffered a sharp and fatal heart attack.

In the world of intellect, few in his generation had achieved more. His theories, as he noted, had been accepted 'even by economists'. His views of practical policy were written into the laws of civilized countries. He had dealt gold, an old enemy, an apparently mortal blow. His labours as a Treasury official during the war and as a diplomat at the war's ending had been unique. Fastidious in his tastes, impatient of party politics, unhappy in the company of fools, Keynes had achieved far more in the world of politics than less gifted men who had devoted their careers to the political arts. He died at a time of triumph and achievement. Late in his life he had expressed a single regret: he had drunk too little champagne.

Those who lived through them had no doubt of the grimness of the 1930s. Nevertheless, for Keynesians the ailment of the age was easy to diagnose and simple to treat. The whole trouble was a deficiency in aggregate demand caused by a feeble, uncertain inducement to invest. Even though Keynesians argued among themselves about the reasons for this pervasive decline in the marginal efficiency of capital and about the possibility of reversing the downward trend, their new doctrine directed them to clear-cut fiscal remedies which were the more appealing because they called into grave question the bankrupt conventional wisdom of bankers and Treasury officials. Usually unwittingly, the spending agencies of the New Deal pursued the deficit-creating programmes which coincided with the intricate analysis of *The General Theory*. Devoted Keynesians were impatient with the New Deal only because its leaders spent too little too seldom.

If anything, the Second World War was a still plainer exemplification of the accuracy of Keynesian analysis and the Keynesian cure. The lavish American and English outlay upon the instruments of modern war created tremendous deficits, rapidly sucked into military uses idle human and non-human resources, and in remarkably short order created economies rejoicing in buoyant demand, factories operating at capacity and overfull employment. The objective of the exercise was victory. The means to victory were the grim public works of modern armies and navies. The financial techniques were above all borrowing and credit creation. And the consequence was the ready achievement of the objective which for a decade had eluded the grasp of policy makers – steady, high employment.

What was to be expected after military spending was turned off? Many if not most Keynesians anticipated a replay of the 1930s: the same deficiencies of aggregate demand, the same sluggishness of investment, the same mass unemployment – indeed, the same evident failure of enterprise capitalism to ensure the public happiness. When reconversion and buoyant markets disproved this simple-minded expectation of repetitive history, Keynesian speculation began to ask whether the reforms of the New Deal in capital markets, the national commitment to high employment written into the Employment Act of 1946, and the new automatic stabilizers* had combined to transform the economic scene by diminishing capitalism's instabilities. Severe depression was now out of the question. Modern monetary and fiscal instruments were adequate insurance that modern economies could operate at satisfactorily high rates of activity, interrupted by only the gentlest and briefest of recessions.

History has an infinite ability to astonish prophets. The last fifteen years of American economic experience are evidence that neither the pessimism of the stagnationists nor the euphoria of the prophets of the new day has been an appropriate position. In actual fact the United States has neither returned to the simple, comprehensible disasters of the Great Depression nor entered the promised land of permanent full employment and perpetual prosperity. Since 1953 the phenomenon which has puzzled economists and politicians has been a rate of unemployment that has fluctuated within a four to seven per cent range – high enough to be disturbing, not high enough to alarm the prosperous majority. The companion of persistent unemployment has been a rate of economic growth not particularly low by historical criteria but far short of the parallel Japanese, West German, French and even Italian experiences. Thus, most Americans have never had it so good; possibly fifteen to twenty per cent of Americans have had it as bad as ever.

It is something of a puzzle. Keynesian theory prepared no one for the American version of the split-level society, most of us on the upper levels but too many of us in the basement. Social science is a puzzle-loving and puzzle-solving activity. Hence there are numerous

---

* These included unemployment compensation, agricultural subsidies, welfare payments and the progressive income tax. Broadly, their common characteristic is to rise in amount as national income declines. A progressive income tax helps to stabilize income by taking a decreasing share of declining income.

proposed solutions to the conundrum. It is worth noting some of the more plausible.

Contrary to the expectations of the 1930s, population has begun once more to rise rapidly. The substantial spurt in births which characterized the 1940s has produced in the 1960s a large increase in the number of new entrants into the labour force. This circumstance above all explains the very high unemployment among the young. This high rate in turn pulls the general unemployment rate upward. The difficulty will afflict the American economy for some time to come. Five years from now the labour force will contain an additional 1·5 million teenagers and an additional 2·75 million twenty to twenty-four-year-olds. By 1970 these two age groups combined will constitute 23·6 per cent of the labour force. In 1964 they were only 20·7 per cent.[13] Therefore, we face a special problem of education, training and assimilation, but not a general condition of inadequate inducements to investment or deficient aggregate demand.

At least since the English Industrial Revolution, technological progress has been a commonplace in the Western world. Over the nearly two centuries which have elapsed since Watt's steam engine and Arkwright's factory, *per capita* productivity has risen persistently, jobs have been redefined and simplified, the division of labour has become increasingly fine, and the traditional craft skills have steadily disappeared. Hand loom weaver, hand compositor, glass-blower and telephone operator – each in his or her day has been replaced by a mechanical device more productive and more dependable than the imperfect human hand and brain. Granted.

But, so the prophets of automation argue, in the 1950s and 1960s the *pace* of this historical process has been accelerating and the *kinds* of skills rendered obsolete have become far more numerous. In contrast with the past, jobs are vanishing in numbers larger than the vacancies created by economic growth. Worse still, a growing proportion of the new jobs which do become available require skills not possessed or readily acquired by the unemployed. In the past new jobs usually demanded less skill than old ones which vanished. The reverse is now true. Vacancies in the ranks of computer programmers in New York are no help to displaced West Virginia coal-miners. Shortages of social workers in Chicago represent no opportunities for the rural unemployed of Appalachia.

And this is only the beginning. Techniques now known make it possible to substitute automated devices for much nursing attendance, medical diagnosis, search for legal precedents and managerial supervision. Middle management is faced with obsolescence. Teachers will be compelled to yield their places to teaching machines. A world without work is over the horizon.

In economics fashions alter quickly. Until the middle of the 1950s, American and European economists in large numbers favoured the view that the world was suffering from a long-run, possibly permanent shortage of American dollars. This sombre assessment was solidly based upon the dilapidated condition of the economies of Western Europe at the close of the Second World War, the remarkable expansion of the American economy during the war years, the depletion of European currency reserves, the concentration of the world's gold in American hands, and – above all – the evident ability of American manufacturers and farmers to produce more efficiently almost everything that the remainder of the world craved. About all that Europe had left to sell travelling Americans was its history and monuments.

From both the American and the European standpoint, the immediate post-war problem was the rehabilitation of the European economies. The British loan was an early attempt to supply the dollars Europe was too weak to earn for herself. The loan's $3·75 billion was soon dwarfed by the Marshall Plan's $11 billion, poured into Western Europe between 1948 and 1951. At our urging, the recipients of aid founded the Organization for European Economic Cooperation (O.E.E.C.). Its success in handling the allocation of Marshall Plan funds and a number of other cooperative endeavours strengthened a European unity movement which led in due course to the formation of the European Economic Community, the Common Market. The dynamic growth of the E.E.C. nations has been a triumph of American economic policy.

There is such a thing as too much success. In this instance the Western European boom has imposed a constraint upon American domestic policy. The reasons are these. Year after year our gold reserves have diminished as American investors, lured by a rich European market, have transferred huge sums to France, West Germany, the Netherlands and Italy. These sums have purchased shares of European corporations. They have erected American-owned factories. Our balance of payments troubles are not being caused, at least in the 1960s, by any loss of competitiveness on the part of our manufacturers, much less on the part of our farmers. They are the consequences of enormous capital exports.

Although these capital exports derive from the strength, not the weakness of our economy, they cannot be permitted to continue. Our gold stock is finite, the claims of foreigners on that stock are substantial, and foreign confidence depends upon our success in controlling the outflow of gold. This need, novel for Americans, to pay serious attention to our balance of payments imposes limits on the expansive nature of our domestic economy. Thus, if we lower interest rates so as to stimulate consumer borrowing and business investment, American capital will flow in still larger amounts to European financial centres which offer higher rates of return. If we stimulate aggregate demand by reducing taxes or increasing public expenditures, we place inflationary pressure upon prices and wages. As a result, American exports become less competitive in European markets, European goods sell in larger quantities in American markets, and the deficit in our accounts rises.

The dilemma before any administration has been the choice between two entirely desirable objectives: full employment and a balance in the international accounts. The dilemma explains the caution of economists and officials. Consider, as an early example, the blue-ribbon committee of economists appointed by President-elect Kennedy in the winter of 1960. Composed though it was of liberal Keynesians, the committee was extremely careful in its advice. When its Chairman, Paul Samuelson, reported to the President in January, 1961, he observed that a recession now existed. In December, 1960, unemployment was 6·8 per cent, and the 4·5 million men and women seeking work were the largest number in any December since 1940. All the same, what the committee recommended was three carefully defined series of measures. The first joined a slight easing of credit to a moderate stimulus of residential building and long overdue improvements in the unemployment compensation system. If the economy remained sluggish, it would be appropriate to move to a stronger measure, a general reduction in personal income taxes, the same policy which Arthur F. Burns, fresh from his service as Eisenhower's Chairman of the Council of Economic Advisers, had recommended during the 1958 recession. If all else failed, Samuelson's committee was prepared to advocate a substantial increase in public works. This was a notably mild policy brew for liberal economists to offer to a liberal President. It would have been much stronger if the balance of payments could have been ignored.

There was another reason for the moderation of the Samuelson committee. This was the unpleasant tendency of prices and wages to rise even *before* complete recovery and full employment. Was the answer to be found in what was dubbed 'cost-push' inflation during the 1950s? There were those who were certain of this explanation. Gardiner Means and John Blair of Senator Estes Kefauver's anti-monopoly sub-committee maintained that in industries like the steel, aluminium, chemical and automobiles, a very few very large corporations were able to raise prices for their entire industries even when market demand was sluggish. During the 1950s the leading villain was the steel industry, which raised its prices far more rapidly than prices in general rose, though much of the time the industry operated at low percentages of capacity. Similarly, powerful unions were able to push wages up even if the cost was unemployment for some of their own members. In concentrated industries inflation might threaten early in economic expansion and accelerate as expansion approached the target of full employment.

If cost-push inflation was really important, then the familiar Keynesian measures designed to operate upon aggregate demand might simply raise prices, or at best combine larger aggregate demand with dangerous price inflation.

In the current generation, the doctrine of secular stagnation has attracted few adherents. The reasons are comprehensible. Population has resumed a rapid growth. Aggregate demand has been high. Investment has been substantial here and abroad. The dire events of 1929 have receded into a past recalled only by the middle-aged and elderly. One prominent personage ever willing to remind his fellow Americans of the 1960s that 1929 really could happen all over again is that impeccable conservative, William McChesney Martin. Although his June, 1965, speech caused the stock market to flutter, administration officials took pains to contradict him, and sober business opinion promptly discounted the warning.

Nevertheless, there is a general sense in which the issues raised by the stagnationists of the 1930s have not really been settled. Does

American capitalism retain enough energy and drive to assure full employment? What would happen to the economy if peace broke out and military expenditure declined from $50 billion to $5 billion per year? What does the long economic expansion of the 1960s prove – that the economy is still buoyant, or that even extended prosperity, repeatedly stimulated by tax reduction, still cannot move the American economy to a satisfactory level of performance?

Thus, the important economic issues of the 1960s are only partially Keynesian in formulation. Pressing hard upon old problems of stimulating aggregate demand and preventing economic stagnation are questions of inflation, balance of payments deficits, automation, cost-push inflation and lagging economic growth. The evolving complexity of economic analysis has stimulated a new sophistication in economic policy. Before his death President Kennedy showed the marks of post-graduate training in economics from his advisers. He tried hard to pass on its fruits to the general public. Much of the thrust of Mr Kennedy's Yale commencement address in June, 1962, took the shape of an assault upon ancient ideological myths. For the myth of the balanced budget he proposed to substitute an appropriate technical approach to the highly technical issues involved in administering a huge economy.

By mid-1965 the application and extension of such political insights had had noticeable effects on the blend of administrative and congressional action which constitutes American economic policy. The place to begin is with the Tax Reduction Act of February, 1964, passed after a year of congressional debate. Conceptually, this reduction is premised upon a refinement of the aggregate demand doctrine – Walter Heller's notion of the tax drag. As Heller explained his invention, a highly progressive tax system tends to produce a budget surplus well short of full employment. This surplus impedes continued expansion and threatens to plunge the economy into unnecessary recession. The mission of a general tax reduction is to remove this drag upon expansion, or, altering the metaphor, to loosen the brake which slows expansion. The continued expansion of the economy in 1964 and 1965 has given credence to the Heller thesis, and encouraged President Johnson to recommend still another tax reduction in 1965 (this one in excises) and reject yet a third reduction in 1966 only because of rising Vietnam expenditures.

The mixture of tax reductions has been the consequence of politics

as well as economics. The reduction in personal income taxes, winning the support of the vast majority subject to these imposts, has
stimulated personal consumption out of larger sums available to
each income recipient. But like good Keynesians, Presidents Kennedy and Johnson have tailored the bulk of their proposals to encourage business investment. The process started early. The Kennedy administration's first tax measure, enacted in 1961, was an
investment tax credit whose effect was a seven per cent price reduction on new tools and machines. In the summer of 1962, the Treasury
liberalized the rules which govern the depreciation practices of
businessmen in such a fashion as to enlarge business profits. Early
in 1965 President Johnson once again relaxed these rules. Finally,
the 1964 tax law reduced corporate income taxes.

Neither Democratic President has been able to stop with the
stimulation of business investment and the creation of moderate
budget deficits. In particular the balance of payments problem has
evoked some complex administrative and monetary responses. The
Kennedy–Johnson administrations, to their credit, have grappled
with the management of interest rates so as simultaneously to promote domestic expansion and ameliorate our balance of payments
deficits. At first glance the objectives appear incompatible. The high
interest rates which attract foreign funds to American financial markets discourage domestic investment and growth. The low interest
rates which stimulate domestic activity increase the flight of funds to
financial centres where interest rates are higher.

The administration answer, the interest rate 'twist' as it became
known, was highly ingenious. One element was the passage by
Congress of an interest-equalization act in 1963. A technically complex measure (which exempted Canada), this tax had the effect of
raising the rates foreigners had to pay in order to borrow funds in
the United States by about one per cent. It was an effective dis-
couragement to foreign use of Wall Street as a means of marketing
new securities. At the same time, this tax had no direct effect upon
domestic interest rates. Indeed, it was argued that the capital kept at
home might well be invested here. Simultaneously, short-term rates
were raised slightly so as to attract short-term foreign funds to New
York. The administration completed its delicate operation early in
1965 by appealing to the business community to keep its dollar
holdings and investments in foreign countries to a minimum. In the
middle of 1965, compliance was remarkably complete, possibly

because of the widespread suspicion that, if voluntary steps failed, compulsion would not lag far behind.

But neither tax policy nor interest rate policy could succeed if inflation damaged the competitive position of American merchandise in export markets. The Kennedy–Johnson administration tacitly accepted the presence of a concentration of power among a few large corporations and a few large unions. Moving on from this acceptance to the reality of cost-push inflation, the administration endeavoured to counter the forces of inflation by enunciating a set of guidelines for both business and unions. As these wage–price criteria were first described in the January, 1962, *Economic Report of the President*, they enunciated, in the opaque language of federal economics, a rule: 'The general guide for non-inflationary wage behavior is that the rate of increase in wage rates (including fringe benefits) in each industry be equal to the trend rate of over-all productivity increase.'[14] Freely translated, the Council's declaration urged unions and employers to negotiate settlements which accorded with national changes in productivity rather than with shifts in the performance of individual industries or individual firms.

If the rule was followed, some business firms would increase prices, others would reduce them, and the remainder would make no changes. The public expectation of an industry which enjoyed an eight per cent improvement in output per man, during a period when the economy in general inched forward at only two per cent, would be a wage increase of two per cent (the national average improvement in productivity) and a six per cent price reduction. Similarly, an industry which stagnated at old productivity levels would still be expected to raise wages two per cent, but it would be permitted to increase prices. The last group of firms could afford both to raise wages two per cent and to hold prices steady. If everything worked out tidily, the general price level would remain constant and inflation would be averted.

The thrust of the Council's policy was unmistakable. Identifying power where power exists, the Council warned its owners to restrain themselves. How effective the guidelines have been is the subject of later enquiry, but it has often been conjectured that the dramatic confrontation between President Kennedy of the United States and President Blough of United States Steel in April, 1962, was in slight disguise an episode of business resistance to the guidelines and presidential insistence upon their relevance.

In their various ways, tax, interest rate and price policies were attempts to diminish unemployment. The more direct assault on unemployment which is implied by area redevelopment, regional rehabilitation, and manpower retraining schemes is at the centre of a continuing controversy, an argument over the nature and causes of unemployment. Led by Professor Charles Killingsworth of Michigan State University, some analysts of labour markets believe that unemployment is for the most part structural, caused by the mismatching of job vacancies and the skills of the unemployed. The structuralists, as the school is called, point to high rates of unemployment among the unskilled and the uneducated and the practical absence of unemployment among college graduates as evidence that those without jobs suffer from a lack of marketable skills. Impressively marshalled by the Council of Economic Advisers, the aggregate demand school is convinced that the bulk of unemployment is caused by a deficiency of aggregate demand. The controversy is closely related to the discussion of why American growth rates flagged (relatively, at least) during the 1950s. In that season of discontent, the United States appeared to be losing badly both the sputnik race and the international growth sweepstakes. Was the cause structural unemployment? Was it deficient aggregate demand?*

When the experts quarrel, a wise politician hedges his bets. Although President Kennedy finally placed most of his chips on the aggregate demand explanation of unemployment, the conflicting voices of his advisers reinforced his initial inclination to treat unemployment as a symptom of human factors – the reluctance to leave a depressed area that is nevertheless home, the absence of education, the presence of racial discrimination or the lack of a marketable skill. Tax cuts are poor cures for such social ailments. In the first year of his presidency, Mr Kennedy persuaded Congress to pass the

---

* Here is one calculation of the international growth race.

RATE OF GROWTH OF PER CAPITA OUTPUT 1950–60 (PER CENT)

Belgium	2·3	Germany	6·5	Sweden	2·6
Canada	1·2	Italy	5·3	Switzerland	3·7
Denmark	2·6	Netherlands	3·6	United Kingdom	2·2
France	3·5	Norway	2·6	United States	1·6

Average 3·1

SOURCE: Adapted from Angus Maddison, *Economic Growth in the West* (New York: Twentieth Century Fund, 1964; London: Allen & Unwin).

Area Redevelopment Act and the Manpower Retraining Act. The emphasis of both measures was upon the preparation of displaced (or never placed) workers for decent jobs in a changing labour market. The training features of the War on Poverty and aspects of the Appalachian programme are natural descendants of these two measures.

As the programmes of the past five years demonstrate, the issue in practical terms is one of emphasis. The sturdiest advocates of retraining concede that unless the economy is buoyant, no jobs will await the graduates of training and retraining programmes. And the most devoted believers in aggregate demand, including the Council of Economic Advisers, recognize some amount of structural unemployment. Argument will no doubt continue about the relative scope of tax reduction, public expenditure and specific measures against structural unemployment.

In this rapid sketch of the economic pathology of the 1960s, there is a final and possibly most important issue implicit in the policy choices that American Presidents have made. For short this might be termed the Galbraithian issue. The central theme of John Kenneth Galbraith's elegant tract for the times, *The Affluent Society*, is the contrast between an economy whose public sector, starved of funds, is pathetic in performance, and whose private sector, bloated with riches, pours out a cornucopia of trivial products. Galbraith urged not greater growth, which he considered fruitless unless public attitudes changed, but social balance – an expansion of production for public purposes and a corresponding reduction in private output. Seen in this context, every tax reduction increases the percentage of the community's resources which is devoted to private production, and every increase in public spending diminishes the private share. In their emphasis on tax reduction, Presidents Kennedy and Johnson have in Galbraithian terms further distorted the relations between public and private output.

These, then, are the matters which provide the agenda for the remainder of this volume – economic growth, automation, tax reduction, wage-price guidelines, balance of payments and the quality of the nation's output. Keynes does not cease to be relevant. He becomes relevant in different ways and in different company.

SOURCE NOTES TO CHAPTER 7

1. Quoted in Alvin H. Hansen, *Economic Policy and Full Employment* (New York: McGraw-Hill, 1947).

2. Quoted in ibid.

3. Quoted in ibid.

4. J. M. Keynes, 'Proposals for an International Clearing Union', Speech in House of Lords, 18 May 1943; quoted in Sir Roy Harrod, *The Life of John Maynard Keynes* (London: Macmillan, 1951). An abridged version of Keynes's original proposals appears in Seymour Harris, *The New Economics* (New York: Knopf, 1947).

5. Ibid.

6. E. A. G. Robinson, 'John Maynard Keynes', in Robert Lekachman (ed.) *Keynes's General Theory: Reports of Three Decades* (New York: St Martin's, 1964; London: Macmillan).

7. Quoted in Harris, op. cit.

8. Quoted in ibid.

9. Quoted in ibid.

10. Quoted in ibid.

11. Robinson, op. cit.

12. Ibid.

13. See Sophia Cooper and Denis F. Johnston, 'Labor Force Projections', *Monthly Labor Review*, February 1965.

14. *The Economic Report of the President* (Washington D.C.: U.S. Government Printing Office, January 1962).

The Keynesian Era

The crisis of the 1930s was concealed from no one. Unemployment, bankruptcy, foreclosures and soup kitchens – these were conditions, not theories. In contrast the political and economic controversies over the growth rate of the 1950s raged among disputants, some of whom challenged the existence of a problem and others of whom judged it trivial or transitory. For many it was an ultimately baffling exercise in rival statistics, American, Russian and Western European. For others it was a chance to berate a Republican administration which basked in the reflected popularity of President Eisenhower. In the near dead-heat run by John F. Kennedy and Richard M. Nixon, the issue of growth was one of the few real differences between the candidates.

Before embarking on waters as stormy as these, it is advisable to start with a few facts about economic growth in the Western world. As long as population increases, a society must increase output at least as rapidly if it desires simply to maintain existing living standards. If it treasures the more ambitious objective of raising these standards, then *per capita* output must expand at a rate higher than the annual population rise. Its failure to do so in poor societies leaves their peoples in continued poverty accentuated by disappointed hope – the condition of countries like Egypt, Algeria, Ghana and India. In traditional societies characterized by unchanging techniques and little hope of personal improvement, the Malthusian checks of famine, disease and high infant mortality tend to keep both population and living standards static.

The situation is different in the West. At least since the Industrial Revolution, in places where industrialization has been institutional-ized, both population and living standards have risen, subject only to cyclical interruptions. This experience has generated a popular expectation of higher and higher real income, which is itself a nineteenth-century innovation. In the United States, Great Britain, Scandinavia and much of Western Europe, actual economic per-formance has come reasonably close to fulfilling the expectation. The trend has been towards a steady improvement in *per capita* productivity, which underlies general rises in living standards.

Even if (and it is debatable) the 1950s truly represented a departure from an historic trend, the performance of the American economy during the past century and a quarter has been commendable. As the distinguished economist Simon Kuznets has summarized the record, 'Over the one hundred and twenty years from 1840 to 1960, population grew at an average rate of about 2 percent per year; labor force at a slightly higher rate of about 2·2 percent; gross national product at 3·6 per cent ... and product per worker at 1·4 percent per year.'[1] The dry numbers had a cheerful meaning: although 1960's population was 10·5 times as large as 1840's, standards of life had risen enormously because *per capita* output was now five times as large.

What has the shouting been about? The *per capita* improvement in output between 1950 and 1960 was only minutely less than the 1913–50 rate and not very different from the average change from 1840 to 1960. Even if the measure used was changes in total output, there was nothing superficially alarming. In the 1950s the gross national product rose 3·2 per cent per year, somewhat higher than the 1913–50 average. On the face of it, the political argument requires more explanation. This is especially so if the simple-minded question is asked, what is so wonderful about growth? Old-fashioned opinion was more divided than modern views. Thus, in stating his preference for an economy with a stable population and output, John Stuart Mill put the issue in words which may still contain some contemporary resonance:

I cannot, therefore, regard the stationary state of capital and wealth with the unaffected aversion so generally manifested by political economists of the old school. I am inclined to believe that it would be, on the whole, a very considerable improvement in our present condition. I confess that I am not charmed with the ideal of life held out by those who think that the normal state of human beings is that of struggling to get on; that the trampling, crushing, elbowing, and treading on each other's heels, which form the existing type of social life, are the most desirable lot of human beings.[2]

Indeed, despite the unpopularity of this attitude in the United States, one might wonder whether growth and size have not been over-emphasized. Elephants are not superior to cats. If the greater height and bulk of the modern Yale man coincides with any increase over their Yale-bred fathers in intelligence, public spirit or humane enlightenment, the change is concealed from an indulgent public. Big cities are not invariably more pleasant than smaller ones. Who prefers Chicago to San Francisco? Large countries are not automatically superior to small ones. Given the choice, who would prefer Russia to the Netherlands or Denmark? The speculation can be extended. Surely the American landscape was pleasanter before the automobile promoted economic growth and the concomitant of highways lined with billboards, refreshment stands, motels and junk-yards. Growth and affluence have defaced inner cities and sprawling suburbs with rare impartiality. Water and air pollution, unbearable traffic congestion, a disappearance of space and solitude, these are all among the corollaries of economic growth here and elsewhere. Even General de Gaulle has been powerless to stem Coca-Colanization, *franglais* and the quick lunch counters cluttering French highways and betraying generations of French gourmets.

In the real world one of Mill's major assumptions is contradicted. Americans grow more numerous each year. Hence unless the economy expands with them, unemployment and idle resources are unavoidable. The sluggishness of the 1950s was the consequence of a growth rate too low to provide the extra jobs that population growth and productivity improvement demanded. The rising tide of new entrants into the labour force, out of the schools and the colleges, adds a million and a quarter net souls to the working population each year. A three per cent annual improvement in *per capita* output eliminates approximately two million jobs each year.* In the Alice in Wonderland economics of growth, it is essential to run as fast as one can, just in order to stay where one is. During the 1950s we ran too slowly.

So much was evident from the moderate but persistent increase in unemployment. During the eight Eisenhower years, unemployment fell below four per cent only in 1953, a period still heavily influenced by the requirements of the Korean conflict. Looked at more closely, the record was still more distressing, for successive business cycles seemed to carry with them higher average rates of

---

* In a labour force of over seventy million persons, a one per cent *per capita* improvement in productivity eliminates 700,000 jobs. A three per cent improvement, not far from recent years' records, means that a given year's output can be produced with two million persons fewer at work than was true the year before.

unemployment. July, 1953, was the peak of a business cycle expansion which began in November, 1949. During the forty-five months of upward movement in the major indicators of business activity, unemployment was less than five per cent in forty-two months, less than four per cent in thirty-five months, and less than three per cent in eleven months. At the cycle's peak in July, 1953, unemployment had fallen to a quite acceptable 2·7 per cent – close to the practicable minimum. Obviously the American economy of recent history could function at levels of unemployment substantially lower than the four to five per cent currently cited by some as the practicable objective.

In retrospect the 1949–53 expansion was the strongest of the post-Second World War years. The next cycle reached its peak in July, 1957, as the culmination of thirty-five months of expansion. In thirty-four of those months unemployment dipped below five per cent, in only three of those months below four per cent and in *no* months below three per cent. At this cycle's peak, unemployment was a much less satisfactory 4·2 per cent. A third cycle reached its high in May, 1960, after only twenty-five months of expansion. In only one month did unemployment fall below five per cent and in no months below four per cent.

These statistics recounted a simple and disturbing tale. Each successive business cycle expansion was shorter than its predecessor. At each peak unemployment was higher than at the preceding cycle's peak, and from cycle to cycle average unemployment rose. No wonder that Nelson Rockefeller campaigned for the Republican presidential nomination in 1960 on the promise to raise American growth rates. No wonder that as an actual presidential candidate John F. Kennedy demanded that we get moving again, and that as President he stressed the theme in words like these:

In the past seven years, our rate of growth has slowed down disturbingly. In the past three and one-half years, the gap between what we can produce and what we do produce has threatened to become chronic. . . . Realistic aims for 1961 are to reverse the downward trend in our economy, to narrow the gap of unused potential, to abate the waste and misery of unemployment. . . . For 1962 and 1963 our program must aim at expanding American productive capacity at a rate that shows the world the vigor and vitality of a free economy[3].

Though demography was the most cogent of the impulses to faster economic growth, it was not the only factor explaining why 'growthmanship', as Richard Nixon once termed what he considered the over-emphasis upon economic expansion, agitated the public and its political leaders. The Rockefeller Brothers Fund's Panel Report on the Economy of 1958 was a typical argument for rapid expansion: 'The first basic conclusion that emerges from our analysis is the very great importance of maintaining a high rate of growth.'[4]

The reasons adduced by the panellists went beyond high employment and rising living standards. They included a long list of national requirements – more defence, liberalized aid to education, more generous welfare aid and enlarged urban public works programmes. The panel's line of argument started with the existing preferences of Americans for something like the 1960 mixture of private and public goods. It proceeded with the assumption that the higher tax receipts generated by an expanding economy would enable public authorities to fill social needs better.

Thus, anyone who favoured more foreign aid or more missiles or a quicker American appearance on the moon or urban renewal or medicare or better schools would, if he accepted the Rockefeller line of analysis, find himself urging faster economic growth upon his leaders. Yet these are only the bread-and-butter explanations of economic growth's popularity. The less tangible are conceivably the more influential explanations. One is the American tradition of expansion. Here is a representative expression of the confidence in dynamism as an integral element of the American experience:

The adventure of the American economy is a continuing reality. The dynamism that has produced the present level of well-being holds out the promise of a still more challenging future. Our nation is dedicated to economic growth. It is also dedicated to full employment. . . . We want to achieve rapid growth and full employment in a free and private economy. The freedom of the economy is fundamental to other freedoms we cherish.[5]

Thus once more the Rockefeller panellists.

The American vision of the future emerges from a past dominated by the imagery of the frontier, the symbolism of the American garden invaded by the conquering machine,[6] and the conviction that the material universe can be mastered by ingenious men. As Seymour Lipset has suggested, America is the first new nation, or at any rate the first nation that has embraced the creative myth of starting from the beginning and making its own history. Americans know, either joyfully or ruefully, that this is the land of youth and novelty, of the bigger and better, of destruction and new construction. For most Americans even temporary stagnation is repugnant, and a permanent halt in the march of progress is an insupportable conception.

Closely allied to this set of attitudes is a national expectation of winning all competitions. The cult of the good loser is an official element of American attitudes. Nevertheless, Leo Durocher's classic 'Nice guys finish last' may evoke still stronger emotional responses in the American consciousness. Within this context of aspiration, the 1950s was a shocking decade. So recently our ailing client, Western Europe expanded at rates far in excess of ours and suffered from labour shortages which coincided in time with our labour surpluses. In a remarkably short period, small European cars won a popularity which jarred Detroit into reluctant emulation and accorded George Romney a public importance which projected him into Michigan's state house and national political prominence. Italian sewing machines and typewriters gave American producers a competitive battle as startling as it was unexpected.* The giant steel industry, less and less successful in export markets and more and more vulnerable to West German and Japanese competition, took to whining about foreign dumping and American trade unions.

This was bad enough, but at least Americans could take solace from the argument that the embarrassing vigour of the European recovery owed much to our Marshall Plan and other aid programmes. Nothing of the kind could insulate us from the shock of Soviet competition. The menace of this rivalry was symbolized by the rapidity with which the Russians matched our nuclear technology, developed intercontinental ballistic missiles, and as a bonus from this achievement manufactured the powerful rocket boosters which orbited the globe for the first time in 1957.

It is difficult to over-estimate the symbolic importance of the sputnik. One of its consequences was a public demand for vastly enlarged American support of space technology, a demand resisted by the Eisenhower administration but embraced by the Kennedy–Johnson administrations. A second was a bout of soul-searching about a favourite national topic, the state of education.† The National Defense Education Act poured federal funds into scientific

---

* When Olivetti acquired Underwood, it sent its management experts to reform Underwood's *American* procedures, just as though the United States was an underdeveloped country.

† Book titles of the *Why Johnny Can't Read* and *What Ivan Knows That Johnny Doesn't* variety expressed the national mood.

schooling. Dr Conant examined the public schools and found them wanting. He visited the teachers' colleges and discovered in them one of the sources of the schools' deficiencies. Teams of eminent mathematicians, physicists and biologists began to devote themselves to the reformation of high-school curricula and the writing of modern high-school textbooks.

Inevitably, the Soviet scientific and technological accomplishments were connected with another Soviet triumph, an exceptionally high growth rate. According to American estimates (the Russian claims were higher still), the Soviet gross national product averaged an increase of 6·8 per cent between 1950 and 1958 and 4·6 per cent between 1958 and 1962.[7] Although the second rate was moderate enough, what caught the imagination was the spectacular performance of the early 1950s.

The fact was that Soviet achievements in space and Soviet rates of growth were not very closely connected. In the calm which has followed the years of hysterical anxiety about missile gaps, sputniks and the Soviet will to world domination, it has been realized that the Soviet growth rates were exaggerated, and the Soviet space successes derived from a single-minded concentration upon one scientific sector which left much of the remainder of Soviet science neglected. Tranquillity was to come. In the meanwhile the Russian example and the Russian threat were useful bogymen.

One result was the construction of an unlikely coalition of liberal advocates dedicated to social improvement and militant patriots devoted to the defeat of communism. It was natural that quite aside from the merits of the case, public concern over lagging growth dominated the politics of the late 1950s. If the 1960 presidential campaign developed any but the covert Catholic issue, it was the question of whether the Eisenhower administration had done all that a government could to restore the American position at the head of all the international league standings – in space, growth, nuclear technology, education and pure science.

An understanding of why the American economy grew too slowly to employ everybody able and willing to work demands an appreciation of the growth process in general. The revival of interest in economic growth is a return to an ancient preoccupation. Although the Great Depression and the Keynesian response to it shifted economists' interest from economic growth to economic instability,

English and American economists from Adam Smith onward have been deeply interested in economic progress, a state usually identified with economic growth. An early and powerful explanation was advanced in *The Wealth of Nations*. Here Smith, cribbing liberally from Diderot's encyclopedia, argued that improvements in *per capita* productivity were caused by the spread of the division of labour. In one of the more famous illustrations in the history of economic doctrine, Smith asked his readers to consider the humble pin:

To take an example, therefore, from a very trifling manufacture; but one in which the division of labour has been very often taken notice of, the trade of the pin-maker; a workman not educated to this business ... nor acquainted with the use of the machinery employed in it (to the invention of which the same division of labour has probably given occasion), could scarce, perhaps, with his utmost industry, make one pin in a day, and certainly could not make twenty. But in the way in which this business is now carried on, not only the whole work is a peculiar trade, but it is divided into a number of branches, of which the greater part are likewise peculiar trades. One man draws out the wire, another straightens it, a third cuts it, a fourth points it, a fifth grinds it at the top for receiving the head; to make the head requires two or three distinct operations; to put it on is a peculiar business, to whiten the pins is another; it is even a trade by itself to put them into the paper; and the important business of making a pin is, in this manner, divided into about eighteen distinct operations, which, in some manufactories, are all performed by distinct hands, though in others the same man will sometimes perform two or three of them. I have seen a small manufactory of this kind where ten men only were employed, and where some of them consequently performed two or three distinct operations. But though they were very poor, and therefore but indifferently accommodated with the necessary machinery, they could, when they exerted themselves, make among them twelve pounds of pins in a day. There are in a pound upwards of four thousand pins of a middling size. Those ten persons, therefore, could make among them upwards of forty-eight thousand pins in a day. Each person, therefore, making a tenth of a part of forty-eight thousand pins, might be considered as making four thousand eight hundred pins in a day. But if they had all wrought separately and independently, and without any of them having been educated to this peculiar business, they certainly could not each of them have made twenty, perhaps not one pin in a day; that is, certainly, not the two hundred and fortieth, perhaps not the four thousand eight hundredth part of what they are at present capable of performing, in consequence of a proper division and combination of their different operations.[8]

As Smith explained and as today's economists still believe, the division of labour promotes efficiency in three ways. It increases individual dexterity. It saves time otherwise lost in moving from one operation to another. And it promotes invention, by agents of the employers if not by workmen themselves as Smith believed. This powerful and beneficent principle operated most effectively as the market broadened. Where the customers are few and widely scattered, specialization on the part of their suppliers is impossible. Where the buyers are numerous (as in any large city), then the sellers can concentrate on the creation and sale of articles more and more specialized.

In Smith's day an array of government regulations hampered the extension of the market. Mercantilist restraints upon foreign trade, domestic investment, free entry into trades and even the liberty of the labourer to move about the countryside conspired to keep the market narrow, impede the division of labour and retard the growth of efficiency and specialization. Hence Smith's basic argument for *laissez faire* hinged on the freedom it gave to each man to pursue his own self-interest. And it was obvious to Smith (said by Walter Bagehot to believe that there was a little Scotsman inside each of us) that human beings conceived self-interest as the maximization of their wages and profits. Since these were maximized only in a progressive society, such a society ran parallel to the extension of the division of labour.

What has survived has been Smith's general conclusions rather than his common-sense analysis. The marginal productivity explanations of wages, rent and interest which came into vogue during the 1870s simultaneously in England, Germany, Sweden and in America focused less on the division of labour (by then taken for granted) and more on the quality of the factors of production which cooperated in the factory process. The implications of this line of analysis for the general welfare were direct enough. Like any other form of income, wages could rise only as the economic contribution of the labourer rose. Similarly, owners of capital could anticipate higher returns when more acute investment of their funds was followed by more substantial increments of output. It followed that increases in total output paralleled increases in the quantity of economic resources employed if the same degree of efficiency was maintained. More rapid increases in total output depended upon an expansion of *per capita* output, rendered possible only by an improvement in the efficiency of the human labour, the fixed capital or the managerial supervision which cooperated to turn raw materials into finished products.

With infinite refinement added, this remains the basic doctrine, the underlying explanation of economic growth. An economy can expand as rapidly in output as in population if the efficiency of the agents of production is constant. It can grow more rapidly when these agents improve in quality. The concrete issues of economic policy can be readily inferred from this somewhat abstract discussion. What can be done to make labour more efficient, capital more productive and space more economical? Almost any public or indeed private policy can be analysed for its impact upon the performance of one or more of these agents of production. An ingenious attempt to make quantitative estimates of the impact of various social policies or social changes has been completed by Edward F. Dennison of the Committee for Economic Development.[9] Although it is a mistake to take Dennison's numbers literally, they are dependable enough rough guides to the effectiveness of a great many different possible actions and public policies.

Dennison's computations allow for the compilation of at least two alternative recipes for growth. One might be termed the welfare package. Here are some of the ingredients, a few readily obtainable, some more difficult to locate, and a few scarcely to be perceived.

If the current mortality rate of people under sixty-five years of age was cut in half, the annual growth rate could be raised by ·1 per cent, for in any economy the death of active workers (quite aside from individual survival preferences) is a waste. This is one of the severe handicaps of developing nations like India, where life expectancies at birth are forty years or less. Known medical procedures applied to more people are capable of achieving this improvement. A ban on smoking might help. We might reap a similar gain in *per capita* output if the work losses caused by accidents and illnesses were halved. In a more utopian vein, Dennison suggests that the elimination of all crime and the reform of all criminals would give society the reward of an additional ·03 per cent growth. Doubling the number of immigrants to the United States is worth ·1 per cent in growth and a great deal in national altruism. Again, if racial discrimination in hiring and advancement was eliminated, the economy's rate of growth would be augmented by ·04 per cent. Parenthetically, the point has begun to be perceived that American industry deprives itself of important sources of executive talent by its systematic exclusion of Negroes, Jews and often Catholics from executive training programmes.* Finally, if youngsters were persuaded to stay in their schools for an additional year and a half, the economy might inch upward by an additional ·1 per cent. Taken together, these policies are capable of raising economic growth a little less than ·5 per cent each year, a figure which is modest enough in size until it is converted into the $3·3 billion of extra goods and services which the improvement is worth when the G.N.P. runs at a $660 billion level.

This route to higher economic growth concentrates directly on the improvement of the quality of the human resources which co-operate in economic activity. Since economics is an austere science, no note is taken of the improved quality of daily life and daily experience that this programme carries with it. There is another way to promote growth. Appropriate public policy can encourage a freer allocation of resources and a more efficient combination of capital and labour of existing qualities. The collection of techniques available might be termed the free market package.

Under this strategy, according to Dennison's estimate, a complete cessation of strikes and lockouts is worth ·1 per cent in added economic growth – a smaller effect than sensational publicity about the damaging impact of strikes might have led the naïve to suppose. Among the other changes tentatively quantified are expanded private investment, the closing of tax loopholes and the equalization of tax burdens, the prohibition of retail and manufacturing price-setting, more rigorous anti-trust enforcement, and an end to feather-bedding, restrictive work rules and union resistance to technological change. In the main these are changes which strengthen competition and weaken protected monopoly positions. There are other possibilities. If farm subsidies were diminished or eliminated, still more families would move to the cities where their labour would contribute larger amounts to the value of the G.N.P. If all firms adopted the practices of their most efficient brethren, growth would rise. A reduction in tariffs and other barriers to trade would increase growth by ·07 per cent. Added up, the total realizable gains are ·6 per cent, somewhat more than those derivable from the welfare package.

Neither growth strategy seriously upsets established political and

* Mr Ray Bliss, in 1965 national chairman of the Republican Party, has extended the arguments to politics. He has posited that one of the reasons for his party's loss of public favour has been its conversion into a nest of WASPS.

economic practices. Private ownership is not assaulted. The existing distribution of income and wealth and the moderate degree of progressive taxation which slightly alleviates inequities in distribution are both tacitly accepted. The welfare proposals fall short of John Kenneth Galbraith's drastic fiscal alterations of the balance between private and public enterprise. Neither strategy calls for wage and price controls, public ownership or national economic planning. What impact these more radical interventions would have is pure conjecture.

Choosing a growth programme involves at best uncertainty about the public estimate of benefit and the public approach to payment. Consider this indictment of the urban environment issued by the Joint Committee on Washington (D.C.) Metropolitan Problems:

Its population is pressing against the limits of such natural resources as water supply. Its growth outstrips the capacity of existing sewage disposal plants. Where growth is most rapid, as at the suburban fringe, the shortage of government facilities such as schools, highways and parks is especially acute. With growing population has come territorial expansion into the metropolitan counties ... and with the metropolitan 'explosion' the decentralization of government employment sectors, retail trade and much other private business. The metropolitan expansion, coupled with fundamental changes in travel habits and transportation technology, has disorganized the older systems of mass transportation .... In the central city forces of social change have been accelerated by unprecedented migrations of population, the disorganization of residential neighbourhoods, shifting land use, and the invasion of vehicles and parking facilities. The congestion and decay of the central city, the shortages and fiscal plight of the peripheral suburbs, the metropolitan transportation dilemma, and the dissipation of our natural resources are all parts of the same interrelated process of urban growth.[10]

The indictment is not overdrawn, and the only answer is communal action. Public agencies supported by public funds improve (or fail to improve) schools, libraries, museums, transportation, zoning, roads, water supply, parks and beaches. Improvement means higher taxes. Is the public prepared to pay them? How will greater public outlays on such objectives affect economic growth? How will the failure to spend more operate upon growth? To these relevant questions the answers are yet to be given.

Nationally, the policies actually pursued during the 1950s accurately reflected the old ideology of a Republican President and a Congress dominated by a coalition of rural Republicans and Southern Democrats. The man who placed his imprint upon the decade was George Humphrey, Secretary of the Treasury much of the time, in private life a phenomenally successful entrepreneur, and in public as in private life a charming but determined economic reactionary. Humphrey's persistent effort was to balance the budget by reducing federal spending, and no Keynesian proclivities complicated his remedies. During the Eisenhower years, strong conservatives – Joseph Dodge, Percival Brundage and Maurice Stans – filled the strategic position of Director of the Bureau of the Budget. Conservatism in a more sophisticated guise found a home in the Council of Economic Advisers, headed in turn by two Columbia professors, Arthur F. Burns and Raymond J. Saulnier, who were sceptical of Keynesian analysis and predisposed in favour of private over public activity. And in the White House, General Eisenhower, untrained in economics, held firmly to the simple moralistic opinions appropriate to the graduate of an Abilene boyhood: deficits were bad for the character, public spending was wasteful, and the national debt was a burden unfairly imposed by one generation on the generations which succeeded it. No amount of free tuition offered by economists persuaded Mr Eisenhower to deviate by a hair from these convictions.

Life in high places would be simpler if events allowed officials to act as they speak. No one could doubt the sincerity of Secretary Humphrey's opposition to a more interventionist fiscal policy:

No, and I am not opposed to that. I just do not believe that – I said a minute ago, I just do not believe that there is any group of men who are so smart that they can tell everybody in America what to do and be wiser than the great bulk of our people who are actuated by an incentive free choice system. I believe with all my heart in an incentive free choice system. I believe it is what has made this country.[11]

Taken at their face value, these words committed the President and his administration to six principles:

1. Federal budgets should always be balanced.
2. Private spending is far more important than public spending, or as W. Randolph Burgess, then Under Secretary of the Treasury, put it, 'When the government spends money, it does not produce goods which the people can buy'.[12]

3. Any federal debt is a burden. A bigger debt is a bigger burden.
4. Taxes should be reduced only in the presence or imminent prospect of a balanced budget.
5. The free choices of savers, investors and consumers determines the national rate of growth. In any event, growth is not the government's business.
6. The federal budget should not be used as an instrument of economic stabilization.

Accordingly, the eight Eisenhower years should have featured eight balanced budgets. Each year's balance should have occurred at a lower and lower expenditure as tax receipt totals in public activities were pruned and private enterprise encouraged to expand. Above all, federal intervention during recession should have been minimal. In fact the economic history of the 1950s turned out to be considerably more complicated than this ideology and conservative expectation hoped.

The Republicans had been particularly explicit during and after the presidential campaign of 1952 about the necessity of reducing federal spending. The new administration started bravely enough. In 1954, 1955 and 1956, the President's budgets pushed the spending total down to $47·5, $45·3 and $45·7 billion from 1953's $58 billion. Although the largest reductions were facilitated by the Korean armistice, the Bureau of the Budget and the Treasury also succeeded in pushing other expenditures down from $9 billion in 1953 to $5·7 billion in 1956.

After 1956 the trend reversed itself, and by 1961 expenditures returned practically to their pre-Republican level, divided between national defence ($49 billion) and other purposes ($8·9 billion) very much in 1961 as in 1952. What had tempered the zeal of the administration? For one thing the exigencies of cold war diplomacy did not permit of military expenditures as low as 1955's $39·1 billion for very long. Then there were the inclinations of a Congress which, fiscally prudent though it was, still responded to constituency spending pressures. And the administration itself was not monolithic in its attitudes. Gabriel Hauge, the President's White House economist; the members of the Council of Economic Advisers; and even Cabinet officials like Secretary of Health, Education and Welfare, Marion Folsom, were friendlier to expenditure than the true believers in the Treasury and the Bureau of the Budget.

For Secretary Humphrey the upshot of this pulling and hauling

was an odd episode in January 1957. At a renowned Press conference, Mr Humphrey said of the Budget which he himself had just
sent down to Congress that it could be cut by congressional action,
and indeed unless it was cut, the country would experience a 'depression that will curl your hair'.[13] This peculiar example of administration posture was rendered still more bizarre by President Eisenhower's open sympathy not with the budget whose ultimate sponsor
is the President but with his subordinate's impromptu denunciation
of a document prepared in his own office.

The frustration of the economizers was comprehensible. As Dr
Neil Jacoby, himself a former member of the Eisenhower Council of
Economic Advisers, pointed out, at the beginning of the Eisenhower
years federal cash payments to the remainder of the economy com-
prised 19·7 per cent of the nation's total spending. Eight striving
years onward the federal share had been pushed down to nineteen
per cent – not much of a conservative revolution.[14]

Did the Republicans at least win the reward for which they
yearned – a balanced budget? Alas, in only three years did the Eisenhower administration balance the national accounts. When the
Republicans left office, the national debt was larger than when they
had assumed it. So much for the vanity of human wishes and the
perversity of human institutions. Even excluding fiscal 1953 (a year
for which the Democrats were responsible), total deficits during the
Eisenhower years far exceeded total surpluses. Thus it was that
between 1954 and 1961 the public debt increased $18 billion. Still
worse, the $12·4 billion 1959 deficit still holds the record as the
nation's largest peacetime gap between income and expenditure.
What gave the screw a final turn was the contrast with the spendthrift
Truman administration, when public debt, despite all charges, rose
a mere $7 billion. The numbers gave no substantiation to Repub-
lican claims to superior fiscal merit.

Did the Republicans at least succeed in checking price inflation?
The short answer is no, for with the exception of 1955, the cost of
living rose steadily. Taking average prices during the years 1957–9
as a base, the consumer price index stood at 93·2 when General
Eisenhower took office. During his last year of service, the index was
103·1. Moreover, the largest part of the increase was suffered between 1955 and 1959, a period also marred by a fairly sharp business
cycle recession. Prudent Republican policy thus presided over a new
paradox, simultaneous recession and price inflation.

It was all a poor reward of principle. The Eisenhower administration had refrained out of conviction from stimulating the economy enough to evoke high growth rates and satisfactory employment totals. Its single tax cut in 1954 was justified not by Keynesian doctrine but by the older ideology of reduced federal influence and expanded private discretion. During the 1957–8 recession, the administration successfully resisted pressure for a tax reduction explicitly aimed at enlarging aggregate demand. What followed was the huge 1959 deficit which resulted from recession declines in tax receipts and statutory expansions of payments to farmers and other subsidized groups. In all probability a deliberate tax cut would have caused a *smaller* deficit than inaction had produced.

Seeking balanced budgets, free markets, active competition and price stability, Republican policy had achieved instead deficits, inflation, recession and lagging growth. The record of frustration appears in the weakening of the nation's recovery from recession. The recovery from the 1949 recession lasted forty-five months, from the 1954 low point thirty-five months, and from 1958 only twenty-five months. By contrast the expansion which commenced in February, 1961, was still continuing in mid-1966. The Eisenhower administration had released (or failed to counter) strong depressive elements. A statistical measure of deterioration contrasts increases in employment and income between the beginning of 1948 and the end of 1955 with similar changes from the beginning of 1956 to the end of 1961.

INCREASES IN EMPLOYMENT AND INCOME (PER CENT)

Period	Total Employment	Personal Disposable Income	Corporate Profits Before Taxes	Unemployment Rate (Average per Period)
1948–55	9·5	37·0	36·0	4·3
Per year	1·2	4·6	4·5	
1956–61	3·5	18·0	14·0	5·6
Per year	0·6	3·0	2·3	

SOURCE: Alvin H. Hansen, 'Four Postwar Cycles in the United States', in Arthur L. Grey, Jr, and John E. Elliott (eds.), *Economic Issues and Policies* (Boston: Houghton Mifflin, 1961).

The contrast is sharp between the expansion of total employment at an average rate of 1·2 per cent in the first period and the expansion at half that figure in the next period. The direct consequence was an increase in average unemployment from 4·3 to 5·6 per cent. The economy simply was not growing rapidly enough to absorb the young men and women who each year enlarged the labour force.

Hence the judgement on the Eisenhower administration must be harsh. By the criteria of the Employment Act of 1946, by the principles of modern public finance, and by the expectations of the general public, the Republican economic policy was a failure. In 1960 the party paid the appropriate electoral price.

SOURCE NOTES TO CHAPTER 8

1. Simon Kuznets, *Economic Growth and Structure* (New York: Norton, 1965).
2. John Stuart Mill, *Principles of Political Economy* (ed. J. Ashley) (London: Longmans, Green, 1909).
3. John F. Kennedy, *To Turn the Tide* (New York: Harper & Row, 1962; London: Hamish Hamilton).
4. Rockefeller Brothers Fund, *Prospect for America* (New York: Doubleday, 1961).
5. Ibid.
6. See Leo Marx's provocative *The Machine in the Garden* (New York: O.U.P., 1964).
7. Harry Schwartz, *The Soviet Economy Since Stalin* (Philadelphia: Lippincott, 1965).
8. Adam Smith, *Enquiry into the Nature and Causes of the Wealth of Nations* (1776) (London: Methuen).
9. Edward F. Dennison, *The Sources of Economic Growth in the United States and the Alternatives Before Us* (New York: Committee for Economic Development, 1962).
10. Mimeographed statement, Joint Committee on Washington (D.C.) Metropolitan Problems, December 1963.
11. Quoted in Seymour Harris, *The Economics of the Political Parties* (New York: Macmillan, 1962).
12. See ibid.
13. Quoted in *The New York Times*, 17 January 1957.
14. See Neil Jacoby, 'Fiscal Policy of the Kennedy–Johnson Administration', *The Journal of Finance, Papers and Proceedings*, May 1964.

The timidity of fiscal policy is less than an adequate explanation of the semi-stagnation of the 1950s. Even after it is conceded that Republican programmes administered less stimulus than the economy required, there remains a crucial question: why did the economy require the stimulus in the first place? Why weren't the impulses of private spending strong enough to employ men and machines fully?

One popular answer to these questions focuses on the nature of technical change and the possibility that the 1950s registered a break in the quality and pace of innovation. The hypothesis incorporates a contrast between the replacement of human muscle by steam engines and electrical energy and the displacement of human craft by machines which do men's work more rapidly and more accurately. It deals with a phenomenon significantly different and strikingly new – automation.

What is automation? Here is Daniel Bell's sophisticated definition:

Automation is a process which substitutes programmed machine-controlled operations for human manipulations. It is the fruit, so to speak, of cybernetics and computers. Thus, the kind of semi-routinized jobs and simple task judgments that a worker performs in the manufacturing process is now taken over by servo-mechanisms, while the sequential flow of work is directed from a computer which is programmed to regulate each step of the operation. Or, in an office, the tasks of recording, posting, or retrieving information, once done by a clerk laboriously using a filing system, are now performed directly by a computer.[1]

In this definition the word *cybernetics* refers to the feedback control simply exemplified in a thermostat. More broadly, the term covers 'any self-adjusting or self-regulating mechanisms or large-scale systems, be they in engineering, cell biology, the brain, or economics'.[2] Servo-mechanisms are self-adjusting or feedback devices which eliminate human machine operators.

Bell's definitions are temperate and free of apocalyptic statement. There are social commentators who are convinced that much of this potential revolution in work has already arrived and that the remainder is imminent. Here is a less mechanistic statement of the meaning of the new technology:

The new development in our technology is the replacement of the human nervous system by automatic controls and by the computer that ultimately integrates the functions of the automatic control units at each point in the production process. The human muscle began to be disengaged from the productive process at least a hundred years ago. Now the human nervous system is being disengaged.[3]

There is no question of the versatility of computer programming or of the power of linkages of computers and servo-mechanisms in the factory. Examples are numerous and hair-raising. As everyone knows a correctly programmed computer can digest, sort and analyse vast masses of data. This is a capacity which implies far more than the relief (or displacement) of countless clerks performing endless computations. It is true that the post office's electro-optical scanner does no more than this, although it is hard not to be impressed by a device which can glance over a printed or typewritten envelope, lock on to the state and city in the address, and tidily place the letter in its appropriate bin.

But there are much more ambitious devices. Consider the Bureau of Standards computer which the Veterans Administration harbours in Washington. Any of the ten V.A. hospitals linked with the computer can transmit a patient's electrocardiogram over ordinary telephone lines. The computer then makes a quicker diagnosis than a mere M.D. could. Moreover, its diagnosis is far more likely to be accurate. Or pause in wonder at the success of the McLouth Steel Corporation in Detroit. This enterprising company has linked a computer with the daily production flow of steel in its mill. McLouth's rolling mill can be programmed to turn out eighty-three different grades of steel in forty-seven different sizes. Another example: American Electric Power Systems uses computers to control generators in fifteen plants scattered over six states. When the demand for power peaks, the computer – a resident of Canton, Ohio – calculates fuel, transmission and operating costs for each plant, and on the basis of these arithmetic feats makes the thriftiest decision about which plant should produce the energy.[4]

Embarrassingly often these machines produce work superior to human effort. They suffer no lapses of attention, no depletion from age, illness or hangover, and no innate defect in character, confidence or discrimination. As one manufacturer of control devices has expressed the point,

There are scheduled to appear new devices which are without friction and which will not wear out; new materials of unbelievable strength and versatility; manufacturing production lines which adjust themselves to each new product; tools which are automatically selected, sharpened, inspected and installed; and warehouses and transportation systems which handle the flow of orders and shipments without human intervention.[5]

It would appear that the prospect pleases or appalls according to one's own role as an agent or a victim of the new technology. What effects, soberly, will such changes have upon employment? One approach to an answer is to start with an extreme position and ask how justified it is. Possibly the boldest predictions are those in the Manifesto of the Ad Hoc Committee on the Triple Revolution. The alliance of political liberals, civil rights activists and independents who were the signers of this declaration argue that productivity has risen much more rapidly in recent years primarily because of the combination of computers and automatic factory controls.* The jump in *per capita* productivity has created surplus factory capacity and rising unemployment. Since the attractions of cybernation are immense, we can anticipate 'a more rapid rise in the rate of productivity increase per hour . . . from now on'.[6] We stand at the threshold of a revolutionary transformation destined before too many years have passed to redefine the nature of work and to render the bulk of the working population superfluous.

This is a statement which has attracted a good deal of attention, especially since it has been linked with a radical social proposal – the guarantee of a minimum income to each American, regardless of his employment status. It is a statement which stimulates four questions:

1. Has there been in very recent years a technological leap, whether termed automation, cybernation or some other label?
2. If such a leap has taken place, has it caused *per capita* productivity to rise?

* The term used in the Manifesto is 'cybernation', practically synonymous with Bell's definition of 'automation'.

3. If *per capita* productivity has risen, is its rise the major reason for the high unemployment rate of the past ten or twelve years?

4. If no technological leap is now demonstrable, or if a real leap has not yet affected productivity and employment, is such a leap and are such effects reasonably to be anticipated in the near future?

In 1810 English weavers were smashing textile machines, burning factories and assaulting factory managers in a desperate attempt to prevent the extinction of their traditional crafts. This was a year in which approximately 100,000 men, women and children operated power looms in textile mills, subject to the discipline of the new factory. Outside the factory system, there were twice as many highly skilled, well-paid and self-respecting hand loom weavers. English authorities took this Luddite rebellion sufficiently seriously to deploy 12,000 soldiers against the machine-breakers, a number larger than Wellington's troops in the 1808 Spanish campaign.[7] As often occurs, the troops had the better of the argument, the riots were repressed, and the process of displacing skilled workers by automatic machines continued. By 1840 twice as many workers attended factory looms as laboured in increasingly difficult circumstances in their own homes. Twenty years later factories employed 427,000 workers, and craftsmen numbered a mere 10,000. Within the lifetime of a single worker, a traditional skill all but vanished. England had traded the virtues of the independent artisan and the small workshop for the huge and efficient factories which guaranteed her half a century of dominance in the world textile markets.

Or shift the scene to the last two decades of the century. In the United States, a German emigrant named Ottmar Mergenthaler invented a new piece of printing equipment, the linotype. The linotype was a machine which could set and cast type anywhere from three and a half to ten times as rapidly as a skilled compositor. Not cheap, at least compared to the prices of compositors' cases of type and other equipment, the machines were originally rented to undercapitalized printers. Nevertheless, the linotype's efficiency was so striking that in a relatively short time the machines entered print shops all over the country. The change had a happier ending for the hand typesetter than the earlier process had included for the hand loom weaver. The International Typographical Union, even in the 1890s an organization to respect, had the muscle and the intelligence to wrest from employers a measure of control over the introduction of the process. The Union won for its members a contractual right to learn to use the new machinery at prevailing union wage rates. The enormous expansion of printing which the linotype facilitated had the effect of actually enlarging printing employment in spite of the leap in *per capita* productivity.

The two illustrations demonstrate a very familiar process, the technological displacement of human skills by more efficient mechanical equipment. When the pace of displacement is rapid, job retraining is the only alternative to unemployment or condemnation to unskilled, casual labour. When the pace is gentler, the attrition of death and retirement eases the pain of the change. In the context of the current debate over automation's meaning and impact, the sharp question is, does automation represent a genuine technological leap, a variety of change which in some major aspects is entirely novel?

The lineage of the computer can be traced back at the least to the nineteenth-century experimenter Charles Babbage. But as an instrument of control and information, it is a very recent development. The linkage of computers and servo-mechanisms in the factory offers the possibility of converting manufacturing into a series of automatic processes requiring little human intervention. Where these potentialities have been translated into factory or office routine, uniform standards are readily defined and followed, such errors as occur are corrected by computers, and junior and even middle managers yield their jobs to computers which can make routine decisions with fewer routine mistakes.

There is another organizational consequence of great importance. Top managers, fed more rapidly with fuller and more accurate information, are able to exert closer control over ever larger organizations. Economists who have been accustomed to basing the continuance of limited competition upon the inability of the most talented executives to coordinate the affairs of a giant enterprise without falling prey to the diseases of bureaucracy must reconsider their doctrine in a world in which computers vastly enlarge the top executive's capacity to receive organized information in good time and to issue orders and directives whose effects can be analysed by the same techniques as the information was gathered. Secretary McNamara's unprecedented capacity to control the affairs of the Department of Defense, expending $50 billion or more each year, testifies not only to his personal force but also to the sophisticated managerial techniques which he has introduced. These techniques are increasingly based on the systems analysis and operations research which the computer has made possible.

Thus, the case for automation's novelty is strong, but possibly less strong than it appears to be. Again, an historical parallel helps us perceive a qualification of automation's importance. In 1939 television was a technological possibility. Indeed, a·few rudimentary television sets were in the homes of the enterprising and the wealthy. These early buyers were gamblers on the future, since all that they got in 1939 were a few primitive programmes transmitted to them four or five hours each week. In 1939 television contained the potential of a revolution in entertainment technology. Its principles were embodied in actual products. But it had very little economic meaning. The product was priced far too high to attract the market that would have persuaded advertisers to support the new medium, broadcasting systems to invest in programme development, and consumers to buy millions instead of hundreds of receivers. As the history of air travel before the Second World War demonstrates, not everything that is technically possible actually occurs.

The gap between technical feasibility and economic viability is a matter of both cost and consumer taste. On the latter point, the present status of the teaching machines, or more accurately programmed instruction, is illuminating. As every school board and college administration knows, it is perfectly possible to teach everything from elementary French conversation to elementary economics by programmed devices which substitute capital for the labour of teachers. Aided by foundation support, attracted by novelty or convinced of financial saving, some education administrators have actually experimented with these devices. Others will certainly follow their example, especially as enrolment pressures on the colleges increase in the next five years.

Why have the substitutions not occurred more rapidly? It is true that teachers welcome changes in the definition of their work about as eagerly as trade unionists embrace new shop rules. But teachers' unions are rarely strong enough to force their opinions upon administrators. In most situations teaching machines are cheaper than human instructors. The reason for the moderate rate of innovation then must be found in the consumer's evaluation of the product. At least in the current state of technology, machines achieve less *rapport* with students than do efficient teachers. Their counsel is less cherished and their office hours less well-attended.

The teaching machine exemplifies a large number of outputs in which automation produces an inferior product. Wherever person-to-person confrontation is a significant element, automation must produce a second-rate result. Machines thus make poor social workers, nurses, recreation leaders, psychiatrists, politicians, Boy Scout leaders, den mothers, military commanders, clergymen, attorneys, Peace Corps volunteers, policemen, probation officers, children's court judges, artists and ballet dancers. The point for the quality of a society is strategic. It turns out that the impact of automation is intimately related to the *kinds* of output that a society emphasizes. A community devoted above all to the expansion of the number and variety of consumer manufactures – automobiles, appliances, clothing, cameras, and so on, and so on – is ripe for rapid automation. On the other hand, a community which employs affluence to improve urban environments, alleviate poverty and inequality, enhance aesthetic experience, and raise the quality of public health and education will devote more and more of its resources to endeavours only minimally subject to automation.

Indeed, a society which follows the second road will experience a growth in employment little disturbed by technological leaps. Whether automation is to be a blessing or a curse depends in part on the pace of its introduction into factories and offices and upon the rate of expansion of employment in the non-automated sectors. As far as the future is concerned, the key questions regard the cost of automated devices and the social valuations of the community.

What has happened so far? How much unemployment has automation caused to date? How villainous has its contribution been to unemployment? On such issues the experts disagree. At least three major positions are identifiable. There is the argument that automation has proceeded sufficiently rapidly and expansion of employment in other sectors sufficiently slowly so that unemployment has been pushed upward. Professor Killingsworth has advanced this conclusion with particular force. The Council of Economic Advisers is identified with an opposite diagnosis which attributes unemployment to a deficiency of aggregate demand, not to the special characteristics of recent technological change. Finally, Professor Yale Brozen of the University of Chicago has concluded that the major cause of unemployment is a wage structure which prices far too many of the unemployed clear out of the labour market. Accordingly for Brozen, minimum wage laws – national or state – are major errors of public policy.

What does the available evidence suggest? One consoling irrelevancy can be dismissed at the outset: that workers who lose their jobs to automated devices will find new ones in the machine-building industry. The record is clear on this score:

EMPLOYMENT IN METAL-WORKING MACHINE PRODUCTION

Year	Workers
1900	29,000
1929	39,000
1939	37,000
1958	37,000

SOURCE: Charles C. Killingsworth, 'Automation, Jobs and Manpower', in Stanley Lebergott (ed.), *Men Without Work* (Englewood Cliffs, N. J.: Prentice-Hall, 1964).

These are the machines which make other machines. All that a half-century of economic expansion, technical improvement and population growth has achieved is an increase of a mere 8,000 workers. Worse still, in the three decades between 1929 and 1958, employment actually shrank, suggesting that technical improvement must have been exceptionally rapid in the industry which produced the means for the improvement of other industries. Whatever jobs automation creates are not in the industries which produce automated devices.

Hence if automation and full employment are to be consistent phenomena, the automated industries themselves must expand very rapidly, the demand for labour in other sectors must increase sharply enough to absorb both the casualties of automation and the net additions to the labour force, or some combination of both movements must occur. Killingsworth's assessment is pessimistic, based in part on his grim expectations of output increases in the automated industries:

Look across the whole range of consumer goods and you will see that our mass consumption society has done a highly effective job of supplying the wants of the great majority of consumers. About 99·5 per cent of the homes that are wired for electricity have electric refrigerators; 93 per cent have television sets; 83 per cent have electric washing machines; and we have even more radios than homes. The only sharply rising sales curve in the consumer-durables field today is that of the electric can opener industry. The electric toothbrush and electric hairbrush industries are starting to grow rapidly too. But the growth of employment in these new 'industries' will not offset the declines in the older, larger consumer goods industries.[8]

Suppose that Killingsworth's claim is valid and consumer durables markets are saturated. Does it matter? There have been substantial increases in the public and private demand for scientists, engineers, mathematicians, programmers, designers and other well-trained individuals. Moreover, increasing numbers and growing percentages of men and women win positions in federal, state or local governments. Displacement is a continuous phenomenon. Some sectors of a dynamic economy will always grow more rapidly than others. The pattern of demand and output can be expected to shift in a free economy.

Why, therefore, should we be more anxious about employment now than half a century or a century ago? One reason relates to the speed of displacement. Although a century elapsed before the steam engine had spread fully to the activities where it was economical, electric power reached maturity in less than fifty years, and events are moving still more rapidly in our day. Although banks installed their initial automatic accounting systems only a decade ago, half the country's banks now possess such systems or are in the process of acquiring them. Good judges in the early 1950s believed that the whole country could profitably employ no more than ten to fifteen large computers for a generation or longer. By early 1966 nearly 27,000 computers were installed and operating, and by 1970 one estimate is that there will be 45,000 in use.

There is a second disconcerting dissimilarity between the past and the present. In earlier years displaced workers frequently found jobs which demanded no more skill or education than the ones they had lost. Frequently, as in the instance of nineteenth-century textile innovations, the new processes required far less training and skill than older handicraft techniques. Only infrequently are today's casualties of technical change equally fortunate. Almost everywhere in labour markets, the demand has expanded for the educated and declined for the ill-prepared. The impact on employment is evident in the differential fortunes of college graduates, high school graduates and school drop-outs.

EDUCATION AND UNEMPLOYMENT OF MALES 18 AND OVER,
APRIL 1950 AND MARCH 1962 (PER CENT)

Years of School Completed	Unemployment Rates 1950	1962	Change, 1950–62
0–7	8·4	9·2	+9·5
8	6·6	7·6	+13·6
9–11	6·9	7·8	+13·0
12	4·6	4·8	+4·3
13–15	4·1	4·0	−2·4
16 or more	2·2	1·4	−36·4
All groups	6·2	6·0	−3·2

SOURCE : Stanley Lebergott, op. cit.

The years 1950 and 1962 were characterized by about the same level of *total* unemployment, but the distribution of that unemployment had changed significantly in a dozen years. The unemployment rates of men and women who terminated their education in elementary or secondary school rose. The rates for the college-trained fell, and the 1·4 rate for college graduates practically speaking signifies a shortage of qualified personnel, in the light of a definition of full employment which allows 2·5 to 3 per cent frictional unemployment. To Killingsworth the pace of technical change, the rising skills required for employment and the shortage of these skills among the unemployed explain past increases in unemployment and enforce a prediction of further unemployment troubles. The likeliest solution is a much enlarged communal investment in education and man-power retraining. The problem is magnified when aggregate demand lags, but even when aggregate demand is buoyant, unemployment will remain uncomfortably high.

This, in brief, is the case for the proposition that automation has already caused a significant rise in unemployment. One of this position's leading opponents is Walter W. Heller, Chairman of the Council of Economic Advisers during the three years of Kennedy's administration and the first year of Johnson's. A persuasive advocate of the primacy of aggregate demand, Heller played a large role in enlisting President Kennedy behind a major tax reduction. He has argued that 'the road to 4 per cent unemployment is clearly open to demand-powered measures'.[10] Writing early in 1964, Heller cited three reasons for his insistence upon the stimulation of aggregate demand as the prime national economic policy. The first was the

operation of the American economy until 1957 at generally satisfactory employment levels. The second was the presence of idle men
and incompletely utilized factories. These unused resources were
proof that consumer and investment spending were inadequate.
Finally, the absence of either wage or price inflation refuted structural arguments, for on structural grounds there should have been
serious bottlenecks caused by shortages of specialized skills. These
bottlenecks were normally accompanied by inflation. As Heller
understood recent American experience, employment was high *before*
1957 because market demand was large. It has been unsatisfactory
ever since 1957 because market demand lagged just at a time when
larger numbers of young people were flooding into labour markets.

Heller did not find it essential to deny the existence of structural
unemployment, an attendant mismatching of skills and demand, and
consequent needs for job retraining. The relevant question was
whether or not structural unemployment had been increasing – the
nub of the controversy over automation's employment incidence.
Looking at data somewhat similar to Killingsworth's, Heller readily
conceded that Negroes, the uneducated, the unskilled and the young
suffer more than their share of unemployment during recessions.
But it was equally true that they enjoy much larger gains during
expansions. Unemployment did increase sharply for vulnerable
groups during the recession of 1960–61, but it decreased still more
sharply during the ensuing recovery of 1961–2:

CHANGES IN UNEMPLOYMENT RATES BY SELECTED
GROUPS AND AREAS (PER CENT)

	1960–61	1961–2
Total	+1·1	−1·1
Non-whites	+1·6	−1·9
Operatives	+1·6	−2·1
Non-farm labourers	+2·0	−2·1
Manufacturing workers	+1·5	−1·9
Miners	+2·1	−3·0
Michigan	+3·4	−3·4
Wheeling, West Virginia	+6·9	−7·8

SOURCE: Walter W. Heller, 'Employment and Manpower', in Lebergott, op. cit.

Thus, the five groups most open to layoff suffered or prospered
essentially as aggregate demand rose or fell. The moral was plain:

a strong fiscal stimulus like a major tax cut (or a large expansion of federal spending) will improve the employment prospects even of the unskilled. In Heller's guarded prose,

We do not conclude ... that a reduction in structural unemployment has occurred. Similarly, however, we do not conclude that the unusually high unemployment rates experienced by teen-agers this year, or the rather low rates experienced by adult males prove an adverse structural shift. In some labour market areas, imbalances have lessened; in others, they have increased. But this does not suggest that the over-all rate of structural unemployment has risen significantly.[11]

There is a final point. If automation has really become important, then *per capita* productivity should be rising at unusual rates. The evidence gathered by the Council of Economic Advisers demonstrates that in fact nothing unusual has yet occurred.

CHANGES PER YEAR IN OUTPUT PER MAN HOUR IN THE PRIVATE ECONOMY, 1919–63 (PER CENT)

Period	Total Private	Agri-culture	Non-agriculture		
			Total	Manufac-turing	Non-manu-facturing
1919–47	2·2	1·4	2·0	3·0	—
1947–63	3·2	6·1	2·6	2·7	2·5
1947–50	4·5	8·8	3·7	4·3	3·4
1950–60	2·7	5·4	2·1	2·0	2·2
1960–63	3·5	5·5	·3·2	3·7	2·9
1960–61	3·3	5·9	2·9	2·6	3·1
1961–62	3·9	3·4	·3·8	5·4	2·9
1962–63	3·5	7·4	3·0	3·1	2·8

SOURCE: Ibid.

If automation had *already* significantly altered the productive process, then these measures of efficiency should have been moving upward unusually fast. The evidence does not show such a condition. While it is true that productivity gains since 1947 have exceeded the 1919–47 average, that average was so drastically lowered by the inactivity of the 1930s that not much can safely be inferred from the comparison. In fact, since 1947 productivity has behaved according to historical precedent. For some periods, notably 1947–50, it has been high. For others, especially 1950–60, it has been low. The 1960s thus far are consistent with earlier years. And over the years, the most striking gains in productivity have been neither in offices where computers have been installed nor in factories where servo-mechanisms have replaced machine minders. They have occurred instead in agriculture, where productivity since 1947 has increased twice as rapidly as in the rest of the economy.

There is still a third diagnosis of the unemployment rate in recent years: Professor Yale Brozen's emphasis on an 'inadequate adaptation of price and wage rates to offset external factors'.[12] A charter member of the Chicago free market school of economic thought, Brozen maintains that when technological innovations displace workers, unemployment need not be the consequence if prices and wages respond flexibly. Workers who accept lower wages in their current jobs retard the pace at which labour-displacing equipment is installed. Workers who agree to lower wages in other occupations also avoid unemployment. For Brozen it follows that any effective minimum wage law causes unemployment by raising wages above free market levels. Similarly, unions which push wages up render inevitable price increases which diminish demand and employment. Brozen is convinced that wage rates have been rising persistently more rapidly than *per capita* productivity. The consequence has been a predictable rise in unemployment, a rise intensified by the reluctance of the Federal Reserve Board (prior to 1960) to expand the supply of money.

The central public policy which emerges from this diagnosis is a more realistic minimum wage law (at best, the repeal of existing statutes). Further, if union pressures for higher wages were resisted rather than encouraged by public officials, employment would rise. If free market forces were permitted adequate scope, neither tax reduction nor manpower retraining would be necessary.

What is the upshot of this argument among the experts? Brozen's free market theory recognizes rather more competition among employers than most students of the economy perceive. It is a posture, whatever its analytic merit, which seems inappropriate to an economy dominated by giant corporations, national unions and powerful public bureaucracies. The choice remaining is between Heller and Killingsworth – aggregate demand and structural unemployment.

Some of the differences are less sharp than argument occasionally makes them. Just as the structural camp admits the necessity of high levels of total spending, the fiscal stimulators concede the need to finance retraining, vocational education and re-location.

Such a bland compromise works badly as far as national economic policy is concerned. Necessarily, administration and congressional controversy concentrates on the mixture (and the financing) of specific policies. Here choices must be made. A presidential pro-gramme which stresses substantial tax reductions simply cannot at the same time demand of Congress very large new programmes of regional development, education, man-power retraining, public works and urban reconstruction. If the structuralists had their way, these proposals would be given priority over tax reduction.

In practice a modern administration programme blends tax favours to the populace with appropriations for a variety of social purposes, which in 1965 included assistance to Appalachia, general school aid, medicare, anti-poverty programmes and rent subsidies. Neverthe-less, the politics of consensus – something for everybody – should not conceal the relative financial weights of the two varieties of action. It should be evident that after an initial flirtation with cautious structural devices, the Kennedy–Johnson administrations have quite literally placed their money on the stimulation of aggregate demand by means of successive tax reductions totalling far more than the new social outlays.

Is this the right way to reduce unemployment? The best answer seems to be yes for now and probably no for later on. The aggregate demand school appears to have the better of the statistical argument as of 1965. The structuralists have not proven their key proposition – that automation has already caused increased unemployment. Neither have they proven that unusually rapid productivity rises have recently occurred. No doubt technological change has been displacing two million or more men and women each year. But this is normal. As always the issue is whether enough jobs are being created to re-employ the displaced and employ for the first time the bumper crop of young people flooding into the labour markets. No convincing evidence has been presented *yet* that the new jobs avail-able are themselves altering more rapidly in nature than in the recent past. Hence the administration stress on aggregate demand has been appropriate. So much should be accepted even by those who prefer an additional $5 billion spent on public housing to a $5 billion

slash in taxes on incomes, automobiles, jewellery, furs and hand-
bags.

But how long will this emphasis continue to be appropriate? At
this point in the argument, even the sturdiest defender of the
aggregate demand hypothesis is likely to shiver in a chilling breeze
of doubt. The prophets of automation may be premature. Still, in the
long run, are they not likely to be right about the potentialities of
computers, automatic factory controls and the linkage of the two?
One should not dismiss too lightly Killingsworth's argument that
technical change is accelerating. If the computers have not yet produced the results which their numbers might promise, the explanation may be teething troubles rather than computer inefficiency.
Again, the attainable cost savings from automated factories have
been translated into fact in only a small number of plants in a smaller
number of industries. It may be that we are at the beginning rather
than in the middle of a larger and more pervasive transformation of
the work experience and the nature of labour markets than that
caused by the steam engine or the harnessing of electricity.

It is worth recalling that nearly three-quarters of a century after
Watt constructed a working steam engine, most Englishmen still
toiled in occupations little affected by the energy revolution. In mid-
Victorian England, the largest single industry was agriculture and
the second was domestic service. While the third most numerous
group consisted of cotton textile operatives in the industry where the
Industrial Revolution had been most complete, building craftsmen
were only slightly less numerous. They actually included more male
workers than did the cotton textile force. The English economy of
1850 still afforded numerous chances of labour to the unskilled; it
still employed hundreds of thousands of artisans and craftsmen who
used traditional tools on familiar materials. Though unprecedentedly
rapid, the pace of change, by mid-twentieth-century criteria, was
nevertheless slow enough to allow attrition to perform the bulk of
the readjustment in the labour force. Change in the modern world is
quicker. It is not sensible to anticipate a spread of computer technology at the majestic pace of the steam engine. Here is the overriding reason to expect that automation will *in the future* cause
employment and output problems of very great complexity. But
not yet.

The cause of the semi-stagnation of the 1950s, therefore, was not
automation. Even if the Eisenhower administration had not opposed

manpower retraining and area redevelopment, tepidly supporting only the most timid aid to education proposals, it is unlikely that the unemployment of the decade would have been substantially reduced by structural measures of the scale projected by liberal Democrats.

There is a more plausible inference from the puzzles of the 1950s. Keynesian fiscal policies evidently were still applicable. The fact that they had not been applied, and the circumstance that in their absence unemployment steadily crept upward, prepared the way for the essays in fiscal stimulus of the 1960s. Perhaps another observation is in order. Economists who had celebrated too readily the conversion of the politicians to contemporary economic theory should have been shaken by the evidences of ideological atavism which at times influenced and at others very nearly shaped the economics of the two Eisenhower administrations.

The 1950s remain a disquieting decade. The Eisenhower administration was indeed guilty of much inaction, but to the issue posed at the outset of this chapter – the need of the economy for stimulation – no answer has been returned. Was there after all something in the doctrines of the stagnationists? Their demography was proven in error. Their frontiers closed at whimsical moments. Technical innovation has not slowed. Nevertheless, the 1950s contained disquieting echoes of the 1930s. Why shouldn't private capitalism generate enough spending pressure to employ everybody? Why should the federal government need to stimulate aggregate demand? Were there still other errors of private and public policy that impeded spending? There were those, as the next chapter will indicate, who were convinced that a new variety of price behaviour influenced aggregate demand and total employment adversely.

SOURCE NOTES TO CHAPTER 9

1. Daniel Bell, preface in Sir Leon Bagrit, *The Age of Automation* (New York: Mentor, 1965).

2. Ibid.

3. Gerard Piel, quoted in Robert Theobald, *The Commonwealth*, 4 September 1964.

4. *Newsweek*, 25 January 1965.

5. Edwin F. Shelly, speech at the annual meeting of the National Council of the Aging, Atlantic City, 12 February 1964.

6. Arthur L. Grey and John E. Elliott (eds.), *Economic Issues and Policies* (Boston: Houghton Mifflin, 1961).

7. See E. J. Hobsbawm, *Labouring Men* (London: Weidenfeld & Nicolson, 1964).

8. Charles C. Killingsworth, 'Automation, Jobs and Manpower', in Stanley Lebergott (ed.) *Men Without Work* (Engelwood Cliffs, N.J.: Prentice-Hall, 1964).

9. Ibid.

10. Walter W. Heller, 'Employment and Manpower', in Lebergott, op. cit.

11. Ibid.

12. Yale Brozen, 'Why Do We Have an Unemployment Problem?', in Lebergott, op. cit.

In the simple world of *The General Theory*, inflation follows full employment. Until resources are completely occupied, increases in business and consumer spending have the effect of raising output and income but leaving prices alone. During much of the 1950s, it proved perfectly possible to suffer from unemployment and inflation simultaneously. Here was something to be explained, especially since the phenomenon complicated economic policy enormously. It was difficult to advocate raising interest rates when unemployment was already substantial, but it was not easy to suggest that the federal government enlarge its deficit when inflation was already occurring.

Were we experiencing a new kind of inflation? Classic, old-fashioned inflation is of the demand-pull variety. It occurs when too many dollars chase too few goods, or, what is much the same thing, when at a given price level the output of consumer and capital goods falls below the sum of incomes available for spending. Classic inflation is likely during or after wars which interrupt the normal course of production for civilian uses. It flourishes under weak or imprudent governments which print paper money instead of curtailing their expenditures or enlarging their tax collections. The classic remedy for the classic malady is austerity. Prudent men of affairs wrest power from spendthrift politicians. Once in office they reform the currency and see to it that their central banks raise interest rates. Public spending is severely pruned, and taxes are raised. No doubt it is hard on ordinary workers, not to mention those who possess large quantities of the old, unreformed currency, but once the fever is cured, then recovery *on a sound basis* becomes feasible.

Unfortunately, the American inflation of the 1950s was disconcertingly different from this venerable model. Prices did indeed rise during the decade and especially between 1955 and 1960, but it was hard to see what caused them to behave so peculiarly. This was a period when government spending increased only moderately (for a spell it actually declined). Under William McChesney Martin's cautious guidance, the monetary authorities succeeded in expanding the supply of money *more slowly* than the gross national product increased. By all the conventional rules, price levels should have declined. The demand-pull explanation of inflation ill suited a peacetime economy which featured moderate defence outlays, high interest rates, a conservative fiscal policy and substantial surpluses of men, factories and materials.

Inevitably, an alternative version of the inflation process, called cost-push inflation, won attention and converts. The analysis started with the institutional organization of American manufacturing. In most major manufacturing industries, there is considerable concentration of control. In steel, aluminium, chemicals, automobiles and rubber tyres, the largest three or four enterprises control the bulk of their industry's output. It is against nature to expect three or four giants to compete with each other in the same fashion as would several hundred or several thousand small entrepreneurs. Locked in complex interdependence (as well as rivalry),* the Goliaths of manufacturing tend to institutionalize pricing decisions rather than entrusting them to the free play of the market.

A common form that this institutionalization has taken is the version of administered pricing known as price leadership. Where price leadership is the accepted pattern, the price leader – in steel U.S. Steel, in automobiles General Motors – announces a set of prices which other companies conventionally follow. Collusion, illegal under the Sherman Anti-trust Act, is unnecessary; the rules are understood by all the players. Agreement on price does not eliminate other kinds of rivalry. The competition, as in automobiles and cigarettes, for instance, tends to focus on quality, service, packaging, style and glamour.

Price leaders and price followers may unite in preferring a high level of prices which generates large profits, even at the cost of surplus capacity, to lower prices which may promise a little more in profit but a great deal more in administrative time and energy. It has been guessed that U.S. Steel endeavours to set prices which enable

* Oligopolistic interdependence, the technical term for the condition, exists when several rivals are large enough to have to take each other's reactions into account before making important price or merchandising decisions. Ford would be guilty of either stupidity or megalomania if its officials priced the company's cars without anxious attention to General Motors' decisions.

it to break even at as low as thirty-three per cent of its capacity. Price leaders may raise prices even when demand is slack or shrinking, out of a wish to widen unit profit margins. And the price leaders are especially tempted by such policies when they are convinced that the elasticity of demand in their market is low.*

In sum, administered prices depend upon the market power of price leaders and their major associates, not upon the intensity of demand for the product or the volume of money in circulation. When the product is as important as steel, price changes spread to the numerous users of the material – automobile manufacturers, home-builders, appliance-makers and packagers.

The importance of administered price inflation is measured by the extent to which price leaders use their market power to raise prices at times when the demand for their products is sufficiently low to cause low operating rates. The key performance of the steel industry is highlighted by Gardiner Means's computations comparing steel price movements with other price changes between 1953 and 1959:

STEEL AND OTHER WHOLESALE PRICE INDEXES
(1953 = 100)

Year	Index of Finished Steel Prices	Index of Wholesale Prices	Index of Prices of Metals and Metal Manufactures	Index of Wholesale Prices Excluding Metals and Metal Manufactures
1953	100·0	100·0	100·0	100·0
1954	104·3	100·2	101·1	99·8
1955	109·2	100·5	105·9	97·8
1956	118·4	103·8	114·2	98·5
1957	129·7	106·8	118·9	100·5
1958	134·2	108·3	120·4	102·0
1959	136·1	108·5	121·6	101·5

SOURCE: Adapted from Gardiner C. Means, *Pricing Power and the Public Interest* (New York: Harper & Row, 1962).

* Elasticity is a measure of the responsiveness of sales to changes in price. Demand is elastic if a one per cent reduction in price causes more than a one per cent increase in sales. It is inelastic where a one per cent reduction in price causes sales to expand by less than one per cent. When an industry believes that the demand for its product is inelastic, it will also be convinced that price increases through the range of inelasticity will actually expand total sales receipts, for a one per cent price *increase* will result in a less than one per cent reduction in sales receipts.

The table tells an interesting story. Wholesale prices, apart from those of metals and metal manufacturers, were almost stable. Metals and metal manufactures rose 21·6 per cent, and finished steel prices soared 36·1 per cent. What moved the wholesale price index (including metals and metal manufactures) from 1953's 100 to 1959's 108·5 was the untypical behaviour of metals and especially of steel.

If the demand for steel was moderate during this period, how did it happen that steel prices rose so dramatically? By the industry's account, the cause was higher wages and fringe benefits. When U.S. Steel announced another price boost on 1 July 1957, its justification was that 'increases in wages and benefits that were provided for in its 3-year labor contract reached with the United Steelworkers of America last summer will take effect beginning next Monday, July 1'.[1] The company wondered at its own public spirit, for these wage increases, it was convinced, might have permitted a still larger price hike. Wage costs were the industry's usual defence.

It was not an argument which won over the industry's most careful student. Gardiner Means debited increased wages with only a little over a sixth of the price increase, on the ground that labour productivity rose rapidly enough during the 1950s to absorb the bulk of increases in hourly rates and benefits. Another portion of the price rise was occasioned by higher raw materials costs faced by steel-makers. However, well over half of the price increase was the simple effect of the widened profit margins which the companies acquired by the deliberate exercise of their market power in a time of moderate to low demand for their products.[2]

One may well wonder how it was possible for the industry to raise its prices so steadily and so publicly in the presence of moderate home demand, declining export sales and rising competition from foreign steel-makers. A portion of the answer was the extraordinary complaisance of a pro-business national administration which out of policy intervened little in the affairs of its supporters and friends. But the industry also operated through a charade. Since the production's run has apparently been ended by the Kennedy–Johnson insistence on wage-price guidelines, it is worth describing this amateur drama.

A performance occurred during each of the four industry-wide steel strikes of the 1950s, the last of them the four-month stoppage of 1959. From strike to strike, the sequence of events varied little. During the pre-strike negotiations, company executives warned that a large settlement would lead inevitably to price increases, loss of export markets and general inflation. Patriotically, the executives pledged themselves to resist the selfish exactions of the steel union. For their part the union leaders called attention to the cost of living and the high profits of the steel companies. Otis Brubaker, then research director of the United Steelworkers, gave a congressional committee assurances that 'The industry's leader, United States Steel Corporation, which initiated the 1957 steel price increase . . . could have put into effect a price cut of $6 a ton, instead of a price increase of $6 a ton, absorbed the cost of the wage increase that occurred in July, and could still have earned greater net profits after taxes in 1957 than were ever earned in the history of the corporation'.[3]

As the contestants verbally escalated the contest, public apprehension mounted, newspapers warned of the inflationary consequences of a large contract settlement, and mediation efforts were intensified. The mediation attempts usually failed, and after frantic negotiations up to a midnight strike deadline, the union pulled its members out of the mills. Blaming each other, both parties remained intransigent. The days, the weeks, even the months passed, and excess inventories of steel were worked off. Finally, the union moderated its demands somewhat, the company raised its last offer, and the industry 'reluctantly' yielded to national necessity and reached a bargain with the union on terms stated firmly by the industry to be inflationary. Then, with many a protestation of regret over the necessity, the industry raised its prices by an amount adequate not only to cover the new level of wages and benefits but also to add pleasantly to the profits of the companies. As Roger Blough, at the time Chairman of the Board of U.S. Steel, put it, 'In our most recent negotiations last year – after a five-week strike – we signed a labor agreement. It was that labor agreement which foreordained our recent price increase.'[4]

So it was that as long as the steel companies were in a position to pass on wage increases and widen their profit margins simultaneously, there existed a tacit community of interest between the United Steelworkers and United States Steel. During the 1950s and perhaps later still, the steel companies were adequately persuaded of the merits of high prices and slack operations to face with equanimity the loss of important markets to foreign producers and important American sales to concrete, aluminium and plastic substitutes. And although the Eisenhower administration repeatedly admonished both contestants to agree on non-inflationary settlements, neither the companies nor the union believed that government concern would move from admonition to action. In this they were correct.

The extent of administered price or cost-push inflation remains in dispute. Certainly the phenomenon was real during the 1950s, and its occurrence complicated monetary and fiscal policy. To start with, this variety of inflation rendered simple Keynesianism simple-minded. As Keynes for beginners (encouraged by Keynes himself) put the inflation analysis, where unemployment is high, both interest rate and fiscal policy are appropriate. By their purchases of government securities in the open market, the Federal Reserve authorities expand the money supply and lower the rate of interest. Lower interest rates compared with existing marginal efficiencies of capital enlarge business investment. The multiplier impact of a larger business investment raises the national income by some amount greater than the investment increment. It may be, however, that borrowers are insensitive to interest changes. If this is so, monetary measures will have little effect, and an intelligent policy will em-phasize fiscal devices. If taxes are reduced, experience teaches that consumers will spend anywhere between ninety-two and ninety-four per cent of the increases in their disposable income. Or if the fiscal stimulus assumes the shape of increased public spending, the flow of funds to government contractors, public employees and recipients of transfer payments (such as retraining allowances, rent subsidies, parity payments, medicare support, old age pensions, and so on) increases incomes and produces much the same effect as major tax reductions.

In a primitive Keynesian universe, these processes work them-selves out without price increases until full employment is actually achieved. Implicit in this analytical confidence is an assumption that the competitive economy is unimpeded in its adjustment by major price or wage setters, and unhampered by bottlenecks caused by shortages of strategic materials or skills. Where such bottlenecks do in fact exist, the wage or price increases which begin with them tend to spread. Since Keynes also assumed that diminishing returns would apply to increased production, he appeared to expect real though not monetary wages to decline in the course of economic expansion.

When pricing and wage-setting power are concentrated in a few hands, significant amendments must be made to this recital. Strong unions represent one danger. They may enforce wage increases which check additional employment. The wage increases may serve partly as a reason and partly as an excuse for price increases by price leaders. And these may restrict the growth of output and sales. Where such behaviour is widespread, economic expansion will terminate long before unemployment is completely eliminated and idle machines are restored to full activity. Wages and prices may rise rapidly enough to evoke inflation in the midst of persistent unemployment. Under such conditions fiscal policy loses much of its potency. If the principal effect of a tax reduction or increased spending is encouragement of enlarged union demands and widened corporate profit margins, then little or no improvement in employment may result.

Some Keynesians, among them Professor A. P. Lerner of Michigan State University, have so interpreted the experience of the 1950s. In Lerner's words,

Attempts by expansionary monetary and fiscal 'aids' to increase employment brought about price increases or inflation, before the unemployment was cured. Attempts to cure the inflation by restrictionary monetary and fiscal 'aids' brought about an increase in unemployment before the price increase was stopped. The Keynesian policy seemed to be calling for expansionary and for restrictionary monetary and fiscal policies at the same time to deal with the unemployment and inflation existing side by side.[5]

Unfortunate politicians, harassed on one flank by the unemployed and their advocates and on the other by inflation's usual enemies, bankers and editorialists, might be excused for veering back and forth between policies designed to sedate the economy and policies designed to stimulate it. During the 1950s it was often not plain whether inflation or recession was the greater danger, particularly when both threatened at once. Stated in these terms, even a liberal administration persuaded of the efficacy of modern economic policy would have had its troubles. An administration which was leery of fiscal policy, and reluctant to advance the sort of price and wage policy that might restrict cost-push inflation, had very little hope of success.

Had these institutional developments invalidated Keynesian public policy? There are good reasons to be sceptical. Important as steel, automobiles and other concentrated industries are, they are less than the whole even of manufacturing. Clothing, commercial printing, furniture and baking, among others, are less concentrated and more subject to the normal pressures of price competition. But more important still, manufacturing is itself a decreasingly important share of total economic activity. Unless it is assumed that what happens in steel and other oligopolized industries produces equally substantial effects in the remainder of the economy, concentration diminishes but does not destroy the efficacy of fiscal policy.

Even within the concentrated industries, the scope of price administration is limited. As Dr Lerner himself has observed, 'When there is great excess of demand over supply, it is difficult for the administrators to prevent prices from rising, because black markets will emerge.... When there is a very great excess of supply over demand, the administrators may be unable to prevent "cutthroat competition".'[36] The administrators in the end are influenced by the state of the demand for their products. What is needed in support of fiscal policy, then, is measures which induce the price administrators to change their prices in ways which more quickly and more closely reflect the state of the market.

Here it is necessary to anticipate the discussion of the 1960s with some account of the 'incomes' policy (the efforts to set standards for wage and price increases) of the Kennedy–Johnson administration. At the beginning of President Kennedy's administration, it was not certain whether he planned to push beyond President Eisenhower's lectures in the attempt to control inflation. The first statement of the wage-price guideposts in *The Economic Report of the President* was susceptible of interpretation either as another exercise of the jaw-bone technique or as a covert intimation of stronger measures in the near future. As usual the issue came to a head in steel.

During the autumn and winter of 1961, the United Steelworkers and the steel industry reached an extremely moderate settlement, a settlement which appeared to promise a halt in the industry's inflation spiral. Since union gains were confined to fringe benefits (many postponed at least a year), little additional cost was imposed upon the industry. Also violating recent precedent, the settlement occurred without a strike, but only after much personal persuasion (directed to his former union associates) by then Secretary of Labor Arthur Goldberg. Both the Secretary and President Kennedy interpreted the settlement as a personal commitment by Roger Blough that the industry would exercise price restraint if the steelworkers settled for modest, non-inflationary gains. The contract which was signed struck most observers as meeting Blough's specifications.

What occurred next afforded a dramatic test of the actual if not the legal powers of a President. On 10 April 1962, shortly after the last steel company had initialled the contract settlement, U.S. Steel's Board of Directors met in New York and raised the company's steel prices by an average of 3·5 per cent, about $6 per ton. *After* the decision had been taken, Blough arranged at short notice a late-afternoon appointment with the President, during which he handed his host a four-page mimeographed statement of the company's action. In the bitter evening of discussion with his aides* which followed this *démarche*, the President delivered himself of a remark that later resounded through the business community: 'My father always told me that all businessmen were sons of bitches, but I never believed it until now.'†‡ The tone of much of the evening's war council was pessimistic as well as angry. The President was simultaneously enraged at the industry's 'doublecross' and gloomy about the chances of reversing the price increase.

In spite of the risk of failure, the President decided that evening to mobilize all the resources of his great office in an attempt to force U.S. Steel to back down. It quickly appeared that these forces were considerable. In the next two days, the administration deployed anti-trust threats and a grand jury investigation, diverted defence contracts, intimated unfriendly legislation, unleashed the willing Senator Kefauver, and made personal appeals to the smaller steel companies. For a time the issue hung in doubt, especially since the next day, Wednesday, 11 April, the major steel companies – Bethlehem, Republic, Youngstown and Jones & Laughlin – dutifully followed Big Steel's lead. At Wednesday's end, only five of the smaller companies, controlling fourteen per cent of the industry's capacity, had failed to raise their prices in concert with U.S. Steel.

Fortunately for the administration, there was one key figure among the smaller companies who was willing to pursue a line of his own. He was Joseph L. Block, chairman of Inland Steel, who before

---

* Among them Secretary Goldberg, Walter Heller, Robert Kennedy and Theodore Sorensen.

† Quoted by Hobart Rowen in *The Free Enterprisers*. I have drawn upon Rowen's vivid account of the incident in the following pages. Sorensen's *Kennedy* substitutes 'steelmen' for 'businessmen'.

these events had already expressed a sympathy heretical in his industry for government intervention in price and wage decisions. In
Block's opinion, 'a contest of strength where the stronger side wins
doesn't prove a thing. Each side has to represent its own interests, but
neither side must be unmindful of the needs of the nation. Who else
can point out those needs but the Government?' Obviously something of a maverick, Block yielded both to his own instincts and to a
concentrated telephone campaign of persuasion from the White
House. On Friday, speaking from Japan, Block declared, 'We did
not feel that it was in the national interest to raise prices at this time.
We felt this very strongly.'[8]

Influenced conceivably by Inland competition in a number of its
markets, Bethlehem then rescinded its short-lived price increase.
This was too much for U.S. Steel, which proceeded to follow suit.
Then the parade of companies who had cheerfully pursued U.S.
Steel up the price ladder now glumly followed their leader down the
same ladder. The moral of it all, at least as the President later drew
it in a late 1962 television interview, was this:

> though I don't like to rake over old fires, I think it would have been a
> serious situation if I had not attempted with all my influence to try to get
> a rollback, because there was an issue of good faith involved. . . . If I had
> not attempted, after asking the unions to accept the non-inflationary
> settlement, if I had not attempted to use my influence to have the com-
> panies hold their prices stable, I think the union could have rightfully felt
> that they had been misled. In my opinion it would have endangered the
> whole bargaining between labour and management, would have made it
> impossible for us to exert any influence ... in the future ... on the great
> labour–management disputes. So I have no regrets. The fact is, we were
> successful. . . .
>
> I just think, looking back on it, that I would not change it at all. There
> is no sense in raising hell, and then not being successful. There is no sense
> in putting the office of the Presidency on the line on an issue and then
> being defeated. . . . Given the problem that I had on that Tuesday night, I
> say I think we had to do everything we could to get it reversed.[9]

Blough found a rather different moral. He explained the President's
actions as motivated by an effort to recover the good will of trade
unions whose proposal for a thirty-five-hour week he had just
opposed. As Blough put it, 'I believe that he and Secretary Goldberg
felt an increase in steel prices...would be viewed as evidence that
the Administration's policies were adverse to labor's interests'.[10]

For economists eager to control inflation, the important lesson of the confrontation was that a determined administration actually could enforce a price policy upon a recalcitrant industry. In this instance the full force of the executive branch was directed towards a goal unauthorized by statute – public determination of private prices. The motives and the manners of the major contestants recede into insignificance when compared with the demonstration of relative power here offered. Its consequences have been considerable. Eisenhower's exhortations to unions and corporations remained just that, because neither the labour unions nor the corporate managers believed that the administration wished (or dared) to enforce its views. The Eisenhower administration indulged businessmen, entertained businessmen and included businessmen, but it simply could not influence businessmen. The Kennedy administration appointed few businessmen and admitted a still smaller number to social favour. It all seems to prove that political power is more important than social empathy.

This digression into contemporary history reinforces a single point. To argue from the existence of administered prices to the obsolescence of Keynesian public policy is mistaken. On the evidence already before us of the policies pursued during the 1960s, Keynesian public finance requires the supplement of wage and price policies, not consignment to the junkyard of antiquated doctrines.

Public control of major pricing decisions does all the same pose a special problem, one of law and politics as well as of economics. It is a problem with which public policy has tried to grapple for more than three-quarters of a century. Legislatively, the Sherman Anti-trust Act was the initial American attempt to extend the common law disapproval of monopoly. It was the congressional expression of rising public concern over the trust movement of the 1870s and 1880s. As a recent historian of the act has put it, 'American economic policy has always rested on two principles: (1) government should play a fairly confined role in economic affairs, and (2) private economic activities should be controlled largely by competition.'[11] In its apparently unequivocal prohibitions of restraints upon trade and attempts to monopolize markets, the Sherman Act simply wrote into statute the sense of case-law precedent. The common law, frequently if not always, judged price-fixing as a conspiracy. The tangled history of anti-trust policy need not delay us long. However, the passage of the Clayton Anti-trust Act and the Federal Trade Commission Act in the first Wilson administration testified to a continuing public concern over the concentration of economic power and the inadequacy of the Sherman Act to control the drift of business firms towards large size via merger and internal growth.

Throughout its history, anti-trust administration has been hampered by congressional reluctance to provide the funds to hire enough lawyers, Supreme Court tendencies to treat large corporations gently and executive puzzlement about whom to prosecute for anti-trust violation. When, the plaintive question might go, does a monopoly exist? It is unusual to find a single firm in control of 100 per cent of an industry's output. Although the concentration of assets and output is indeed substantial,* each industry is likely to include three, four, half a dozen, or even a dozen large units, and quite a few midgets. What number and what size distribution constitute *de facto* evidence of monopolistic behaviour? Indeed, what varieties of behaviour should be defined as monopolistic? The difficulty of making the distinction helps explain the inconsistencies of the Department of Justice and the courts.

Nevertheless, the anti-trust laws are far from a dead letter. If anything, recent events have diminished traditional doubts about their effectiveness; some impressive testimonials to the Department of Justice's role could probably be offered by numbers of enraged businessmen. For instance, the Anti-trust Division halted the projected marriage of Bethlehem Steel and Youngstown Sheet & Tube on the ground that the merger would diminish competition in steel. It compelled the movie companies to choose between film production and film distribution. Most sensational of all were the jail sentences imposed by Judge J. Cullen Ganey in a Philadelphia courtroom upon a group of electrical appliance executives in 1961. What the twenty-one colluding corporations, among them General Electric, Westinghouse and Allis Chalmers, had confessed to was a systematic rigging of government bids on turbines, switch-gears and other items of heavy electrical equipment. Although the sentences

* In 1962 the twenty biggest manufacturers owned $73·8 billion, one-quarter of the total for all manufacturing. The fifty largest corporations controlled thirty-six per cent, the one hundred largest forty-six per cent, and the thousand largest almost seventy-five per cent of all manufacturing assets. The remaining 419,000 manufacturing corporations shared the residual quarter. (See Estes Kefauver, *In a Few Hands: Monopoly Power in America* (New York: Pantheon, 1965; Harmondsworth: Penguin).)

were only thirty days and good behaviour reduced them by a week, it is not often that a General Electric vice-president, not to mention six lesser executives, finds himself subject to a criminal penalty.[12] The $825,000 in fines which accompanied the jail sentences was a fleabite on the corporate hide, but the damage suits promptly initiated by overcharged customers cost the conspirators many millions of dollars.

In the wake of the electrical case, it is possible that businessmen in this industry and others have been more hesitant about making price agreements in restraint of competition, especially since collusion on prices is one mode of behaviour about which the Supreme Court has been utterly consistent. The Aldyston Pipe case of 1899, the Trenton Potteries case of 1927, and the Madison Oil case of 1940 are three of the legal landmarks which state plainly the Court's position that no economic necessity, prior legality or altruism towards struggling competitors justifies collusive price-fixing.

However, overt collusion is generally a sign that more legal expedients have momentarily failed. Ordinarily price leadership will do the job of stifling price competition. As one commentator has put it, 'A covenant signed with blood, an agreement signed with ink, an understanding without written words, concerted acts approved with a wink or a nod, a common course of action followed without physical communication, these may be different forms of collusion, but the differences are irrelevant, if the effects are the same'.[13] Diminished price competition, it is worth recalling, derives not from the special depravity of corporate executives in the concentrated industries but from the innate logic of oligopoly. In the industries where a few large units are dominant, each cannot help knowing that the prices it sets influence the sales and profits of other firms.

Prevailing anti-trust concepts have not solved this problem of oligopoly. Yet the concept itself seems to suggest a consistent solution. If in the spirit of Justice Brandeis we truly admire the small and distrust the large, the clean-cut remedy is to fragment corporate giants. Using the criteria of size and function as guides, the Department of Justice might carve large corporations into five or more parts, much as the 1911 Supreme Court decree divided Standard Oil into several successor organizations. General Motors' automotive divisions alone might yield five smaller companies, each of them more than adequate in size to reap all possible technical efficiencies of scale. Ford, by the same logic, might be succeeded by three smaller automotive companies. In other industries similar multiplications are feasible. The great gain of fragmentation is the increase in the number of competitors and the corresponding decline in the power of any one of them to influence the prices of all.

How plausible is such a proposal? From a technical standpoint, probably little would be lost, though the answer varies industry by industry. Our largest companies have long since exceeded the necessary scale required to minimize factory production costs. If the full technical economies of mass production in automobiles are available to the assemblers of half a million units annually, there is no pressing engineering reason to maintain General Motors' capacity to turn out five million or more units every year. For that matter the considerable decentralization of decision and the managerial autonomy conventional in that company[14] imply that the largest corporations are compelled to pretend to be confederations of smaller ones in order to avoid strangulation by their own bureaucracies. The advantages which make the giant companies profitable are financial, advertising, marketing and political rather than technical. The dubious or negative social utility of advertising and the legitimate questions about the constructiveness of industry's political influence suggest that social gains might be reaped from a decrease in the size of corporations.

These social gains are several. Genuine consumer choice might be widened by the increase in competition. If the power of the large corporation was lessened, the extensions of union and government size and functions which have historically paralleled the rise of the great corporation might also be checked or even reversed. Thus, fragmentation is in close harmony with that strand of American tradition which distrusts all concentrations of power, whether private or public.

All the same it is probable that few Americans are sufficiently moved by this tradition to support a reorganization of the country's industrial life. By now the large corporation has got a good grip on the American imagination in alliance with another American tradition, a liking for size. The corporation has successfully identified itself with economic progress and rising standards of living. In the generation since the Great Depression, industry has told its story too well for its severest critics to have much chance of a successful hearing. Moreover, it is a recital which has gained credibility from the popular exaggerated confidence in the efficiency of very large-scale operations. In this world of large units, therefore, a proposal to return to smaller ones has a touch of the utopian, even the un-American about it. The probabilities, then, favour the continued application of anti-trust statutes to overt collusion, less consistent attention to-proposed mergers and rare invocation of the extreme remedy of divestiture and fragmentation.

The historical companion of anti-trust action has been the public utility concept, the notion that there are certain activities which by their nature possess a public interest and require a public presence. The clearest class of enterprises subject to public utility regulation is the natural monopoly. Natural monopoly characterizes telephone communications, electricity, gas and sometimes transportation, because competition carries with it a conspicuous waste of resources. The thought of several Consolidated Edisons competitively installing their equipment simultaneously is probably enough to indicate the horrors of rivalry among the public utilities.

Yet ever since the birth of the Interstate Commerce Commission in 1887, it has equally been recognized that a public utility can be endowed with a local monopoly only under the supervision of an appropriate public authority vested with control over rates and standards of service. Although regulatory principle has persistently stated that the monopolist should be held to lower profits as the proper rent of his sheltered situation, actual regulatory experience offers substantial ground for hesitation about extending the public utility concept to large manufacturing corporations. Definitions of fair rates of return on capital investments have invariably involved extensive litigation and uncertain outcomes. The public utility commissions established by the states have often been weak and sometimes corrupt.

Broadening public utility regulation would multiply the difficulties in the path of its success. A single instance is illustrative. If public utility regulation was extended to the steel industry and it was decreed that all major units would be allowed to earn no more than a stated return on their investment, *different* prices would have to be fixed for each company, since the companies vary in efficiency. Moreover, since the product mixture varies over time, any commission would encounter almost insuperable difficulties in multi-product pricing.

If neither anti-trust action nor a simple extension of public utility regulation is the indicated programme, evidently a certain creative cleverness is desirable. Since oligopoly is apparently a stable organizational form and the anti-trust laws can do little to compel price competition, the most sensible reconciliation of aspiration and possibility may be an amalgam of surveillance, investigation, publicly stated standards of performance and equally public pressure, rather than the older blend of inertia, prosecution and occasional punishment. The beginning of wisdom is the open recognition that wage and price decisions in a small number of strategic industries are matters of public interest, both because the industries are themselves large and because they set examples to others.

What may be required is new institutional machinery suitable for observing industries like steel and automobiles. A wage and price board, initially armed with the power to investigate price and wage decisions in enumerated industries, might represent the public interest, act as an institutionalized representative of the President and evolve criteria of judgement. Indeed, until firm criteria emerge from the case load of such an agency, its decisions should be pieces of advice rather than legal orders.

The transitional device which has actually worked with reasonable success has been the wage-price guidepost. Originally proposed in the Kennedy years, the guideposts urge unions to limit their demands to average annual productivity gains, even if a union's particular industry has improved its efficiency more rapidly than has the nation at large. A price guidepost instructs businessmen to maintain existing prices if productivity in their enterprises matches the national average, raise their prices if they have done less well, and lower them if they have reaped efficiency gains more substantial than their fellows.

In several regards the guidelines are a compromise. They tacitly maintain unaltered the existing division of income between labour and capital, simply sharing the gains of enlarged productivity between the major economic partners. Administratively, the weapons available to the President are his own persuasion and implicit power (after the Kennedy–Blough flare-up, much more credible) and the publicity which he and his advisers can give to the recommendations of the Council of Economic Advisers in specific negotiations.

By no means have the guidelines always guided successfully. The contract settlement between the United Automobile Workers and their employers in 1964 resulted in gains of 4·9 per cent for the workers at a time when the wage guidelines recommended 3·2 per cent. For their part the automobile manufacturers, whose spectacular productivity gains eventuated in very large profits, failed to lower their product prices according to prescription.

Nevertheless, the guidelines have been a sufficiently strong pressure upon negotiations and price decisions to restrain inflation and prevent a return to the cost-push era of the 1950s. And aided by this relative price stability, the two Democrat Presidents of the 1960s have been freer to apply monetary and fiscal remedies to a sluggish economy. Like the other major industrial nations, the United States in the 1960s has had to declare an incomes policy. How far that policy will extend towards legal control of key wage and price decisions will depend upon the success that the present device maintains.

SOURCE NOTES TO CHAPTER 10

1. Quoted in Gardiner C. Means, *Pricing Power and the Public Interest* (New York: Harper & Row, 1963).

2. Ibid.

3. Quoted in ibid.

4. Quoted in ibid.

5. Abba P. Lerner, 'Keynesian Economics in the Sixties', in Robert Lekachman (ed.), *Keynes's General Theory: Reports of Three Decades* (New York: St Martin's, 1964; London: Macmillan).

6. Ibid.

7. Quoted in Hobart Rowen, *The Free Enterprises* (New York: Putnam, 1964).

8. Quoted in ibid.

9. Quoted in ibid.

10. Quoted in ibid.

11. William Letwin, *Law and Economic Policy in America* (New York: Random House, 1965).

12. See Robert Lekachman, 'Who Should Set Prices?' *The New Leader*, 13 March 1961.

13. Estes Kefauver, *In a Few Hands: Monopoly Power in America* (New York: Pantheon, 1965; Harmondsworth: Penguin).

14. On General Motors' corporate government, the most illuminating account is Peter Drucker's *The Concept of the Corporation* (Boston: Beacon, 1960).

How completely has Keynesian fiscal policy swept away older notions of public policy? Enthusiasm for Keynesian ideas requires some tempering when the British and American records are examined. One fact is central as far as British policy is concerned: every post-war prime minister has taken pains to maintain very high employment. In England the known penalty of failure is speedy political disaster. Nevertheless, in balance of payments crisis after balance of payments crisis, both Labour and Conservative cabinets have reacted in ways distressingly reminiscent of the antediluvian wisdom of the Treasury and the Bank of England. Sometimes it has seemed that the spectre of Lord Norman walks Westminster's battlements, tediously lecturing his countrymen on the need to create as much unemployment and as much business recession as might be required to check and reverse adverse balances in Britain's trading accounts.

Now, it is fortunate that no post-Keynesian British government has dared to create very much unemployment or initiate very much recession. All the same there was something depressingly familiar in the 'stop-go' tactics of Conservative Chancellors of the Exchequer between 1951 and 1964 as they invoked increases in domestic interest rates, slashes in public spending and higher taxes on consumer purchases, all in the attempt to choke off imports, expand exports and put the roses back in the cheeks of the pound sterling. During those years the Labour Party severely criticized such policies as fatal to stable economic growth, high business investment and productivity improvements.

For the Labour Party, the sequel has been rueful, for when a Labour government headed by an adept economist won office in October, 1964, its actual policies resembled much more than they departed from the Conservative model. The day after they took office, Harold Wilson and his associates might have devalued the pound and placed the blame on the Tories' thirteen years of financial mismanagement; but they didn't. Alternatively, the government might have imposed a really effective protective tariff; instead, it added a temporizing fifteen per cent surcharge to existing imposts. The charge was sufficient to infuriate England's major trading partners but not nearly large enough to rectify a large import surplus. Keynes might well have approved of either of these steps, not because devaluation or tariff protection was in itself desirable, but because either would have freed the government's hands and allowed it to take those domestic measures which it judged essential to the reform and revitalization of a sluggish economy, hampered by many vested inefficiencies and addicted to far too many restraints upon innovation.

Like any of his Conservative predecessors, however, the Prime Minister decided instead that he must protect the present value of the pound at all costs. The costs to a Labour government are larger than they are to a Conservative administration for the persistent psychological reason that international bankers and treasury officials automatically suspect the financial soundness of 'radical' politicians. As it turned out, the price that the British Government had to pay for international support of its currency included an increase in the bank rate to the crisis level of seven per cent, curtailment of domestic welfare programmes, harsher mortgage terms for home buyers, stiffer instalment charges for car purchasers, increased borrowing burdens for investors and postponed socialist legislation ranging from steel nationalization to larger pensions for the elderly. When even these measures failed to make the desired impact, the Labour government in the summer of 1965 further curtailed government spending.

Such responses to economic adversity squared poorly with Keynesian preferences. Keynes had endlessly emphasized the desirability of placing domestic expansion ahead of balance of payments necessities. As a patriotic Englishman, he had yearned to release his native land from the bondage of gold and the foreign bankers who controlled the bulk of its supply. This thread in Keynesian thought can be traced back to his writings in the 1920s – to the *Tract on Monetary Reform* and the *Essays in Persuasion*. From a Keynesian perspective, therefore, it was doubly sad to observe even a leftist British government allowing the weakness of its international trading position and the precariousness of its currency's valuation to dictate the size of its defence programme, the shape of its foreign policy, and above all the quality of its domestic monetary, fiscal and welfare legislation. In 1964 and 1965, it was hard not to speculate that Keynes's scepticism about the Labour Party's capacity to govern England would have been enlarged by his distress at this spectacle. Keynes might well have accepted his old friend Sir Roy Harrod's judgement that 'the low growth rate in Britain has been due to the authorities holding actual interest rates above their natural level'.[1] All his life Keynes favoured low interest rates even if their price was moderate inflation.

A Keynesian is entitled to make an additional comment upon Britain's commercial crisis. If Englishmen and especially Americans. at Bretton Woods had accepted Keynes's proposals for an International Clearing Union, the plaguing liquidity shortages which have afflicted both Britain and the United States in the last decade or so could have been averted. As recent events have once more proved, Keynesian public policy in a major trading nation will always be impeded by the state of exports and imports unless the international currency medium is made a good deal more elastic and a good deal more responsive to the growing demands of an expanding world trade.

For Keynesians there is some hope of improvement. Discussions begun in 1965 among American, French and British financial officials may lead to the creation of an artificial supplement to gold as an international medium. If this supplement actually does emerge from present negotiations, then Britain may win permanent relief from the repetitive crises which have marred her post-war economic performance and the United States will no longer be handicapped in the pursuit of rapid growth and high employment. But in Britain the Treasury knights are not yet completely vanquished. Although their power is reduced and they dare not create the serious recessions which were once the 'incidental' effects of repressive policies, they still have their moments. October, 1964, was one of them.

In the United States also, post-war public policy was less than completely Keynesian until very recently. In fairness to several post-war administrations, it should be said that American officials have refused to allow continuing gold outflows caused by repeated deficits in the balance of payments to raise domestic interest rates and cause serious general recessions. However, during the Eisenhower years and the first portion of the Kennedy administration, the Presidents and their advisers, fearing adverse international repercussions, did hesitate to recommend fiscal and financial policies expansionary enough to curtail unemployment and reduce the quantity of idle resources. Employment policy has been the glaring weakness of post-war economic management in the United States. The obvious success of the 1964 and 1965 tax abatements in reducing unemployment rates in 1965 points the moral that fiscal policy in the 1950s and even the first years of the 1960s was much too timid, far less vigorous than the American economy required in order to move from the five to seven per cent unemployment typical of the 1950s to the more appropriate and efficient 2·5 – 3·0 per cent levels which in 1965 still had not been reached.

Thus, American economic policy has had its flaws until only yesterday, even according to the single criterion of economic expansion. There is little favourable to be said of the policies of the 1950s; but the 1960s deserve their fame in the record of public action as the years in which Keynesian economics became the open as well as the implicit national premise upon which two Presidents based their fiscal recommendations. This is the decade which has converted an esoteric theory into the annual exercise of distributing a fiscal surplus between tax reduction and social welfare. Possibly more startling still was business's discovery that economic expansion was assisted by the termination of the traditional civil war between Democratic national administrations and the business community. Business's recognition that prudent Keynesian fiscal policies actually promote larger markets and higher profits has had an unexpected effect. Keynesian prescriptions, the monopoly of reformers and radicals during the 1930s and 1940s, have very nearly become the favourite medicines of the established, propertied interests in the community.

This too is very recent. It is unlikely that even ten years ago any business periodical would have expended editorial space in praise of a tax-slash which further unbalanced a budget in deficit, and then gone on to give direct support to the policy's underlying principle. Yet in *Business Week*'s considered judgement, 'The 1964 tax cut was not a one-shot achievement that forever more solves the nation's growth problems. On the contrary, the lesson of 1964 is that fiscal policy needs to be used actively and steadily if balanced long-term growth is to be achieved.'[2]

The institutionalization of Keynes is an indispensable element of the Great Society programme as well as an aspect of President

Johnson's highly successful efforts to generate national consensus on a wide range of public issues. But the beginnings of the process are located in 1961 and the short administration of President Kennedy. When John F. Kennedy entered the White House, he was still sceptical about the capacity of budget deficits to stimulate economic expansions. As a result his early approach to fiscal and monetary policy was cautious and exploratory. His initial recommendations to Congress, based largely upon the minimum proposals of the Samuelson task force report released in the interregnum between the November election and the January inauguration, included neither a tax cut nor very substantial increases in public spending. As matters turned out, the first expenditure increases to win presidential approval were military; and there was a short time during the summer of 1961, in the midst of the menacing Berlin crisis, when the President actually contemplated a tax *increase*, designed to finance larger military programmes and incidentally to answer those Americans who were eager, after hearing their President's inspiring inaugural address, to find out what they could do for their country.

As his associates have recalled the change, Kennedy's conversion to a modern, Keynesian position resulted from the disappointing failure of the economy to respond to the very limited schemes for manpower retraining, area redevelopment and the extension of unemployment compensation which Congress enacted in 1961, or even to the investment tax credit which Congress approved in the same year. During the first twelve months of that administration, the most notable economic events were controversies rather than new policies, in particular the argument between the advocates of fiscal stimulation and the counsellors of caution. Led by Chairman William McChesney Martin of the Federal Reserve Board, occasionally assisted by Secretary of the Treasury C. Douglas Dillon, the prudent camp pointed to the dangers of domestic inflation and the menace of continuing gold losses to Western Europe.

The expansionists were themselves divided into two groups. The Galbraith group strongly urged a substantial expansion of public spending. As Galbraith analysed the needs of the time, the public spending would not only stimulate the economy but would also feed the starved public services and do something to rectify the existing social imbalance between public and private spending. This was the theme of Galbraith's influential *The Affluent Society*. Theoretically, however, it is just as possible to stimulate a sluggish economy by reducing taxes as by enlarging social welfare programmes or, for that matter, military spending. Hence the second expansionist school, organized by the Council of Economic Advisers, committed themselves with growing urgency to the superiority of a tax reduction over a public spending policy, partly on technical administrative grounds and partly on arguments of political feasibility. As stimulating devices, tax cuts produce their effects much more rapidly than new spending programmes, which take time to get started. On the political front, Congress was believed much more receptive to tax reduction than to additional government spending, even when the budgetary impact was identical.

As this controversy within his own household proceeded, the President gave increasing public signs of his own advancing economic education. The most notable piece of evidence was that same Yale commencement address of June, 1962, which has appeared before in this account. What attracted most attention was the presidential assault on the economic 'myths' which retarded congressional action and darkened public understanding. In the course of his attack, Mr Kennedy expressed a new personal distaste for balanced budgets. 'The myth persists,' he declared firmly, 'that federal deficits create inflation and budget surpluses prevent it.' Against this myth the President opposed recent history: 'Yet sizable budget surpluses after the war did not prevent inflation and persistent deficits for the last several years have not upset our basic price stability.' From the record, Mr Kennedy inferred the sensible moral that 'Obviously deficits are sometimes dangerous and so are surpluses. But honest assessment plainly requires a more sophisticated view than the old and automatic cliché that deficits automatically bring inflation.'[3]

As he administered national instruction, the President just for good measure sought to distinguish the administrative budget (upon which public comment continues to centre) from two more illuminating budget concepts, the cash and the national income accounts variants, both of much more interest to economists.* He had a sharp word to say as well about the real significance of the national debt:

* The former records all government transactions which have an effect upon the flow of cash through the economy, including the purchase and sale of public assets and the transactions of the huge social security, government retirement and road construction trusts funds. The latter provides a still more sensitive measure of the economy's actual trend by treating some taxes and all profits on an accrual rather than a cash basis.

'There are myths about our public debt. It is widely supposed that this debt is growing at a dangerously rapid rate. In fact, both the debt per person and the debt as a proportion of our Gross National Product have declined sharply since the Second World War.'[4] Strongly as the President spoke, he evidently thought it prudent to stop short of the standard textbook proposition that the size of an internally held public debt is of little importance since its handling amounts to no more than a series of income transfers among citizens of the same political jurisdiction. Certainly, there is no sense in which the public debt represents the sort of burden upon the community that a private debt does upon an individual.

The direction of Mr Kennedy's thought was unmistakable. By December 1962, Chairman Walter Heller of the Council of Economic Advisers had succeeded in convincing him of a still more novel corollary of the fiscal stimulus doctrine. Heller's corollary was that the progressive nature of the federal tax system had the effect of moving the federal budget first into balance and then into an actual surplus well before economic expansion had engendered satisfactory levels of output and employment. As these surpluses began to pile up, they inevitably acted as a drag on further expansion, for the federal government took more and more money out of the economy and failed to increase the sums which it pushed out into the economy. Once the President accepted this analysis and applied it to the then current business expansion, he was prepared to take the bold political step of advocating a major tax reduction in the midst of a business cycle upturn, the very time when older counsels focused upon higher taxes and increased interest rates.

For the public and Congress, the argument was new and somewhat suspect. Sensibly, therefore, the President took the opportunities available to him before Congress reconvened in January, 1963, to preach it to the unconverted, of whom he had been one until so recently. In a major speech in December to the Economic Club of New York, a group of generally conservative businessmen, the President phrased his commitment to the Heller doctrine of tax drag in the assertion that 'Our true choice is not between tax reduction . . . and the avoidance of large federal deficits'. No, regardless of which political party governed the nation, 'An economy hampered by restrictive tax rates will never produce enough revenues to balance our budget, just as it will never produce enough jobs or enough profits'. The true causes of deficits were not 'wild-eyed spenders' but 'slow economic growth and periodic recessions'. President Eisenhower's Secretary of the Treasury George Humphrey had been certain that large deficits would cause the sort of recessions that would 'curl your hair'. For his part Mr Kennedy warned of the precise opposite: 'Any new recession would break all deficit records.'[5] Here was something indeed to make the President's staid audience sit up and take notice. Deficits, their guest told them, came because taxes were *too high*, not because they were *too low*. In the 1960s the President of the United States was doing his distinguished best to differentiate public finance from household finance.

This speech signalled John F. Kennedy's commitment to a stimulating tax cut as the centrepiece of his 1963 legislative programme. The Tax Act of 1964, which more than a year later translated a version of the President's wishes into law, has already assumed a symbolic meaning to both fiscal conservatives and fiscal modernists.

In the view of the first group, the act continues to threaten the financial moralities upon which the public reputation and the international credit of any government are founded. Only a year or so earlier, Secretary Humphrey had given pungent voice to such views when he had expressed doubt that we could 'spend ourselves rich'. Many congressmen quite sincerely believed that our present danger was of spending our way instead to 'bankruptcy' or even 'destruction'. As the journalist Theodore White has put it, 'Scores of Congressmen and Senators, Democrats and Republicans, are viscerally terrified that the unbalanced Budget will destroy the dollar, the life savings, insurance policies and civilized life of Americans all together'.[6] Certainty that the fears are utterly irrational does nothing to relieve a President of the need to overcome or soften such widely dispersed emotions.

To the fiscal modernists, the tax measure was a test of the possibility that a young, magnetic, intellectually alert President could move a conservative Congress and an apprehensive public (both apparently more worried about the size of the national debt than the slow rate of economic growth and the large amount of unemployment) in the direction of twentieth-century fiscal policy. Not all the fiscal modernists had originally preferred tax cuts to spending increases. However, by now the tax cut was administration policy. As such, it was the only feasible means of economic stimulus and the chief instrument for making fiscal policy seem to the public what it really was – an important modern technique of economic management, as ideological in its implications as a dental drill.

As the bill which was the focus of these views emerged from the White House, it was a combination of tax reduction and tax reform measures, an omnibus attempt to enact simultaneously Walter Heller's release of the tax brake and the reform objectives of Secretary Dillon, Assistant Secretary Stanley Surrey, Commissioner Mortimer Caplin of the Internal Revenue Service and, far from last in significance, Chairman Wilbur Mills of the House Ways and Means Committee. Upon the good will, personal influence and legislative artisanship of Mr Mills depended the shape and the future of the administration measure. Since Congressman Mills had conducted lengthy hearings on tax reform in past congressional sessions and had publicly avowed his attachment to overhauling the entire tax system, it was inevitable that the President's original bill would defer to Congressman Mills's known preferences. Thus, initially the prominence of the reform features impaired somewhat the clarity of the political argument as a match between the economic Neanderthals and the advocates of the twentieth century.

As a reduction plan, the President's bill sought three major changes. One was a reduction in individual income tax rates from the 20–91 per cent range down to a 14–65 per cent range. Although in fact probably no one enterprising enough to earn an income which would locate him in the ninety-one per cent tax bracket actually paid that top percentage, still, the very existence of such rates was a subject of grievance among conservative Americans. More importantly, the rates led to much tax avoidance and the waste of a great deal of highly talented legal energy on tax finagling. Next, businessmen were offered a curtailment of corporate income tax rates, from fifty-two to forty-seven per cent. As many noted, this change converted the Internal Revenue Service from senior to junior partnership in corporate profits. A third alteration was designed to do something especially pleasant for small businessmen. The corporate income tax applicable to the first $25,000 of profit was dropped from thirty to twenty-two per cent. In addition, the administration proposed some complex revisions in the tax treatment of capital gains, with an uncertain impact upon the size of federal tax receipts after the revisions. The rate reductions were to be spread over twenty-four months and to total $13·6 billion, $11 billion for individual taxpayers and $2·6 billion for corporate taxpayers.

Equally prominent and still more complicated was the second portion of the bill, a series of reforms aimed at increasing the equity of the tax system and producing $3·4 billion in additional revenue. At the 1963 level of the gross national product, the net reduction in taxes after the reforms were taken into the reckoning was expected to be $10·2 billion. The reforms themselves were far from perfunctory. On the contrary they were the fruit of some of the best tax thinking of tax-law specialists, law-school teachers and public officials. One of the reformers' major objectives was a reversal of the erosion of the tax base, which decades of chipping by particular interests had reduced alarmingly. A second aim was more nearly equitable treatment of taxpayers in similar circumstances, and a third was the closing of some of the loopholes which devoted lobbying had opened over the years. Even in this summary fashion, it should be clear that goals which threatened as many special interests as these were certain to start a large number of heated arguments.

One debate was over the proposed five per cent ceiling on deductions for interest payments, medical expenses and charitable contributions. The reform afflicted most severely middle- and upper-income families, especially the home-owners among their numbers who were equipped with heavy (and currently deductible) property taxes and mortgage interest payments. To the financially privileged, scarcely less irritating was the administration's desire to tax stock option profits at ordinary income tax rates instead of at the comforting twenty-five per cent capital gains rate then applicable. Of all executive fringe benefits, stock options have been the most valuable. The reform thus threatened a major corporate recruiting device. Moving from outrage to outrage, the bill next sought to end the dividend credit and exclusion, an Eisenhower concession to stockholders. Almost boldest of all, there were even a gingerly attempt to control some of the grosser benefits of oil-well ownership, a curb on the excessively generous depreciation treatment enjoyed by real estate, a tightening of the rule controlling holding companies and, with much the same objectives, many minor alterations of the tax code.

Taken together these provisions increased Treasury receipts by striking hard at the special privileges of the wealthy. In contrast a few of the remaining reforms would have cost the Treasury comparatively minor sums of money. Liberalised income-averaging

arrangements, slightly more generous child-care allowances to working mothers, and marginally more favourable treatment of the
elderly were justified both by the gains in equity and by the long
history of effort by the experts to make them law. If that most conspicuous offender against tax justice, the oil company, got off lightly,
the presence of a Texas Vice-President and potent Texas and Cali-
fornia delegations in Congress made it astonishing that the administration had tried at all.

Most reasonably impartial students of American tax history considered the reforms well conceived and well drawn. If enacted they
promised to move the tax code measurably nearer justice and consistency. In the main tax liberals were pleased by the President's
programme. Even though lower personal and corporate tax rates
provided solace to the wealthy, the leaks in the tax system were too
numerous for anyone to take seriously the old schedule of personal
income tax rates. What counted in the new measure was the
closing of tax havens and the plugging of loopholes. Although
there were tax radicals who evaluated the Administration programmes as excessively timid, the concensus of the moderate
was that this was the fairest tax bill proposed by a President in a
generation.

*

However, there now remained the task of persuading Congress to
enact the bill without damaging alterations. Even a masterful President has his troubles piloting a tax bill through Congress; this
combined political and economic exercise twangs far too many sensitive financial nerves. As President Kennedy analysed the 1963
alignment of political forces, it appeared to him that the best way to
secure tax reduction was to enlist the energies of those who preferred reform to reduction. Similarly, the way to get tax reform was
to persuade the supporters of tax reduction to fight for the whole
package.

Nevertheless, it was clear to the President's Council of Economic
Advisers and to the President himself that the imperative of the hour
was tax reduction. The priorities were set by consideration of the
economic outlook. In January 1963, the United States was well into
its third year of continuous business expansion. By past precedents
the boom would not last very much longer. If Walter Heller's tax
brake doctrine was valid, the boom's existence was even now being

shortened by excessive tax collections. Hence it might be critically important that Congress approve tax reduction rapidly.*

On the question of timing, the President himself was specific and exigent. As the President saw it, the first principle of congressional action was prompt enactment of the 'entire tax revision programme' in the shape of a 'single comprehensive bill'. In the customary soaring language of legislative proposals, the administration's preamble to the bill promised an enlarged national income, faster economic growth, reduced unemployment, improvement in the balance of payments, higher living standards and enlarged business investment. The aspirations were unremarkable. What was to prove astonishing was the substantial accuracy with which the administration predicted the results of its favourite programme.

Accompanying the rhetoric were some down-to-earth calculations. If the estimates of the 1963 *Economic Report of the President* were accepted as reasonable, the gap between full employment and the 1963 levels of employment and output would be greatly narrowed. If the existing plant and equipment were really capable of turning out $30 to $40 billion worth more goods than in 1963, if the combined value of the multiplier and the accelerator was truly put at three, and if the net tax cut finally approximated the administration's $10 billion, then the total impact of quick congressional action might very well be a $30 billion expansion of the gross national product, possibly just enough to gather up the existing economic slack and push the economy very close to full employment. Thus ran the Keynesian reasoning of the Council of Economic Advisers.

Congress did not yield readily even to logic so persuasive. It was February, 1964, nearly three months after its great champion's assassination, before the tax bill ultimately became law. Intricate battles remained to be waged, and President Kennedy's early hope of welding tax trimmers and tax reformers into one huge coalition soon became a casualty of the fray. In the end the reforms were almost completely jettisoned by the President who had proposed them, a concession which enraged veteran tax reformers like Illinois's Senator Paul Douglas. In a full-dress, embittered Senate address delivered

* The persistence of the boom, even though Congress took another full year to pass the administration bill, does not disprove the Council's analysis. Almost certainly, consumer and business anticipation of final congressional action increased business optimism, enlarged investment and stimulated consumer instalment buying.

in August 1963, Douglas reproached President Kennedy for promising 'a comprehensive tax reform program' in 1961, postponing it in 1962, finally presenting it in 1963, and then abandoning reform hastily 'in the interest of quick enactment of a tax cut'. Yet in the course of his speech, Senator Douglas himself identified the fear of recession as the strongest pressure upon the administration.

The primacy of anti-recession action was accepted even by some of the liberal groups who had been most devoted to equitable reform. Although the National Planning Association and the Committee for Economic Development, two moderate groups, both favoured the original reform-plus-reduction package, the American Federation of Labor–Congress of Industrial Organizations, more fearful of unemployment than eager to see the tax code rewritten, preferred a quick tax slash in 1963 and a postponement of reform until the following year. Among business supporters of tax change, enthusiasm for the closing of tax loopholes was understandably restrained. The administration's highly prized Business Committee for Tax Reduction, whose co-chairman was Henry Ford II, sincerely favoured tax reduction and equally fervently opposed the decrease of tax privileges high in cash value to the Committee's own constituency.

In the end, possibly unavoidably, the man who did the most to kill the reform was the President himself. The President had never really concealed his own views. In his December, 1962, Economic Club speech, again in the tax message to Congress, and still more candidly in a February, 1963, address to a Washington meeting of the American Bankers' Forum, President Kennedy emphasized both his interest in tax reform and the higher priority he attached to tax reduction. To attentive hearers it was evident that the President was willing, however reluctantly, to accept from Congress tax reduction by itself, if this was the best he could get. It is possible that he might have secured rather more tax reform if he had not revealed his own heart so openly.

This is conjecture. The outcome was always uncertain, and the practitioners of coalition politics move in a tricky milieu. When the affluent start brooding about their loss of privilege rather than potential reductions in tax rates, when the poor begin to reflect upon the large percentage of the benefits flowing to the business community, and when each special interest commences to place its own claims above a shared concern for continued prosperity, then the most carefully constructed alliance begins to disintegrate. Each group concentrates upon what it *doesn't* like; nobody speaks for what he admires.

In this instance the prospect of complete frustration was the greater because the public at large displayed amazing apathy and even hostility towards tax reduction. Walter Heller was not the only one astonished at the strength of the Puritan ethic in a free-spending, high-borrowing nation. Apparently there were large numbers of Americans who were more interested in balancing the federal budget, reducing the public debt, and curtailing federal spending than in improving their own financial condition. A Harris poll released on 1 September 1963, revealed that sixty-three per cent of the population did indeed welcome a prompt tax reduction, but thirty-six per cent virtuously preferred to see the budget balanced first (in direct negation of the expansionary principle underlying the administration programme), and another twenty-three per cent were uncertain about the whole issue. This was one occasion at least when a good many people were fully prepared to dislike Santa Claus.

To make matters worse, the congressional spokesmen for ancient ideas were in positions of great power. Senator Harry F. Byrd, chairman of the tax-writing Finance Committee, was an unequivocal budget balancer, deeply committed to the belief that private activity was good and federal spending was wasteful. Although Congressman Mills was far more temperate and in the event far more flexible in his opinions, he too was a long distance from an outright Keynesian position. On taxes he adopted the conservative position that 'The function of taxation is to raise revenue. ... I do not go along with economists who think of taxation primarily as an instrument for manipulating the economy.'⁷ If Mr Mills had acted in the light of this statement, the administration bill would have perished in the House Ways and Means Committee.

The President did still more to soothe his baulky Congress. Himself a belated convert to the deficit gospel, Mr Kennedy responded to the political pressures upon him by placing increasing emphasis on the restraint of federal expenditure. Again and again he came close to promising a ceiling on all government programmes except defence and space. For social welfare proposals, 'fiscal prudence' and 'economic necessity' became the guiding criteria.

In pursuit of this tactic, as Congress continued its apparently interminable deliberations, the President sent a highly conciliatory letter to Chairman Mills on 19 August 1963. In it he sacrificed all but the barest essentials of fiscal stimulus in language which implicitly conceded a good deal to the economic myths which he had so recently been engaged in publicly dispelling. He started with a declaration of budgetary piety: 'Our long-range goal remains a balanced budget in a balanced, full-employment economy.' Even though tax reduction was now essential in order to enlarge national income, it 'must . . . be accompanied by the exercise of an even tighter rein on Federal expenditures, limiting outlays only to those expenditures which meet strict criteria of national need'. The President promised that 'as the tax cut becomes fully effective and the economy climbs towards full employment, a substantial part of the increased tax revenues will be applied towards a reduction in the transitional deficits which accompany the initial cut in tax rates'.[8] Mr Kennedy wound up with a promise that if Congress did enact the tax programme, his next budget would plan a smaller deficit than the $9·2 billion estimated at the time for the fiscal year 1964.

The President's careful conciliation of contrary opinion, the diminishing support for tax reform, and the increasing pressure for congressional decision all began to shape the final accommodation between the opposing tax camps and between the chief executive and Congress. The tax reforms were almost completely deserted. The exemptions, privileges and loopholes soothing to executives, home-owners, oil prospectors, real estate operators, organizers of charities, foundations and universities were preserved. Even the expense account route to workaday affluence was left practically untouched. As for the tax reductions themselves, they gave all taxpayers something, but the large dollar gains made by the middle- and upper-income groups were no longer offset in part by diminished tax privileges.

Possibly not in intention but certainly in effect, the Tax Act of 1964 was a consistent extension of the policies of an administration which had somehow acquired the reputation of being anti-business, just conceivably because a vivacious President adjudged most businessmen dull conversationalists. As politics is played in the United States, it is questionable whether a Republican administration, traditionally allied to business interests and accordingly eager to conciliate other groups, could have ventured to do as much for business as the Kennedy administration's combination of investment tax credit, liberalized depreciation, lowered corporate tax rates and diminished progression in personal income taxes. To achieve his *détente* with conservatives, the President had gone even further by promising to control federal spending and limit his requests for new social welfare programmes. This was the price he had to pay for the acceptance of modern fiscal policy by those who clung to an older faith.

The act which became law was very different from the bill which President Kennedy had sent to Congress. What is a fair judgement on the new law? Passed in a year of economic expansion and existing budget deficit, amounting to the largest dollar tax reduction in American history, was it really, as *Business Week* proclaimed, 'an historic event in U.S. public policy?' Were the periodical's editors accurate in labelling the act 'the triumph of an idea'? Was 'Keynes himself . . . the intellectual godfather of the tax cut'?[9]

Whatever the reservations of tax reformers and the regrets of partisans of public spending, it is difficult not to answer yes to all three queries. Even though in shape the new programme favoured established interests, a new principle of economic policy had indeed won through, a rare event in human affairs. The effects of the victory will be felt for a long time, but the continued expansion of the economy during 1964 and 1965, the steady downward drift of unemployment, and the gratifying increase of sales and profits gave immediate support to the claims of the new public finance and justified the slash in excise taxes enacted in June 1965. It is as certain as such things can be that never again will an American government profess helplessness in the face of unemployment, recession and lagging economic growth. Rational fiscal policy expressed in the use of taxes as stabilizing agents and the acceptance of deficits without guilt may be a belated achievement but not the less treasurable because it comes a generation after the birth of the doctrine which justifies the public action.

In the calm which has followed a new national consensus, it is possible to see at last that Keynesian economics is not conservative, liberal or radical. The techniques of economic stimulation and stabilization are simply neutral administrative tools capable of distributing national income either more or less equitably, improving the relative bargaining positions of either unions or employers, and increasing or decreasing the importance of the public sector of the economy. Keynes's personal history and the early affiliation of liberals and radicals with Keynesian doctrine have obscured this vital point. In the United States, the fact is that two Presidents and two Congresses have chosen to stimulate the country's economy not by expanding public activity but by encouraging more private activity. Indeed, every tax reduction diminishes the federal government's relative share of the gross national product and correspondingly increases the relative importance of the private economy. Each tax cut contains the implicit proposition that dollars released to private discretion achieve benefits more valuable than could be attained by public expenditures of the same amount. Quite probably expressing a national preference, President Kennedy and President Johnson have placed a large bet on the capacity of business to produce the right goods in the right quantities and to distribute them to the right people.

The 1964 presidential campaign disguised this as it did other issues. Promoting neither himself nor public enlightenment, Mr Goldwater ran a straightforward pre-Keynesian campaign. In it he advocated, *inter alia*, less federal spending, further tax reduction and budgets balanced in all save extraordinary circumstances, of which recession was not one. He opposed labour 'monopolies' and attacked the public use of fiscal policy as a stabilizing tool. It was all too consistent with a Senate voting record which featured opposition to the Reciprocal Trade Agreements Act, the Kennedy Trade Expansion Act, agricultural price supports, social security protection, medicare, minimum wage legislation and all the other 'interferences' in free markets which the enemies of liberty (Republican as well as Democratic) had forced upon the country. Under the circumstances President Johnson had no political reason to advance a detailed economic programme or to discuss the genuine issues which now confront him and his constituents.

The major economic question which faces Americans in the Keynesian era is no longer a matter of whether modern fiscal policy should or should not be employed. For the reasonable, this is an issue finally resolved. It has been superseded by a much harder set of choices dependent on social valuations more complex than the simple preference of prosperity to depression, growth to stagnation, and progress to retrogression. These are the choices which were foreshadowed by the controversy in the Kennedy administration over the best way to stimulate the American economy. When a President and a Congress acknowledge the need for fiscal stimulus, *how* should this stimulus be supplied? The practical choice, the major social valuation, and the continuing political argument focus upon the two routes to economic expansion which are open, the twentieth-century liberal route and the twentieth-century conservative alternative.

The modern economic conservative is no longer a budget balancer; he is perfectly willing to recognize deficiencies in aggregate demand as they present themselves. He may well accept the current diagnosis that the economic *malaise* of the 1950s and early 1960s was the consequence of insufficient private investment and a tax structure which withdrew the fruits of economic expansion too quickly and too copiously from the pockets of consumers and entrepreneurs. Defining the problem in this fashion, the conservative expansionist is prone to pin his hopes on a refashioning of the federal tax system and periodical infusions of fiscal stimulus in the shape of additional tax reductions. He is likely to be wary of large expenditures on social welfare and still suspicious of the enlargement of federal influence. Nevertheless, more and more he esteems the federal government as a partner in business prosperity.

As many of the preceding portions of this volume suggest, the thrust of two Democratic Presidents' legislative programmes and administrative actions has been at the least consistent with the expectations of modern economic conservatives. The familiar roster of liberalized depreciation, investment tax credit, reduced corporate income tax rates, moderated personal tax progression and excise tax alteration all have amounted to direct or indirect attempts to stimulate business confidence, enlarge private investment and emphasize the significance of private economic production. The Kennedy and Johnson appointments to the federal regulatory agencies and the Cabinet, and the decision to vest control of the communications satellite in private corporate hands, are additional acts of solicitude for business feelings and preferences. It is accurate rather than invidious to term the faith of modern businessmen commercial Keynesianism, and it is only sensible to welcome the perception by intelligent businessmen that private activity can be aided by a government sympathetic both to business and to high employment. Commercial Keynesianism is a giant step beyond older policies preferred by the business community.

Nevertheless, the opposing contemporary position also has its just claims. The liberal expansionist stance owes a debt to the Galbraith of *The Affluent Society*, the Harrington of *The Other America*, and the unemployment analyses of Charles Killingsworth. Liberal expansionists unite in denying that commercial Keynesianism is capable of meeting adequately the economic challenges of the next decade. By itself expansionary policy will not prepare the nation for a changing labour market.

One of the major concerns of liberal expansionists is the slow growth of manufacturing employment and output. Computers and servo-mechanisms are eliminating unskilled, semi-skilled, and even skilled positions. Education requirements for steady employment are rising too sharply to allow much hope for many of today's unemployed. The uncertainties and dangers of the new market for human skill and energy are such that even advocates of tax reduction perceive that their favoured device is less than the whole answer to unemployment. Testifying on poverty in 1964, Walter Heller phrased the position eloquently: 'Open exits mean little to those who cannot move – to the millions who are caught in the web of poverty through illiteracy, lack of skills, racial discrimination, broken homes, and ill health – conditions which are hardly touched by prosperity and growth.'[10] On this front the alarmists insist upon the imminence of a transformation of production and employment larger in scale and more devastating in impact than the Industrial Revolution of the eighteenth century. Such is the diagnosis advanced by the signers of the Manifesto of the Ad Hoc Committee on the Triple Revolution, among them Michael Harrington and Gunnar Myrdal. But even the more cautious structural analysis of Charles Killingsworth implies the need for a good deal more than the simple stimulation of aggregate demand by tax reduction.

Clearly the persistance of poverty, the presence of structural unemployment and the looming menace of automation all demand specific programmes of public intervention. So also does the fact, in the Galbraithian view, that Americans allocate far too many resources to private activity and far too few to public purposes. What concerns Galbraithians is the number of places in the United States like Perry County, Kentucky, whose teachers start at a salary of $74.42 a week; Washington, D.C., whose Ludlow Elementary School contains one wash-basin for its 260 students and whose General Hospital compels indigent patients to wait even in emergencies three to six hours before they can see a doctor; and even rich New York City, whose decades of experiment with public housing have not eliminated the slums of Harlem. Liberal expansionists are convinced that the nation's schools, houses, hospitals and social services will never be so high in quality as its automobiles, cosmetics and detergents until large amounts of resources are shifted from low-priority private uses to high-priority public uses. The practical import of the judgement is that in a time of prosperity as in a time of recession, the role of the federal government should increase, not decrease.

Therefore, whether they emphasize poverty, structural unemployment or the starvation of the public services, liberal expansionists favour public spending over tax reduction. It is exactly at this point in the practical politics of fiscal policy that they part company from conservative expansionists. Since each time taxes are reduced it is harder to achieve larger federal appropriations, liberal expansionists must in logic be the opponents of tax cuts and the friends of larger expenditures on urban redevelopment, regional rehabilitation, vocational education, manpower retraining, public recreation, aid to education and low-cost, federally assisted housing. Liberal expansionists dislike tax reduction because they perceive it as the inevitable competitor of the superior policies which assist the unemployed young, the victims of segregated education, the technologically displaced, and the miserably housed.

The art of democratic politics often lies in blurring the issues, not sharpening the definitions as intellectuals are fond of doing. It would be naïve to expect a successful President to define his programme in clear-cut ideological terms. Moreover, final judgements upon functioning political leaders are risky. As this is written, Lyndon Johnson has been President in his own right only a year and a half. The ultimate shape of his own programme preferences and accomplishments will depend on many factors, a number of them outside any President's control. The urgencies of foreign affairs, the necessities of the defence establishment, the temper of Congress and the behaviour of the economy are among the important variables which will influence presidential economic policy. Any present assessment must be provisional, the more so because 1965's Great Society legislation contains sufficiently varied emphases to permit of a number of different sequels during the next three or possibly seven years of President Johnson's administration. All the same it is useful to examine Mr Johnson's unusually varied programme up to now in the framework of liberal and conservative expansionism.

To begin with, the President's policies are often continuations of Kennedy, Truman or even Roosevelt initiatives. The lines of development between the Kennedy and the Johnson years are particularly numerous. Originated by President Kennedy, the tax cut was enthusiastically embraced by President Johnson. The preliminary plans for the War on Poverty had already been laid by the Kennedy staff before President Johnson adopted the War on Poverty as the initial identifiable programme of his own new administration. President Kennedy had urged Congress to enact medicare and aid to education. Assisted by a huge Democratic majority, President Johnson pressed the measures through Congress. The wage-price guidelines which appeared first in *The Economic Reports* of the Heller Council of Economic Advisers have been reiterated by the Council headed by Gardner Ackley.

It is style rather than legislative substance which separates the two Democratic Presidents. That Mr Johnson has won business confidence seems to be the joint consequence of the demonstrated success of fiscal policy and Mr Kennedy's apparent 'hostility' and Mr Johnson's evident sympathy to businessmen and their problems. The tragi-comedy of President Kennedy's relations with the business community has already been told. In the months which preceded the assassination, there were signs that the President and business were moving towards reconciliation. Still, it is doubtful whether even proper courtesy between businessmen and their President could have been achieved. Rapport seemed a distant hope. A recollection of Theodore Sorensen's may exemplify the feelings on both sides. Mr Sorensen cites the President as commenting caustically to him after addressing the Business Council that this was the only audience which did not stand when the President of the United States entered the room.[11]

Birthplace, experience and temperament have combined in President Johnson to produce a different set of feelings. Like any other successful Texas politician, Mr Johnson, first as Congressman and then as Senator, had to reach an accommodation with the major economic interests of his region. Although Lyndon Johnson entered Congress as a New Dealer, the personal protégé of Franklin Roosevelt, and voted consistently for New Deal measures, he sought also to protect the tax advantages of his state's oil interests. Moreover, in his own private affairs, he entered into partnership with his wife in one of the period's more speculative industries – television. The

texture of Mr Johnson's personal experience equips him to understand concretely, directly and intimately the financial and tax difficulties of ordinary businessmen. His experience also gives him insight
into the way businessmen regard the regulatory agencies and the
federal bureaucracy. His past activities have developed in him a taste
for business company and business conversation. The presidency is a
great symbolic office, and these small details of its present occupant's
career can have large consequences.

One of them indeed has been the unexampled extent of business
approbation of Mr Johnson. It has been a long time since so conservative an organ as the *Monthly News Letter* of New York's First
National City Bank could say publicly the kind of thing it said of this
Democratic President's 1965 congressional programme, that 'These
reports and messages indicate a marked evolution toward a more pro-
nounced pro-business attitude, combined with an increasing stress
on free enterprise and market competition in the allocation of
resources'.[12]

The body of messages and reports which the writers of the en-
comium were commending were portions of the Great Society
programme. They offer an excellent opportunity to examine the
quality of the expansionary programme of this activist President. The
chance is the better because the 1965 Congress was more nearly under
the complete control of the chief executive than any has been since
1933. President Johnson made full use of his fortunate situation to
press through Congress an unusually varied list of measures, covering
topics ranging from highway beautification to immigration reform.
Even though this legislative programme is not the President's final
word, it is an impressive first chapter.

Let us consider its elements. The documents which sound the
major legislative themes are the budget message and *The Economic
Report of the President*. The latter began with an account of the successes of the past twelve months. Nineteen sixty-four had been a year
of expansion in which employment had risen by a million and a half,
the gross national product had increased from $584 billion to $622
billion, corporate profits had continued a four-year ascent, and personal income *per capita* (after taxes) had touched $2,288 per year, up
17·5 per cent in just four years. Any administration would have
pointed proudly to another characteristic of its stewardship – the
price stability which had accompanied economic expansion.

In allocating the credit, *The Economic Report* tactfully began with the 'businessmen, workers, investors, farmers and consumers' whose investing, spending and planting decisions had combined to stimulate economic growth. Then came the last partner, 'Government policies which have sustained a steady, but non-inflationary growth of markets'.[13] The President stated his belief 'that 1964 will go down in our economic and political history as the "year of the tax cut"'.[14]

From the attractive economic record President Johnson drew a semi-Keynesian lesson, that 'Purposeful expenditure, stimulative tax reductions, and economy in government operations are the three weapons which, if used effectively, can relieve our society of the costs and consequences of waste'.[15] How the President intended to use the first two weapons rapidly emerged in his concrete legislative proposals.

The 'stimulative tax reductions' included the remainder of the reductions already mandated under the 1964 tax measure – some $3 billion in personal tax benefits and another $1 billion in corporate tax remissions. The new tax item substantially reduced some excise taxes and eliminated a good many others. In combination these tax changes were a continuation of the fiscal stimulus initiated in 1964 by the passage of the Tax Reduction Act.

The 'purposeful expenditure' list was an interesting agglomeration. It included enlargements of old programmes like social security and the War on Poverty as well as initial financing for some new programmes. The latter were a varied lot – aid to education, the rehabilitation of Appalachia, the construction of regional medical centres, rent subsidies, and medical assistance to the aged. Although so many programmes were new (as objects of legislation if not of repeated proposal), requests for increased spending amounted to only a modest total. In fact, as a fiscal exercise, what unified this programme of tax reduction and welfare extension was a constraint – the President's promise that both tax benefits and welfare spending would be financed out of the normal growth of an expanding economy. Both types of benefits depended upon the capacity of a growing economy to create a fiscal dividend each year to be distributed to its citizens.

Emphatically, the architects of this legislative design did not intend to reallocate the community's resources in the direction of greater public influence. During his first two budgets, President Johnson's insistence on not exceeding the $100 billion expenditure mark attested to the importance which he attached to keeping government activity within limits. It appears likely that the President would have recommended still greater fiscal stimulus in each of the budgets if he had not been restrained by his concern for the size of federal spending. That concern was itself related to the President's wish to retain within the boundaries of his political consensus the business support which he had won. In the end the implicit check on the size of social welfare expenditure delimited the amount of intervention that the business community was willing to accept.

The President's choices between tax reduction and larger spending continued to emphasize the former. Even after 1964's major tax surgery, the President offered new benefits in 1965 and intimations of future reductions in personal income levies. Only the escalation of the Vietnam war transformed administrative discussions and created the possibility of tax increases. As a result, even though the 1965 congressional record was startlingly enlightened by comparison with earlier congressional performances it remained true that the combined increases in old social programmes and initial appropriations for new ones amounted to less than the reductions in personal income taxes, corporate imposts and excises.

From the standpoint of the liberal expansionist, this was bad enough, but the distribution of the tax benefits and even the new public spending raised still livelier apprehensions for him. Like 1964's tax harvest, much of 1965's improvements would be realized by prosperous corporations and wealthy individuals. Reduced corporate income tax rates generated additional dividends and capital gains which flowed for the most part to upper-income investors. The same group would enjoy a very large percentage of the gains from additional reductions in personal income taxes. Some portion of reductions in excise taxes would be retained as extra profits by corporations which were already turning in highly satisfactory earnings records.

The design of the expenditure programmes also raised a number of questions about who precisely benefits from welfare policies besides the direct recipients of assistance. The interests of specific business groups sometimes appear to influence the shape of programmes as much as the needs of the ostensible beneficiaries. Thus, the major innovation of the 1965 omnibus housing measure, the rent subsidy plan, undoubtedly enables a number of families, ineligible under other programmes, to escape the slums and move into a decent environment. At best rent subsidies modestly promote housing integration. However, local governments have long known that under such programmes financial benefits accrue to landlords and builders, helping them maintain the existing structure of building costs and apartment rentals. This is another way of saying that the rent subsidies tend to support the existing customs of an industry usually considered backward in both its technology and its social practices.

The Appalachian programme raises somewhat similar issues. No reader of Harry Caudill's affecting *Night Comes to the Cumberlands* will question that most of Appalachia's inhabitants live in abject misery, nor that public help is unqualifiedly desirable in a region that has manifestly lost a grip on its own troubles. All the same, it is hard not to pause and wonder why the most expensive of the components of the administration programme is a major road-building effort. Certainty on its merits is not easy, for in the long run, new roads in the appropriate places may indeed open the region to the tourist trade, promote the internal mobility of labour and encourage industrialists to establish new plants. However, what appears all too likely in the short run of the next few years is that the road contractors will reap the major gains. There will be little immediate increase in local employment because of the highway construction. By now road-building has become so skilled a trade and uses so much expensive equipment that much of the labour force employed on the new Appalachian highways will be imported from other more prosperous regions.

Not even the poverty programme is totally exempt from the same reservation, that it contains an excessively generous tendency to distribute some portion of the available largess to the unneedy. The ample scale on which local poverty officials are paid has already aroused a quantity of sour humour about the identity of the programme's major beneficiaries. This point may be comparatively minor administratively though it is surely significant psychologically. However, it can reasonably be argued that high salaries attract abler and more inventive human types into social welfare specialities than the social service bureaucrat who now dominate the field.

A more serious question about the goals and strategies of the War on Poverty concerns the participation of major corporations like Litton Industries, Philco and International Telephone & Telegraph in poverty ventures which they define as commercial opportunities.

These and other firms have signed up as operators of new job camps for unemployed youths. Although there is no reason to quarrel with the sincerity of either portion of a Litton executive's remark that 'We got into the poverty war for two reasons, one the opportunity to serve the community, the other the business opportunity',[16] serious issues are tied up in business sponsorship of training programmes. Will the training become a variety of publicly subsidized preparation for semi-skilled jobs with little future in the sponsoring corporations? Will a firm's concept of training necessarily or even usually coincide with the interests of either the trainees or the community? Will the commercial limitations of even the best-intentioned business ventures really lead to the social transformations which in its more visionary moments the poverty programme promises? Once more it is difficult not to wonder whether the Administration programme, intentionally or unintentionally, does now offer as many benefits to the successful as prospects for the poor, the rejected and the hopeless.

Under the circumstances it is not astonishing that many businessmen have extended substantial support to the administration's housing, poverty and regional development plans. Thus far, at any rate, the total outlays required are small enough to be financed from that portion of the growth of federal tax receipts not pledged to tax reduction. The programmes are so constructed as to favour existing agencies and interests. To their credit, a generation of more sophisticated business leaders have come to see that active fiscal policy and limited social welfare improvements are themselves conducive to business prosperity. Perhaps still more to their credit, many businessmen have come to identify themselves sufficiently with their employees to recognize a common interest in higher wages and steady employment.

When all this is said, the administration's programme can be realistically appraised only within the context of a consensus whose limits are defined by the business community, not by trade-union leaders or liberal intellectuals. In some areas these limits are narrow. In 1965, the repeal of Section 14(b) of the Taft–Hartley Act, the section enabling the individual states to outlaw union shop agreements, was put at the top of the A.F.L.–C.I.O.'s legislative agenda. Congress, which cheerfully passed a variety of Great Society proposals, stopped abruptly at the presidential request for the deletion of Section 14(b), and repeated its action at the start of 1966's congressional session. A similar reluctance to raise minimum wages and extend coverage to migratory farm workers and other unsheltered groups attests to the reluctance of influential portions of the business community to shift the existing balance between labour and industry.

Possibly the best illustration of all brings us back to the continuing shortage of low-income housing. This is a huge problem. As President Johnson sketched its dimensions, 'In the remainder of the century ... urban populations will double, city land will double and we will have to build in our cities as much as all that we have built since the first colonist arrived on these shores'. As the President went on to observe, the cities are already overcrowded, the nation contains 'over nine million homes, most of them in cities, which are run down or deteriorating', and 'many of our central cities are in need of major surgery to overcome decay'. The concluding sentence of Mr Johnson's diagnosis – 'The old, the poor, the discriminated against are increasingly concentrated in central city ghettos'[17] – is both accurate and eloquent enough to command the agreement of most students of city affairs, not to mention the unfortunate city residents themselves.

Just here appears most glaringly the gap between the accurate description of a large problem and the means which the limits of business-defined consensus permit to be used. Although the 1965 Housing Act contains many commendable features, including the rent subsidy innovation, it fails at two crucial points. The amounts allocated to the rent subsidy programme are very small, as are the benefits that the big cities, the accepted focus of the problem, can anticipate in 1965, 1966 and 1967. New York City, for example, can expect no more than 3,500 units of low-income housing each year. Indeed, Mrs Hortense Gabel, in 1965 the City's rent control administrator, observed that the federal government planned to spend less on all housing programmes in New York City than it did four years earlier in 1961.

No one denies that improving housing and eliminating slums are enormously complex matters, made more difficult by the accumulation of past failures and the existence of contemporary prejudices. Nevertheless, successful advancement requires the creation of a huge, expensive and coordinated programme of urban renewal and public housing – and a willingness to upset comfortable commercial, union and political practices. In the past the failures of urban renewal measures have flowed partly from the perversion of the programme into a series of subsidies to luxury-builders, real estate speculators, and business promoters; partly from municipal decisions to set the quite legitimate expansion needs of great universities like Chicago and Columbia ahead of the equally legitimate (and much more acute) housing requirements of displaced residents; and partly, perhaps mainly, from the circumstance that adequate quantities of public housing – attractively designed, socially mixed and suitably located – were never supplied. In New York the consequence has been that at the end of a generation-long boom in private construction, there is still no decent place where most Negroes and Puerto Ricans can live. Though unenviable, this is a record readily matched by Chicago, Philadelphia, Los Angeles, Saint Louis and Detroit.

Thus, in relation to need, the administration programme is minute, far below Senator Robert A. Taft's goals for a smaller population and a poorer nation two decades ago. Yet where consensus is the objective, existing practices must be respected, and benefits are likely to accrue according to the relative weight of the different groups joined together in mutual accommodation. The real if very limited benefits to the poorly housed which present programmes offer are provided in ways which please the construction industry, assist middle-income families also, elevate banking profits, enlarge city real estate tax rolls, and unfortunately leave in their present plight the mass of wretchedly sheltered urban slumdwellers. This judgement is less a moral statement than a summary of the fact that in this important sphere, established practices and social objectives are in conflict.

Even medicare, the triumph of an aspiration thirty years old, has its conservative, prudential aspects. A complex piece of legislation, this is the first extension of major significance to social security since the passage of the Social Security Act in 1935. Benefits to the elderly are enlarged, and existing child health and aid to dependent children programmes are expanded. But the basic innovations are in the medical provisions. Henceforth social security pensioners are automatically entitled to payment of the expenses of hospitalization, post-hospital care, nursing home treatment and home health visits. Moreover, a voluntary supplementary plan pays the bulk of medical and surgical costs incurred in clinics, homes and medical offices.

In 1967 the programme's first full year of operation, the entire medicare package will cost about $6 billion – $2·2 billion for the basic health care plan, an additional $1 billion for the supplementary plan, $2·3 billion for increased social security benefits to the elderly, and the remaining $500 million for the liberalization of existing public assistance programmes. Particularly by comparison with recent social welfare spending, the scale of the new measure is generous. More welcome yet are the relief from anxiety and the gain in human dignity finally accorded the old. That this programme has taken so long in the coming detracts nothing from its very substantial merits.

However, this legislation also contains certain checks on benefits and on their extension to other age groups. Throughout, financing is exceedingly conservative. A case in point is the voluntary programme. The premiums set are $3 per month per covered individual, adjustable upward as medical costs rise. Rise they will. If the precedent of the post-war history of Blue Cross premiums holds true, the elderly must anticipate rapid increases in these initially modest premium payments. Worse still, other portions of the programme will be financed overwhelmingly by increases in payroll taxes, which are now scheduled to rise to 5·5 per cent *each* for employer and employee in the next fifteen years. This bite will be the more ferocious because soon the first $6,600 of earned income will be assessed instead of the $4,800 now taxed.

Reliance upon payroll taxes has unfortunate consequences. Fiscally, these taxes are as much a drag on economic expansion as any other impost. From the standpoint of social fairness, they are inequitable, regressive imposts which will remove smaller percentages of total income from those who will earn over $6,600 each year than from those who will earn less than that sum or derive their income from property. This rise in payroll taxes, coupled with recent decreases in personal and corporate income tax rates and progressions, involves a shift towards greater inequality of income distribution after taxes. Finally, the reinforcement of the precedent that social security benefits are to be financed only out of social security payroll taxes renders it exceedingly difficult to extend the benefits of medical protection to other age groups. Further increases in payroll levies may well arouse the opposition of ordinary wage-earners on whom these deductions are an irksome present burden.

What can be achieved by the consensus of the major interest groups in the United States is very substantial. The flood of legislation in 1965 verified the possibility of moderate improvement within the fiscal limits set by business predominance in the administration coalition. In short, conservative expansionism is really capable of making American society tolerable for most Americans. Nevertheless, its limitations are such, its powerful tendencies to favour the prosperous are so dominant, and its suspicion of the public sector is still so strong that it will take a more vigorous path of government action, the road of liberal intervention, to convert even an enlightened commercial community into a Great Society – to move from Keynesian fiscal policy to the Keynesian vision of a rational community.

SOURCE NOTES TO CHAPTER 11

1. Sir Roy Harrod, in Robert Lekachman (ed.), *Keynes's General Theory: Reports of Three Decades* (New York: St Martin's, 1964; London: Macmillan)
2. *Business Week*, 24 July 1965.
3. John F. Kennedy, *The Burden and the Glory* (ed. Allan Nevins) (New York: Harper & Row, 1964; London: Hamish Hamilton).
4. Ibid.
5. Ibid.
6. Theodore H. White, *The Making of the President, 1964* (New York: Atheneum, 1965; London: Jonathan Cape).
7. Quoted in ibid.
8. Charles C. Killingsworth, 'Automation, Jobs and Manpower', in Stanley Lebergott (ed.), *Men Without Work* (Engelwood Cliffs, N.J.: Prentice-Hall, 1964).
9. 'Special Report', *Business Week*, 19 February 1966.
10. Killingsworth, op. cit.
11. Theodore C. Sorensen, *Kennedy* (New York: Harper & Row, 1965; London: Hodder & Stoughton).
12. First National City Bank, *Monthly News Letter*, February, 1965.
13. *The Economic Report of the President* (Washington, D.C.: U.S. Government Printing Office, January 1965).
14. Ibid.
15. Ibid.
16. *The New York Herald Tribune*, Financial Section, 25 April 1965.
17. 'Special Message on Housing', 9 March 1965.

Epilogue

Among his many roles in English life, Keynes was treasurer of the Camargo Ballet Society. The story is told that he was once consulted on a ticklish billing problem – the familiar tale of a performer who insisted that her name precede all others. Keynes was asked whether the cast should be permitted to settle such issues by itself. His reply was in the spirit of a man experienced in the manifestations of the artistic temperament: 'That will be all right, if you will provide the ambulance.'

Keynes was a man who believed in the expert management equally of artistic groups and larger human societies. Indeed, one of the threads of consistency running through his career was a growing sense that to allow the major participants in complicated modern economies to settle their own financial affairs was to invite mayhem. As early as his 1919 *Economic Consequences of the Peace*, Keynes glimpsed the precariousness of the Victorian and post-Victorian *laissez-faire* arrangements to which he was born. Later events strengthened this vision. England's disastrous efforts in the 1920s to return to the pre-war gold standard and the calamity of the Great Depression clarified for Keynes a need for more intelligent public policy and more conscious direction of economic affairs.

Thus, the path to *The General Theory of Employment, Interest and Money* was really a search for increased rationality in economic policy. In its contemporary applications, Keynesian economics is essentially a description of the ways in which an alert government, by taking thought, can tame the business cycle and alleviate the miseries of personal insecurity. If Keynes could be said to have possessed an ideology, it was a confidence born of the humane Locke–Hume–Mill tradition that intelligence in human affairs is both essential and possible.

A good society is a society open to personal choice. Keynes laboured to control the business cycle and improve the lot of the average citizen, not alone because prosperity is preferable to depression and employment to idleness, but because 'A man can be neither a saint, nor a lover, nor a poet, unless he has comparatively recently had something to eat,' as another enlightened Englishman, Philip Wicksteed, remarked earlier.[1] Since for Keynes society was made for man, the social arrangements which won his admiration were those most capable of preserving the virtues of individual action even as they mitigated the hardships of mistaken choice. Keynes was far too discriminating a human being to accept public paternalism as a proper human fate. It is not the least of the complexities of Keynes's character that the believer in state intervention was an equally dedicated individualist. Few conservatives have been as eloquent:

individualism, if it can be purged of its defects and abuses, is the best safeguard of personal liberty in the sense that, compared with any other system, it greatly widens the field of personal choice. It is also the best safeguard of the variety of life, which emerges precisely from this extended field of personal choice, and the loss of which is the greatest of all the losses of the homogeneous or totalitarian state. For this variety preserves the traditions which embody the most secure and successful choices of former generations; it colours the present with the diversification of its fancy.[2]

In this context Keynesian economics is the purge of individualism's 'defects and abuses', and accordingly the friend of 'personal choice', 'variety of life, and rich tradition. Both realist and optimist, Keynes would scarcely have been astonished at some of the choices Englishmen and Americans have made in the Keynesian era.

SOURCE NOTES TO EPILOGUE

1. Quoted in Robert Lekachman, *A History of Economic Ideas* (New York: Harper & Row, 1959).
2. J. M. Keynes, *The General Theory of Employment, Interest and Money* (London: Macmillan, 1936).

Index